Ghana Democratic Governance.
Transitioning Routes.

Author
Justice Danquah

SONITTEC PUBLISHING. All rights reserved. No part of this publication may be reproduced, distributed, or transmitted in any form or by any means, including photocopying, recording, or other electronic or mechanical methods, without the prior written permission of the publisher, except in the case of brief quotations embodied in critical reviews and certain other noncommercial uses permitted by copyright law. For permission requests, write to the publisher, addressed "Attention: Permissions Coordinator," at the address below.

Copyright © 2019 Sonittec Publishing
All Rights Reserved

First Printed: 2019.

Publisher:
SONITTEC LTD
College House, 2nd Floor
17 King Edwards Road,
Ruislip
London
HA4 7AE.

Table of Content

TABLE OF CONTENT 4
THEORETICAL 1
CHAPTER ONE 3
    Introduction.. 3
STATEMENT OF THE PROBLEM AND RESEARCH QUESTIONS: POLITICAL PARTIES AND DEMOCRATIC DEVELOPMENT 5
CHAPTER OUTLINE 8
CHAPTER TWO 12
THEORETICAL FRAMEWORK 12
    Introduction.. 12
COMPARATIVE THEORETICAL PERSPECTIVES ON DEMOCRATIC TRANSITION AND CONSOLIDATION 14
COMBINED CONFRONTATION AND NEGOTIATION THEORIES 15
INSTITUTIONAL THEORY 18
NEGOTIATED TRANSITION THEORY 21
INTERNATIONALIST THEORY 24
CONSTRAINTS OF NEO-LIBERALISM AS A WEAKNESS OF THE INTERNATIONALISTS' THEORY 25
DEMOCRATIC CONSOLIDATION THEORIES 29
BEHAVIOURAL DIMENSION: THE STATE, INSTITUTIONS AND REGIME PERFORMANCE .. 31
ATTITUDINAL LEVEL: PROMOTING SOCIALIZATION, TRUST AND COOPERATION 35
CONSTITUTIONAL LEVEL: STRENGTHENING CIVIL-MILITARY RELATIONS, LEGITIMACY AND INSTITUTIONALIZATION OF THE POLITICAL SYSTEM 36
EXAMINING THE DEMOCRATIC TRANSITION AND CONSOLIDATION THEORIES 42
PARTY DEVELOPMENT: A CONCEPTUAL FRAMEWORK 50
PARTY INSTITUTIONALIZATION AND PARTY DEVELOPMENT 54
PARTY ORGANIZATION AND REPRESENTATION FUNCTIONS 55
PARTY BEHAVIOUR AND PARTY DEVELOPMENT 57
DEMOCRATIZATION AND PARTY DEVELOPMENT 60
ANALYSIS OF THE PARTY DEVELOPMENT THEORIES 63
    Methodology 64
CHAPTER THREE 80
    Introduction.. 80
FROM AUTHORITARIANISM TO MULTI-PARTY DEMOCRACY IN GHANA 81
EXTERNAL PRESSURES FOR DEMOCRATIC TRANSITION 84

INTERNAL AGITATION FOR DEMOCRATIC CHANGE THE ORIGIN AND ROLE OF CIVIL SOCIETY IN GHANA'S DEMOCRACY 90
CIVIL SOCIETY AS A DESTABILIZING FORCE TO DEMOCRACY IN GHANA................. 97
HISTORICAL PERSPECTIVES ON THE DEVELOPMENT OF THE PARTY SYSTEM AND DEMOCRACY IN GHANA... 102
POLITICAL PARTY TRADITIONS AND IDEOLOGIES 104
POLITICAL PARTIES AND THE 1992 DEMOCRATIC TRANSITION 110
Conclusion.. 110
CHAPTER FOUR 114

Introduction 114
THE LONG JOURNEY TO THE EVOLUTION OF MULTI-PARTY DEMOCRACY IN GHANA 115
THE MODALITIES FOR THE 1992 DEMOCRATIC TRANSITION AND ELECTIONS IN GHANA 117
THE 1992 ELECTION AND ITS AFTERMATH 119
THE 1992 ELECTION'S DISCONCERTING OUTCOME AND THE ISSUE OF NDC LEGITIMACY 123
THE 1996 ELECTION AND THE ELECTORAL REFORMS 133
THE ESTABLISHMENT OF AN INDEPENDENT ELECTORAL COMMISSION (EC) 134
THE FORMATION OF THE INTER PARTY ADVISORY COMMITTEE......................... 139
INTRODUCTION OF ELECTION MONITORING BY SOME CIVIC GROUPS.................... 142
ESTABLISHMENT OF THE NATIONAL MEDIA COMMISSION AND ROLE OF THE MEDIA 144
THE OUTCOME OF THE 1996 ELECTION: PRE AND POST ELECTION PROBLEMS 148
Conclusion.. 155
CHAPTER FIVE 157

Introduction 157
THE 2000 ELECTION AND THE QUESTION OF CONTINUITY OR CHANGE: GHANA'S DEMOCRACY AT THE CROSSROADS.. 158
The 2004 Election: Continuing the Trend toward Democratic Consolidation 163
REASONS FOR THE SUCCESS OF THE 2000 AND 2004 ELECTIONS 167
POLITICAL PARTIES' ROLE IN ELECTORAL REFORMS AND DEMOCRATIC CONSOLIDATION 168
THE END OF NDC'S POLITICAL ADVANTAGES, SECESSION OF THE NATIONAL REFORM PARTY AND POWER STRUGGLES WITHIN THE NDC PARTY................................. 169
ELECTORAL REFORMS IMPLEMENTED BY THE ELECTORAL COMMISSION AND THE INTER-PARTY ADVISORY COMMITTEE... 171

Change in Public Perception of the Political Parties and Active Participation of the Public in the 2000 and 2004 Elections.......................173
The Role of Election Monitoring Groups 175
The Role of the Media 179
Some Problems that Hinder Elections in Ghana 184
Election Irregularities and Conflicts among Party Supporters 184
Abuse of Incumbency Advantages by Ruling Parties................................185
National Democratic Congress 186
New Patriotic Party 189
Shortage of Election Logistics and the Issue of the Bloated Voters' Register...192
CHAPTER SIX 196
Introduction..196
The Rawlings Tradition: National Democratic Congress 209
The Nkrumahist Tradition Parties: The Convention Peoples Party and the Peoples National Convention..214
Political Party Strategies for Recruiting Members 218
Political Parties Financing..223
Factors that Shape Party Development and Democracy in Ghana
Candidate Selection Methods in the Political Parties............................231
Internal Party Democracy: Democratic Procedures in the Parties' Organization..236
NDC and Internal Party Democracy 238
NPP and Internal Party Democracy..244
Patronage and Patron/Client Relations in Membership Drive and Elections
....246
Weaknesses in the Party Financing and Declaration Law........................250
Lack of Participation in the Parties' Structure and Organization 256
Conclusion 261
CHAPTER SEVEN...263

Introduction..263
NDC and Society Linkage: 1992-2000...264
NPP and Society Nexus: 2001-2008...273
MPs as Representatives of the Political Parties and the People 286
Challenges to Ghana's Democratic Consolidation 290
Problems Associated with MPs Representation Functions, the Office Holders' Assets Declaration Law and the 1992 Constitution....................290

Under-representation due to Uneven Distribution of Parliamentary Seats 297
Corruption and Abuse of Power by Party Leaders and Public Officials 299
NPP's "Zero Tolerance" Policy on Corruption 303
Is the NPP's "Zero Tolerance" Policy Working? 305
Institutional Corruption and Inequitable Administration of Justice 308
Police Abuse of Power 309
Judicial Abuse of the Rule of Law 311
Weaknesses in the Anti-Corruption Bodies' Mandate 312
Conclusion 314
CHAPTER EIGHT 317
Summary 317
Some Major Findings of the Study in Comparative Perspective 318
Similarities in the Political Parties' Organization 318
Leadership and Ethnicity in Ghana's Party System 324
Variations in Party Organization 328
Candidate Selection Methods and Democratic Procedures 328
Ghana's Party System and Democratic Consolidation, and the Impact of Democratization on the Political Parties 332

Theoretical

At the time of the Ghana's independence in March 1957, a democratic system of government was instituted, but the process of political development was derailed and often interrupted by frequent coups. This is evident in the interchange of military and civilian regimes in the last fifty-one years. While in the post-independence era, the development of democracy, the party system and democratic institutions in Ghana has taken many twists and turns due to the persistent military interventions in politics, as part of the third-wave of democratization, in 1992, under Ghana's Fourth Republic, a new democratic system was re-introduced in the country under the National Democratic Congress (NDC) government. The opening of political spaces for the political parties and civil society organizations in the last two decades has witnessed the resurgence of political parties of different sizes and ideological orientation under various political traditions, which has led to the strengthening of Ghana's party system.

This, in turn, has immensely facilitated the country's democratic development, which was evidenced in the 2000 power alternation that led to the election of the New Patriotic Party (NPP) to power. Since the emergence of the third-wave of democratization, there have been numerous theoretical approaches by democratic transition and consolidation theorists on the role of political parties in the nurturing and consolidation of democracy in the third-wave countries. This study examines the internal organization of parties and their role in Ghana's democratic transition and consolidation. On the basis of the evidence presented in this study, it can be concluded that while the political parties have been the bedrock for Ghana's democratic transition and consolidation processes, there are a number of key issues such as internal party democracy and candidate selection processes that needed to be resolved by the political parties in order to strengthen Ghana's democratic consolidation process.

Chapter One

Introduction

The decades of the 1960s, 1970s and 1980s were periods of major political upheaval in Ghana due to the dominance of authoritarian regimes, mainly one party state and military regimes, which created political instability in the country for decades. The interchange of democratic and authoritarian regimes shows that Ghana's effort to promote the party system and practice democracy has had a tumultuous ride over the past fifty years, due to constant regime changes and the tenacious military intervention in politics. As a result of the unstable political development in Ghana's postcolonial history, the end of the 1980s was marked by the intensification of popular struggle and increasing opposition to the authoritarian regime, which set the stage for the re-introduction of democratic rule in Ghana. The change in state-market-society relations in the wake of liberalization and globalization in the 1980s and 1990s also changed the dynamics of political discourse and practice in many developing countries such as Ghana. Hence the last two decades of the twentieth century witnessed unprecedented political transformations and advancement of democratic values in many countries in Africa, Latin America, Asia and Eastern Europe. Theorists such as Samuel Huntington have labeled the change from predominantly authoritarian regimes to a proliferation of democratic governments as the "third wave of global democratization."Although the extent of transition differs from one country to another, there is a general consensus among many democratic theorists that the 1990s was the decade of renewed agitation for, and revitalization of, multi-party democracy in many developing countries across the globe. In sub-Saharan Africa alone, between 1990 and 1994, thirty- one out of the forty-one countries that had never held a multi-party election and about seventy-five percent of the authoritarian regimes in African sought to revitalize their rule through multi-party elections. For example, in Benin, Mali and Niger, the authoritarian regimes were dismantled by a national referendum and were later defeated in legislative and presidential elections. In countries such as Ghana, Gabon, Kenya, Senegal and Guinea, although multi-party democracy was re-introduced, the incumbent authoritarian leaders managed to hold on to power. In other countries such as Nigeria, the authoritarian regimes managed to hold on to power until the late 1990s when they were compelled by internal developments and external pressure to handover power to an elected civilian administration. The rapid spread of democratic regimes has led to the widespread perception that democracy provides lasting solutions to the political, economic and social problems facing developing countries like Ghana.

Increasing academic interest in the democratic transition and the power alternation that occurred in the last decade of the twentieth century have sparked some major debates on the democratic character of reforms in the "third wave" democracies and dominated political science research across the world. In the case of Ghana, in the 1980s and 1990s there was increasing internal and external agitation for multiparty rule.

As will be discussed in this chapter, the authoritarian political environment and the austerity economic policies pursued by the Provisional National Defence Council (PNDC) government, coupled with lack of participation, consultation and accountability in public policy-making, sparked a wave of internal pressures from civic groups, which was re-enforced by external pressures from Ghana's external donors and led to the re- introduction of multi-party democracy in Ghana in 1992. While political parties played minor roles in the transition processes, since parties were banned in the pre-transition era, remnants of the banned parties came together to form pro-democracy movements such as the Movement for Freedom and Justice (MFJ) to contribute to the internal pressure on the PNDC regime to return the country to multi-party democracy.

Statement of the Problem and Research Questions: Political Parties and Democratic Development

Since Ghana's democratic transition in 1992, the country has made significant in- roads in consolidating its democracy, and there have been a number of significant changes and improvements in its democratic system. This trend suggests that the country is gradually developing a strong and workable multi-party democratic system. Ghana is among a few of the about thirty "third wave" transition countries in sub-Saharan Africa where the momentum for democratic transition in the early 1990s has been sustained. The remarkable progress in the country's democracy has also exposed some inherent problems not only with the democratic system, but also with the political parties in their role as one of the key promoters of democracy. One of the major challenges facing many "third wave" democracies centers on how to build more effective mechanisms to promote participation and representation in the party system and government in general. The four major political parties, namely, the National democratic congress (NDC), the New

Patriotic Party (NPP), the Peoples National Convention (PNC) and the Convention Peoples Party (CPP), were selected for this study because of their size, composition, organizational strength and level of participation in all the general elections that have been held since the 1992 transition.

The central objective of the study was to examine the role of political parties in Ghana's democratic development, particularly during the country's democratic transition and consolidation processes. Since political parties and elections are central to the promotion of liberal democracy, it is important to examine how the dominant political parties that have consistently participated in the 1992, 1996, 2000 and 2004 elections have contributed toward the promotion of free and fair elections and strengthened Ghana's electoral system. Apart from the promotion of free and fair elections, other aspects of the parties' contribution to democracy that will be examined in the study are participation and how they have enhanced representation in the country's post-transition era and contributed to the consolidation of Ghana's liberal democracy. A secondary objective of this study was to examine how political parties are organized in terms of the organizational and structural characteristics of political parties in Ghana, such as membership recruitment, how they promote participation in candidate selection and internal party democracy.

Many democracy theorists in Africa have often overlooked the significant impact party organization has on democratic development and the importance of issues such as how political parties are organized, how election campaigns are financed, and how election procedures and practices are followed by political parties and ruling governments. Despite the immense role political parties play in Ghana's democratic development, they have structural and organizational problems such as lack of internal party democracy and participation in decision-making and candidate selection processes, as well as the concentration of power in the hands of the parties' leadership. This relates

to the marginal role played by the grassroots members in the rural and urban areas, as opposed to the dominant role played by the affluent and well-educated in Ghana's party system. For example, lack of internal democracy was one of the factors that led to the disintegration of the Nkrumahist CPP political tradition into fragmented parties during Ghana's Second, Third and Fourth Republics. This problem is more pronounced in parties like the NDC, in which one person identifies himself as the owner of the party. Based on the issues raised, the study focuses on two main questions, namely, how do political parties contribute to Ghana's democratic development? And how are political parties in Ghana organized? The questions posed in the study are interrelated and have significant impact on Ghana's democratic consolidation process, and therefore, will be discussed in detail in the subsequent chapters to show how well the parties have contributed to strengthening the party system and Ghana's democracy in general.

Chapter Outline

In line with the research questions discussed above, the study is divided into the following chapters:

Chapter two starts with a review of the literature on democratic transition and consolidation theories, based on the different perspectives on some of the main factors for a democratic transition and consolidation. The chapter further discusses some key theoretical arguments and explanations on party development to serve as a prelude to the empirical evidence on political parties' activities in Ghana. Analyses of the theories show some of the arguments raised by various theorists about the underlying factors shaping democratic transition and consolidation processes, and party development in Ghana. These theories are of key relevance to the study because they provide a basis for a critical analysis of the questions raised in the study. The chapter also discusses the methodology and sources of data used in the study.

Chapter three discusses the background to Ghana's democratic transition. It begins with a brief analysis of Ghana's post-independence political economy and the emergence of the PNDC government to power and some of the problems posed by the authoritarian regime to the development of the party system and Ghana's democratic system in general. This inevitably led to internal and external pressure on the PNDC to re-introduce democratic rule in Ghana. It also discusses civil society's contribution to democratic development in Ghana and its role in destabilizing democracy under various constitutional governments especially in Ghana's second and third republics. The chapter also provides a historical perspective on the development and the roots of Ghana's party system, party traditions and ideologies and a discussion of the contribution of the political parties in the transition process through the activities of some members and groups loyal to the defunct political parties to oppose the authoritarianism of the PNDC. The chapter also examines the role of the external pressure exerted by Ghana's international donor countries and organizations on the PNDC to democratize the state. All these factors immensely contributed to the introduction of the decentralization system in 1988 and eventually helped to facilitate the re-introduction of democracy in Ghana in 1992.

Chapter four discusses the role of political parties in Ghana's transition to democracy and in the 1992 and 1996 elections, preparations made toward the 1992 election, and some of the basic problems encountered during the election process that led to the opposition parties' boycott of the parliamentary election. The chapter further looks at the mechanisms and major changes that were implemented prior to, and during the 1996 election to bring the parties back to the negotiating table, and how the Electoral Commission (EC) managed the 1996 elections to put Ghana's democracy back on track and eventually made the 1996 election relatively peaceful and successful. Examples of these changes are the establishment of substantive electoral institutions, the formation of the Inter-Party Advisory committee (IPAC) by the political parties in collaboration with

the EC, and the introduction of election monitoring by some civic groups. Finally, some of the main problems that continued to hinder Ghana's democratic development after the 1996 election are also examined.

Chapter five focuses on the role of political parties in the 2000 and 2004 elections, with regard to how the political parties have contributed toward consolidating Ghana's democratic system. Apart from the role of the political parties, there are other alternative explanations for Ghana's effort in moving toward democratic consolidation. The chapter examines the role of non-party factors such as the role of the EC, and CSOs in Ghana's democratic consolidation process by discussing the new policies that were implemented by the EC after the 1996 election to make the 2000 election and power alternation that followed a success, and placed Ghana's democracy on the path to consolidation. The chapter further discusses the successes of the 2004 election and the efforts that are being made by the political parties, the EC and CSOs to consolidate the country's democratic system. The last section of the chapter focuses on the reasons for the success of the 2000 and 2004 elections to show how far election processes in Ghana have significantly improved since the 1992 transition, and some of the problems that still need to be addressed by the EC, civil society, the government and political parties, to further enhance the conduct of elections in Ghana.

Chapter Six discusses Ghana's political parties' structure and internal organization. While the party system has gained roots in Ghana, particularly in the last decade, many democratic analysts of Ghana's party system have not critically examined their structure, organization, and sources of funding. The chapter therefore discusses the structure and organization of the political parties in Ghana's Fourth Republic in terms of their membership drives. It further examines the level of participation of the party members with regard to the extent to which the political parties have promoted participation and inclusiveness in decision-making processes. The chapter also examines

the level of internal democracy within the political parties and how the parties have followed democratic principles in their internal organization, such as in the selection of leaders and parliamentary candidates within the political parties that are the main agents of democracy in Ghana. It also discusses some of the main challenges and variations in party development and organization in Ghana. The chapter further discusses how parties solicit funding, the sources of funding available to them and the rules governing their fundraising activities.

Chapter seven examines the political parties and MPs role as representatives of the people and their relationship with their constituents and society in general and the level of participation and inclusiveness in the parties. While the relationship between the parties, MPs, the state and society has improved significantly since the 1992 democratic transition, there are many outstanding issues such as the relationship between members of the respective parties, media/party relations, the role of MPs in their constituencies, state institutions/parties/society interaction. Strengthening state/society relations in Ghana continues to pose some major challenges, despite the country's transition to democracy almost two decades ago.

The concluding chapter discusses some of the major findings of the study in comparative perspective, the role of parties in democratic consolidation and how democratization strengthens the party system, as well as the concluding remarks. The findings from the research will hopefully contribute to the scholarly literature and practice of democracy in Ghana and other new democracies in Africa as well as the developing world in general.

Chapter Two

Theoretical Framework

Review of the Literature on Democratic Transition, Consolidation and Party Development Theories

Introduction

This chapter focuses on the theoretical perspectives on democratic transition and consolidation of the fledgling third-wave democracies in the developing world. The 1990s witnessed the proliferation of democratic transitions in Africa, Latin America, Asia and Eastern Europe. Contemporary democratic theorists such as Samuel Huntington and Robert Dahl's concept of polyarchy emphasize electoral competition, participation and a set of basic rights as the yardstick for an electoral/liberal democracy. Hence they measure democracy as a political system based on periodic free and fair multiparty elections through universal adult suffrage; the existence of freedom of speech, the press, and association; and respect for human rights and the rule of law. Democratic theorists also base their views on institutional standards, such as the enactment of constitutional provisions through which the government and politicians are required to uphold and abide by a clear separation of powers through checks and balances, the independence of the judiciary and the key role of parliament in the legislative process. Some theorists on Africa's democratic development such as Richard Sandbrook and Mamadou Diof argued that despite certain inherent limitations, the liberal democratic system ensures certain rights even to the underprivileged, since it promotes freedom, the rule of law, representation and pluralism. Writing on democracy in Africa, Michael Bratton and Donald Rothchild also argued for the existence of some basic elements such as an electoral system, democratic political institutions, a transparent legislative system and independent courts in order to determine how democratic a society is. Another fundamental argument put forward by proponents of the liberal democratic view is that political parties are key instruments for promoting democracy and serving as a link between the government and the people. Political parties are thus regarded as the main agents for mobilizing people for participation in elections, and for aggregating the peoples' interests in the formulation of public policy. Since elections are central to liberal democracy, the role of political parties in ensuring free and fair elections, and in democratic transition and consolidation is indispensable.

The first part of the theoretical framework focuses on the debates put forward by democratic transition theorists on the factors that paved the way for democratic transitions in most developing countries at the turn of the twenty-first century. One issue that democratic theorists have grappled with since the 1990s is identifying the factors that facilitated the transitions in the third-wave democracies in Africa and the developing world in general. While one group of theorists attribute the third-wave democratic transitions to the agency of political parties, other theorists regard external donors and civil society as the main agents for the transitions. Apart from the arguments put forward by transition theorists, consolidation theorists have also grappled with the basic requirements or standards to determine whether the new democracies are on the path of consolidation or consolidated. It is therefore necessary to analyze the democratic transition and consolidation theories as a framework for the empirical evidence in chapters three, four and five.

Since the role of political parties in democratic development constitutes an important feature of this study, the second section of the chapter also discusses the literature on party development in terms of the factors that are crucial for the development of a political party. For this reason, theories of party development are discussed as a framework for the empirical information in chapters six and seven. These theories are central to the study, since they set the framework for analysis of the empirical evidence in the subsequent chapters and provide a basis for a critical analysis of Ghana's democratic system and its consolidation process. The chapter concludes with a discussion of the methodology, in terms of the research design, techniques employed and how the study resolved the problems that arose in the course of the research as well as sources of data used in the study.

Comparative Theoretical Perspectives on Democratic Transition and Consolidation

Democratic Transition Theories

Democratic transition and consolidation are two phases of political transformation and involve multifaceted processes. A democratic transition occurs when a democratic government replaces an authoritarian regime. This process may be partial, such as in a situation where the authoritarian rulers reserve some powers for themselves and/or share power with the new civilian administration, or take part in the transition process and assume control of power after the transition, as occurred in Ghana in the 1992 transition. In a full transition, the military is fully subjected to the new civilian administration's control. As Juan Linz and Alfred Stepan noted, a democratic transition is completed only when the freely elected government has full authority to design and

implement new policies, and thus the executive, legislative and judicial powers under the new democratic government are not constrained by law to share power with the military. Hence one of the main challenges that faced the third-wave countries in their agitation for multi-party democracy was how to force the authoritarian regimes to change the political system to democratic rule and defeat the incumbent regimes in elections in order to achieve a successful and full transition. As Guillermo O'Donnell noted, democratic transition is the stage of regime change that ends with the establishment of a civilian democratic government. The following literature on the third-wave democratic transitions in the 1990s shows the diverse views that have been expressed by various theorists on the factors that successfully facilitated these political transformations in many countries in the developing world.

Combined Confrontation and Negotiation Theories

The combined confrontation and negotiation theorists such as Nancy Bermeo and Andreas Schedler argue that political parties were instrumental in the third-wave democratic transitions. According to this school of thought, the successes of the third- wave transitions were due to a combination of negotiations and successive confrontations between the supporters of the opposition parties against the authoritarian regimes. For example, some transition experiences in Africa and Latin America such as in Ghana and Mexico, show that a combination of cooperation and confrontation strategies between the opposition and the ruling parties promoted democracy in these countries since both opposition negotiations and confrontations, as well as pressure from civic groups, increasingly opened political spaces for the opposition parties and the public.

In the case of Ghana, while parties were banned by the PNDC, supporters of the parties organized into civic associations such as the Movement for Freedom and Justice (MFJ) and the Alliance of Democratic Forces (ADF), to oppose the PNDC regime and to push for the re-introduction of multi-party democracy. For example, confrontations between the supporters of the opposition parties and civic groups in Ghana and Mexico against the PNDC and Institutional Revolutionary Party and (PRI) ruling governments respectively, attracted international attention and compelled the authoritarian regimes to agree to negotiations with the opposition parties. As Schedler noted in the case of Mexico, the combination of "cooperative and conflictual strategies" through negotiations and street mobilizations allowed the opposition parties in Mexico to gain some concessions from the PRI government under Presidents Salinas and Zedillo, which inevitably strengthened the opposition's electoral competitiveness and helped the National Action Party (PAN) to break the PRI's electoral stranglehold in the 2000 elections. In a similar way, negotiations and confrontations enabled the opposition parties to extract concessions from the ruling P/NDC in the 1990s and led to the NPP's 2000 election victory in Ghana.

Whereas this theory offers a plausible explanation for the third-wave transitions in terms of the strategies that were adopted by the opposition political parties to gain concessions from the incumbent authoritarian regimes, it failed to take into account external pressures, which created the enabling environment for the opposition parties and civic groups in their struggle for political spaces and concessions. Hence the road to democratization in the third-wave transitions, such as in Ghana, Mexico and South Africa was made possible by authoritarian regimes and opposition parties bargaining dynamics, which was facilitated by external donor influences and often occurred in the form of behind the scenes negotiations. This enabled the opposition parties to restrain some of the incumbent authoritarian regimes' monopoly of political power. Faced with growing social and political pressures, the regimes bowed to the opposition parties' demands for a return to democratic rule by paving the way for multi-party elections. This study argues that unlike the case of Mexico and South Africa, Ghana has a different transitional experience in terms of the extent to which political parties in Ghana were directly involved in the transition process. Due to the ban on political parties by the PNDC regime, parties played limited roles in the process of securing multi-party democracy during the transition process. Nonetheless, supporters loyal to the banned parties formed pro-democracy movements to oppose PNDC rule. Hence the role of the supporters of the banned political parties was instrumental in restoring multi-party democracy in Ghana.

Institutional Theory

Whereas the confrontation and negotiation theories argued that parties were instrumental in the democratic transition, some institutional theorists such as Juan Linz and Alfred Stepan attribute the third wave democracies to the agency of civil society. They argued that at all stages of the democratization process a vigorous and independent civil society with the capacity to generate political alternatives and monitor government policies and accountability is invaluable because they not only help start and push transitions to their completion, but also help consolidate democracy. One predominant school of thought put forward by democratic theorists such as Robert Putnam is that a strong civil society forms an essential foundation for the transition and consolidation of fledgling democracies. In *Making Democracy Work*, and *Bowling Alone*, Putnam argued that membership in civic groups helps individuals to better socialize and interact as well as mobilize to achieve societal socio-economic and political goals, such as the use of mass protests in reversing authoritarian regimes restored to multi-party democracy and bringing about governmental accountability. Theorists such as Guillermo O'Donnell, Philippe C. Schmitter and and Lawrence Whitehead recognize the crucial role of civil society in bringing down authoritarian rule and in building pressure for democratic transition in many African and Latin American countries. Some African democratic theorists who support the institutional theory such as Emmanuel Gyimah-Boadi, Mamadou Diouf and Jean Francois Bayart also attributed the shift toward democratization in Ghana and other African countries mainly to the resurgence of civil society. They argued that grassroots or popular political action were the fundamental reasons for the democratic resurgence in Africa. In this regard, the decisive role of civil society as a reaction to political repression and human rights violations led to increased resistance and an end to authoritarian rule in many of the third wave transition countries. Civil society played an enormous role in the process of securing the third-wave democratic transitions through various strategies of confrontation, street demonstrations and negotiations. For example, in Ghana, members of the MFJ and other pro-democracy groups were instrumental in ending PNDC authoritarian rule. The theoretical perspective on the role of civil society in democratic development shows that the unprecedented resurgence of civil society is a major development in the expansion of the third wave democracies in Africa. African civil societies have emerged as key forces for democratic change and public empowerment. Perhaps no single factor more readily contributed to the resurgence of the third wave democracies than the contribution of resurgent civil societies in mobilizing society to resist, and ultimately helped to overturn military domination in politics.

In spite of the significant role civic groups play in the third-wave democratic transitions, they could also serve as a destabilizing force to democratic development. Whereas advocates of civil society have widely applauded it as the foundation of stable and vigorous democracies and the main agency in the third-wave democratic transitions, another school of thought promoted by some democratic theorists such as Thomas Carothers and Omar Encarnacion argued that civil society could obstruct and/or destabilize democratic development. As Encarnacion noted, in the absence of strengthened and reliable state institutions, a revitalized civil society "can be a major source of chaos, social unrest, political instability, and even antidemocratic behaviour. "The role of some civic groups in supporting authoritarian regimes to destabilize democratic governments shows that regardless of the immense positive roles that civic groups play in democratization, they can have both positive and negative influence on a country's democracy, depending on their interests and orientation. As Robert Fatton noted, while civil society is a potential liberating factor, it can also be politically undemocratic and incapable of replacing the state in the provision of public goods. It is not the all-encompassing movement of political empowerment as portrayed by its advocates. In support of these views, Rita Abrahamsen also noted that although civil society is generally regarded as a check on state power that curbs authoritarian practices and corruption, it cannot be seen as inherently democratic or undemocratic, rather, its character may vary across time and space.

Although the intensification of civic groups' activities through resistance to authoritarian rule in many developing countries was instrumental in pressuring the authoritarian regimes to democratize the state institutions, the role of the external forces, such as the World Bank and some developed countries like the United States were highly important in forcing the authoritarian regimes to comply with the popular request for democratic governance. This study argues that both the internal and external factors served as important catalysts in promoting democracy in the third-wave transition countries. These combined strategies to loosen the authoritarian regimes' control over power show that it is inadequate to attribute the third-wave democratic transitions that occurred in many developing countries to a single theory. While it is apparent that some civic groups played destabilizing roles in the process of developing democracy in the third-wave countries, there is no doubt that civil society was very instrumental in most of the transitions that occurred in the developing world.

Negotiated Transition Theory

Another view advocated by some negotiated transition theorists such as Adam Przeworski, Guillermo O'Donnell, Philippe C. Schmitter, Stephen Haggard and Robert Kaufman attribute most third-wave transitions to the agency of the elites in the incumbent authoritarian regimes and the opposition parties. Rather than focusing on the initiatives of civil society, the negotiated transition or structural theory, also termed the agency approach, sees democracy as created by conscious, committed actors, such as elites, who either compromised voluntarily or were forced by internal and external pressures to introduce multi-party democracy in their respective countries. A 1986 analysis of democratization by Philippe Schmitter, Guillermo O'Donnell and Lawrence Whitehead, titled *Transition from Authoritarian Rule,* became the key reference for transition studies. This study focused on the processes of democratization by examining the negotiations and bargains reached between authoritarian leaders on the one hand, and the donors, civil society and opposition parties on the other hand. According to this school of thought, transition and consolidation occurs when there is either a sudden "elite settlement" or an "elite convergence," which turns disagreement over basic political rules into consensus and structural unity. Hence agency-centered perspectives have devoted relatively little time to the analysis of civil society and socio-political struggles in the resurgence of the third-wave democracies. As Jean Grugel noted, many of the transition perspectives take a rather vague attitude to the role of civil society in democratization and regard civil society as unimportant for democratic transition and consolidation. For example, Przworski argued that in some cases, popular mobilization has been detrimental to democratization since it threatened the interests of powerful elites who then went to considerable lengths to close down the tentative experiments in political liberalization.

The negotiated transition theory's main argument is that internal political structures, such as the authoritarian regimes themselves were the main instruments of third-wave democratic transitions. Under such circumstances, opposition parties and civic groups demand for political reforms or change of government only buttressed the negotiations between liberal elites in the government or those who were in favour of a return to multi-party democracy on the one hand and conservative elites, or those who desired to preserve the status quo on the other hand. This is often possible when reformers in the ruling government who are willing to change the status quo are stronger than conservatives, who may want to maintain the status quo, and when there are stronger moderates than radicals in the opposition. In this regard, the ruling government manages to preserve its power by controlling the transition processes. For example, prior to Ghana's transition there was a break up in the PNDC, since there were those who favoured a return to multi-party democracy and the adjustment policies, and those who opposed these goals. This led to divisions and break up in the composition of membership in the PNDC. The key role played by the PNDC in the transition process also helped the regime to preserve its power after the transition.

Theorists such as Charles Hauss have termed the situation whereby democratic transition occurred due to the "joint action by elites in the authoritarian regime and opposition groups as the "hurting stalemate". In this case, the two sides – ruling and opposition parties – come to realize that neither can win without negotiations, because the benefits of negotiating far outweigh the cost of continuing the confrontation. As a result, both parties recognize that they need to cooperate with the other to attain a smooth and peaceful transition. Other theorists like Linz have termed the process whereby the elites in power took the lead in bringing about democracy as "reforma." Without doubt, negotiations and political pacts between the authoritarian regimes and the opposition parties set the pace for the landmark power alternation that brought the opposition parties such as the NPP in Ghana, National Action Party (PAN) in Mexico, Senegalese Democratic Party (SDP) in Senegal, African National Congress (ANC) in South Africa, and National Alliance Rainbow Coalition (NARC) in Kenya, as well as the People's Democratic Party (PDP) in Nigeria, to power.

The main strength of these theorists' argument is that it was due to incremental structural changes made by the elites in the authoritarian regimes that led to democratic elections in many of the third-wave transitions. One of the weaknesses of the negotiated transition theory is that it partly explains some of the fundamental negotiations and arrangements that were put in place to facilitate the reforms and transition processes in some of the third-wave democracies. Nonetheless, the theory does not fully explain the pressures from the international bodies, opposition parties and civic groups as well as confrontations that were brought to bear on the authoritarian regimes, which compelled them to institute democratic reforms in the respective countries. While negotiations by elites in the authoritarian regimes and opposition parties contributed to the transition process, it did not constitute the main driving force behind the transition. For example, a combination of elite negotiations and pressure from civic groups, and Ghana's donors compelled Rawlings to give up power, after his two terms in office.

Undoubtedly, democratic reforms benefited some incumbent authoritarian regimes, since it reduced the number of street protests against the authoritarian regimes, and helped to legitimize their rule, as well as improved their relations with the opposition parties and other domestic opponents such as civic groups. In my opinion, the theory does not fully explain all the factors that led to, and accelerated the democratic reforms and transitions in the third wave democracies since it ignores the international pressures and the role of the political parties and other local actors such as civil society organizations. Rather than gradual voluntary top-down changes by the incumbent governments, a more plausible explanation for the third-wave transitions is the combination of international pressure and domestic agitation by the opposition parties and civic groups that were not taken into account prior to the negotiation phase, which greatly restrained the authoritarian regimes from impeding the evolving democratic transformation.

Internationalist Theory

Some internationalist or interventionist theorists such as Samuel Huntington and Francis Fukuyama argued that changes in the international political economy in the 1980s, such as capitalism's triumph over socialism led to the end of the Cold War coupled with the economic crisis of the 1980s in the developing countries led to the third- wave democratic transitions. The thrust of this argument is that the crisis in the international political economy in the 1980s provided the impetus for increasing demands

by the developing countries for financial assistance from the IMF and the World Bank and some developed countries like the United States and Britain. The donors, in turn, increasingly took advantage of this opportunity to increase their demands on recipient countries to adopt multi-party democracy as a precondition for financial aid. In many of these countries, the structural adjustment policies imposed by the IMF and the World Bank led to major internal political crisis and social pressure on the authoritarian regimes, which led to the intervention of the international financial institutions (IFIs). In response to the internal and external demands for multi-party democracy, a set of preconditions from the IFIs were instituted to facilitate democratic development in the developing countries that experienced the third-wave democratic transitions. For example, in the late 1980s and 1990s, the constitutional assistance policies, which were introduced by donors such as the IMF, the World Bank, the United States and Britain, were based on political conditionalities alongside the promotion of macro-economic policies, for the purpose of integrating developing economies into the global economy. These policies became the yardstick for financial assistance that was brought to bear on many developing countries ruled by authoritarian regimes, compelled them to change to multi-party democracy.

Constraints of Neo-liberalism as a Weakness of the Internationalists' Theory

Whilst all the above theories explain the democratic transitions in the third-wave countries from different perspectives, the most contentious issue in the arguments about democratic transition is the internationalist theory and the role of the external donors in the third-wave democratic transitions. Since the internationalist theories focus on the donor countries and organizations' influence in the third-wave transitions, it is necessary to discuss the negative impacts of their effort to promote democracy in the developing world. While the international donors have played significant roles in promoting democracy in developing countries, they have also served as agencies through which Western political and economic interests are promoted. One critical issue is the extent to which the third-wave governments are free from subordination to the donors' influence and the perception that their relationship with the donors is not based on principles of democracy, partnership and transparency. Despite the international donors' efforts to encourage democracy, their role is undermined by the desire to promote the free-market capitalist system in the developing world. Some critics of neo-liberalism such as William Graf pointed out that while pressure from foreign donors has promoted democratic development in the developing world, the form of democracy that is being promoted in countries such as Ghana is tied to the ideology of capitalism. Abrahamsen also termed this trend of promoting neo-liberal policies alongside the promotion of democracy as "disciplining democracy".

This study argues that the new democratic governments, such as Ghana's are put under extreme international pressure from the IFIs and the advanced capitalist countries to promote free market policies alongside democratic systems of government. For example, the World Bank's view of "good governance" is guided by a narrow meaning of governance, which requires recipient governments to reduce corruption, decrease the public sector workforce and vigorously pursue market-led policies. Theorists such as Barry Gills and Joel Rocamora argued that liberal democratic regimes are always to some degree capitalist oriented systems because production and distribution of goods are determined mainly by the free market system rather than by the state and there is significant private ownership of the means of production. The IFIs argued that the implementation of SAP could help resolve the growing developing countries' payment deficits, reduce poverty and bridge the gap within and among nations hence, countries that implemented SAP policies tend to be better off than those that did not implement adjustment policies.

While the IFIs praised Ghana for having experienced unprecedented economic growth and being the most successful case of structural adjustment in Africa, the adjustment policies created serious development problems for the country, such as decreasing standards of living, augmented unemployment rate, increasing poverty and inequalities, and reduced access to basic services. This was due to the failure of the donors to invest an equal amount of capital in programs that could promote equity and social justice in Ghana and other new democracies. Recipient countries like Ghana are pressured to open their economies for close integration into the global capitalist system. Thus, "neo-liberalism defines the ideological and institutional parameters of democratic development. "As Kathleen Schwartzman noted, the current multiparty democratic system seems to be more conducive to the creation of an enabling environment for the implementation of capitalist policies in developing countries. Whereas, at the macro level, SAP policies achieved some level of success in Ghana, at the micro level, the implementation of SAP was a failure because it brought undue hardships to the people.

As John Dryzek noted, democracy within the liberal democratic state is partly a means of inducing recipient countries to accept the dominant political and economic order. The influence of neo-liberalism in Ghana's democratic system has immensely influenced the policy agenda of political parties in Ghana. Like parties in many developing countries, in contemporary times, rapid changes in the world economic systems and international political economy from the 1980s and 1990s have affected policies of parties and governments irrespective of their ideology. While there has been some improvements in the government's policy-making machinery since the transition, there is a perception that social and economic policies implemented by Ghana and other third-wave countries' are based on neo-liberal principles, such as financial and market liberalization, privatization and fiscal discipline, which are purposely designed to serve Western economic and political interests and the interests of global capital. Party leaders interviewed on the issue of donor influence on government policies also reinforced the view that the continued linkage of democratic reforms to economic liberalization and the influence of the donors over the country's domestic and foreign policies often restrict the government's policy agenda. Despite the promotion of the interest of global capital, however, there is no doubt that external initiatives and influences by the donors' played very significant roles in Ghana and other developing countries' transition to democratic rule and the various bilateral and multilateral donors' initiatives continue to contribute immensely to Ghana's democratic consolidation processes.

Another problem with the internationalist/intervention theory is that while it argues that the regimes were forced by external influences to make political concessions to the opposition parties and the public, in most cases, as it occurred in Ghana, the transition processes were ultimately designed and controlled by the ruling governments.

One criticism of the internationalist view is that while it effectively addresses the role of the external factors, it failed to acknowledge the role of the internal agents of democratization, such as the pro-democracy and human rights oriented civic groups, and activities of the members of the then banned political parties, all of which aroused international concern. In spite of the controversies surrounding some of the theoretical perspectives on the third-wave democratic transitions, some of which have already been discussed above, it could be argued that all the arguments put forward by the various transition theorists regarding the role of civic groups, political parties and the international donors greatly contributed toward the successful democratic transition in the third-wave countries.

Democratic Consolidation Theories

Another major challenge that faces new democracies after a successful transition is the consolidation of democracy. In the 1990s the consolidation of democracy became the principal focus for research in terms of how political culture, institutionalization and other factors shape democratic outcomes. Democratic consolidation is the strengthening of democracy to a point where it becomes unlikely that anti-democratic forces can interrupt the democratic process. Thus a democratic regime is consolidated when all politically significant groups regard its key political institutions as the only legitimate framework for political contestation, and adhere to democratic rules of the game. In situations where most conditions of consolidation are met, democratic consolidation normally follows democratic transition. As Larry Diamond noted, democratic consolidation is thus a process of completing regime change or cementing the transition, which involves not only agreement on the rules for competing for power, but also fundamental and self-enforcing restraints on the exercise of power. Democratic consolidation is thus an important concept of democracy and an essential political goal for the fledgling third-wave democracies in the developing world because it shows the extent to which a countries democratic system is stabilized, and how far the democratic culture is deeply rooted in all political actors and the people within the society. Democratic consolidation thus requires various processes of political change, institutional reforms and change in the political culture of the people.

The main distinction between transition and consolidation is that the transition process is the building of the foundation of democracy, during which the democratic system is not well established, and the consolidation stage is when democracy becomes firmly rooted in the society's political culture, in which all political actors obey laid down democratic principles and procedures and accept them as the only way to change the government. In *Problems of Democratic Transition and Consolidation*, and also in *Themes and Perspectives*, Linz and Stepan offer a conceptual framework for consolidation, which entail stabilizing the behaviour and attitudinal foundations of democracy through which democracy becomes routinized and deeply ingrained in the society's social, institutional, and even psychological life. They argue that democratic consolidation is a discernible process by which all political actors must come to regard the laws, procedures and institutions of democracy as the only viable and legitimate frameworks for seeking and exercising political power to govern the society, and aggregating the people's interests. At this stage, democracy as a complex system of institutions, rules and procedures becomes "the only game in town".

While it is possible that in a consolidated democracy, there may be problems of governance, widespread disapproval of the government's policies, a major breach of the constitutional provisions or intense conflict between political opponents in consolidated democracies, it does not lead to any political or social actors' attempt to derail the democratic process by undemocratic means. Rather, all actors in the society and the public in general overwhelmingly believe that democratic procedures and institutions are the most appropriate ways to govern or to change the ruling government. Linz and Stepan categorizes the process of democratic consolidation into a number of variables, namely attitudinal, behavioural, institutional and constitutional levels. In this regard, a consolidated democracy is best understood not as a regime, but as an interacting system comprising five major interrelated areas, namely, a free and lively civil society, a relatively autonomous political society, the rule of law, a usable bureaucracy, and an institutionalized society each of which is influenced by the others. Democratic consolidation is advanced by institutional, behavioural, attitudinal changes and other factors discussed below. In this regard, a variety of interconnected and mutually reinforcing conditions have to be met for a democracy to be consolidated. Among these are the behavioural dimension, the attitudinal level, the constitutional level, promoting legitimacy of the government, institutionalization of the political system and other factors that facilitate party development.

Behavioural Dimension: The State, Institutions and Regime Performance

One of the requirements for democratic consolidation is meeting the behavioral dimension, which involves strengthening of the state and its institutions, intensification of its relations with society and improving its performance. At the behavioral dimension, social organization by social and political groups and their participation in decision- making processes is promoted and not hindered by political actors. One model termed the influence relations between government institutions and society, or intra-societal relations model advocated by theorists such as Plasser, Ulram, and Waldrauch argues that it ensures the concrete implementation of basic civil liberties and political rights. The behavioural level focuses on the practice of the rule of law and the degree to which security forces respect human rights, as well as the practices of state institutions, which aim at curtailing pluralism by excluding certain parties and interest groups from political participation. The relations between society and government institutions model also relate to a situation in which the elites and the public internalize the democratic principles and understand that elections are the central and inevitable channel of influencing political decision making. As Grugel noted, a consolidated democracy is one that has institutions that translate citizen preferences into policy, have effective states that act to protect and deepen democratic rights and principles, and count on a strong participatory and critical civil society, and in which these frameworks are firmly routinized and widely accepted by all political and civil actors. Democratic consolidation also describes adaptations of performance and attitude such as the effective functioning of the state and its institutions in order to stabilize the basic principles of democracy. Its goal is to strengthen and safeguard democratic institutions under conditions of democratic competition and thus reduce insecurity. For example, one of the crucial and commonly overlooked areas of state strengthening in Ghana and many third-wave democracies that hinder democratic consolidation involves the administration of justice by the judicial system and especially how state institutions such as the police that are charged with maintaining law and order carry out their duties and responsibilities to the state and to the people in general.

At the institutional level, the state should have administrative institutions in their functional and/or organizational dimensions because a state that has the administrative capacity to perform the essential functions of government such as maintaining law and order, constructing infrastructure, and defending the national borders plays a crucial role in democratic consolidation. As Linz and Stepan argued, a state with "a usable state bureaucracy" strengthens it for effective policy implementation and successful economic reform. Unless the behaviour of public officials are constrained by a network of laws, courts, independent review and control agencies as well as civil-society norms of transparency and accountability, democracy will be diminished by political abuse and cynicism, and political actors will fail to commit themselves to the rules of the game. Where weaknesses in state structures precede the end of the authoritarian regime, as was the case in Ghana, state building often emerges as a central challenge for democratic consolidation. In such a situation, state institutions, and the rules and procedures that promote democratic values must be developed and strengthened. Due to the institutional weaknesses of many third-wave countries, theorists such as Jack Snyder argued that there is a need to delay democratization until there are well-developed parties and state institutions. While this view may have some credence, it must be noted that it is not a valid argument because many of the third-wave countries have made effort to develop their institutions after the transition to democracy. For example, since Ghana's democratic transition, there have been consistent efforts to develop and strengthen its political institutions and procedures, which have greatly contributed toward its democratic consolidation process.

One other important aspect of the behavioral level of democratic consolidation is regime performance. This concept measures how successive governments under democratic regimes produce sufficiently positive policy outputs to build broad political legitimacy by designing and implementing policies that meet the needs and interests of the people, and for which the government was given a mandate to rule. This also helps to enhance a government's authority and prevent resistance to its legitimacy. Some democratic consolidation theorists such as Diamond argue that combating corruption is a major challenge to regime performance in the process of democratic consolidation, which requires political institutionalization and an effective civil society. According to Diamond, democratic consolidation must also address the challenge of strengthening three types of political institutions. These are the state administrative apparatus or bureaucracy, the institutions of democratic representation and of governance, which are influenced by the political parties, the legislature and the electoral system. They also include structures that ensure horizontal accountability and constitutionalism as well as the rule of law, such as the judicial system and oversight agencies to audit the activities of governmental institutions. Thus, strengthening political institutions should not only be based on capacity building and resource allocation, but also designing policies that fit the country's circumstances and meet the peoples' political and socio-economic interests as well as aim at eradicating administrative and political corruption.

Attitudinal Level: Promoting Socialization, Trust and Cooperation

Democratic consolidation also requires an increase in trust and cooperation among political competitors, and a socialization of the general population through education and involvement of civil society to shape citizen attitudes. The importance of the intra-social model to democratic consolidation leads to one key variable in political culture, which is trust. Theorists such as Diamond, Whitehead and Dahl discussed the central importance of civil society as a driving force behind democratic consolidation. Hence democratic consolidation requires the emergence and a shift in the peoples' democratic political culture. As the democratic transition process advances, a wide range of political actors assume democratic behavior, which leads to a transition from instrumental to principled commitments to the democratic framework in which deliberate efforts are made to promote growth in trust and cooperation among political competitors, and socialization of political actors and civil society. As Plasser et al noted, trust has an integrated effect because it widens the scope of action and serves as an incentive for political parties to cooperate. Some democratic theorists such as Putnam argued that the emergence of a rich civic culture is indispensable for democratic consolidation since it leads to the development of trust relations. While democratic cultures may vary across countries in terms of the extent of the level of internalization of democratic values by the society, unless democratic institutions embrace such broadly shared norms such as political trust, tolerance, willingness to compromise, and above all, belief in democratic principles, those institutions will be vulnerable to breakdown whenever a political crisis arises. The importance of trust and tolerance as part of the democratic political culture, and the willingness of all political actors to cooperate is invaluable to democratic consolidation. For example, during the initial stages of Ghana's transition, mistrust and suspicion among the political parties led to the opposition parties' disillusionment in the transition process and refusal of support by the parties and the public for the democratic process. These developments culminated in the opposition boycott of the 1992 parliamentary election, which almost derailed the democratic process. Hence manifestations of the declining public support for democracy could lead to increasing threat to democratic stability. However the increase in trust and cooperation among the political parties and civil society in Ghana has led to the stabilization of the country's democratic system and contributed to its democratic consolidation process.

Constitutional Level: Strengthening Civil-Military Relations, Legitimacy and Institutionalization of the Political System

The constitutional level requires the acceptance of the constitutional provisions and the new government by all political actors. One of the most critical issues in democratic consolidation is the need for civilian control of the military and the establishment of cordial civil-military relations. When a country has a long tradition of military intervention such as in Ghana, it is often a difficult challenge to consolidate democracy. Nonetheless, recent trends in many third-wave countries in Africa show that

they have made significant in-roads in the process of consolidating their democracies. As Huntington noted, many third-wave democracies have handled civil-military relations better than what they have achieved in other challenges they face and civil-military relations in these countries generally are in better shape now than they were under the previous civilian regimes. Democracy cannot be consolidated in many third wave countries, unless the military is subordinated to the civilian government and the latter promotes good governance and the civilian government respects and honors deserving military personnel for their service to the state and provides the military with good salaries and logistical resources.

In Diamond's view, establishing civilian control over the military is a complex and typically a protracted process, requiring many of the factors that promote democratic consolidation in general, which include skilled political leadership, unity among political parties' actors, across the partisan divide on national security matters is also vital for maintaining the legitimacy of a ruling government. For example, while there is the challenge of democratizing civil-military relations in Ghana to reduce the likelihood of a military coup, the NPP government has so far, successfully implemented policies such as demobilizing and disarming paramilitary and security forces set up under the PNDC/NDC governments, as well as restoring professional discipline in the armed forces. Besides, the government has strengthened intelligence work in the civilian-run defence and the national security departments, and restricted the military to their professional duties and peacekeeping assignments. Civilians have replaced military officers in high profile positions, there are limitations on political involvement and other

constraints have been imposed on the military to curtail military abuses of human rights, which was prevalent under the PNDC regime. All these measures contributed to the government's success in subordinating the military to civilian control.

In addition, the emergence of security sector specialists and civil society organizations such as the African Security

Dialogue and Research in Ghana and other countries in Africa have greatly enhanced civil-military relations in the third-wave democracies in Africa. For example, a 2000 study on the state of civil-military relations revealed that in general, civilians appreciate the role military is currently playing in protecting the territorial integrity of the country and for ensuring peace and security, as well as ensuring political stability. The study shows that 84% approved of a standing army, 69% were impressed with the character of a Ghanaian soldier, and 90% approved of the military's role in international peacekeeping. Some local and international non- governmental bodies work in partnership with the Ghana government to organize workshops and seminars to train and educate the armed forces. This trend toward enhancing military ethics and professionalism as well as strategies to subject the military to civilian control is increasing progress toward strengthening civil-military relations in Ghana and many third-wave democracies in Africa.

The constitutional level of democratic consolidation also requires that all relevant political actors accept the constitution of the state and its provisions as the guiding principle for ruling the country and as the only means through which the government can be changed. In many of the newly introduced democracies in the developing world such as Ghana, strengthening civil-military relations and subjecting the military to civilian control have major implications for legitimacy. Most theorists of civil–military relations such as Diamond and Huntington focus on legitimacy as their level of analysis of

democratic consolidation. They argued that the best way for a democratic regime to deter a coup is by governing effectively and maintaining broad legitimacy. In this way, all political actors regard the constitution as the only framework for governing the country and the only means through which a legitimately elected government could be removed from office. The importance of legitimacy to democratic consolidation is evident in the necessity for all the opposition parties and the military to accept the election results and the authority of the new government. The level of a government's legitimacy shows the willingness of the political parties, the military and other actors in the society to cooperate with the government to protect the democratic system and to promote the stability of the newly established political system. Lack of legitimacy could have negative consequences on democratic consolidation and could result in undemocratic forces taking over power.

Legitimacy also implies abiding by the rule of law and legal frameworks as the basic principles on which the state is governed. Abiding by the principles of democracy such as respect for civil liberties and the rule of law thus help promote the government's legitimacy. Unless the state, military and people in the society are constrained by laws, courts, and an independent judiciary, there will be lack of political and social justice in the administration of justice. The issue of legitimacy also means that democracy can thus be consolidated when no significant collective actors challenge the legitimacy of democratic institutions or regularly violate its constitutional norms, procedures, and laws. Despite the fact that there may be opposition to the promotion of democracy from marginal undemocratic groups, especially in the military, where the overwhelming majority of the people, elites and civic groups support the democratic system and believe that the political system is worth obeying and defending, it helps facilitate the process of consolidating democracy. Hence the deeper and more universal the belief in democratic

legitimacy and commitment to abide by the rules of the democratic system, the higher the possibility that democratic consolidation will occur successfully. This study argues that democratic consolidation involves internalizing the norms and procedures of democracy so that actors routinely conform to rules of the game, even when it conflicts with their interests or they are faced with intensely political competition.

Another prerequisite for democratic consolidation is institutionalization of the political system and political parties because they play significant roles in democratic transition and consolidation processes. Since political institutionalization is crucial for the democratic consolidation, strengthening the formal representative and governmental structures of democracy also helps them become more accountable and thus more effective in the discharge of their duties to the people. In the view of Plasser, Ulram, and Waldrauch, institutionalization is central to the entire process of democratization because the type of government that preceded an authoritarian regime, its institutions, and internal organization could serve as valuable elements of continuity after the transition. Their regime model focuses on a schematic representation of the levels of behavioural stabilization during the consolidation process. This model shows different behaviour patterns such as the relations on the level of government institutions, in terms of the stabilization of procedures in government institutions in accordance with democratic principles to promote accountability between the executive, parliament and judicial bodies. This insulates the democratic system from turning into what O'Donnell termed a "delegative democracy," a situation where the executive branch of government refuses to cooperate with other branches of government to promote responsible governance. Whenever such a situation arises, conflict between the branches of government could result in the derailment of the democratic system by authoritarian enclaves. As Diamond noted, by defining clear and workable rules of the game to which contending political actors can credibly commit themselves, and by establishing more authoritative proficient and dependable structures for mediating political conflicts and concerns, institutionalization enhances trust and cooperation among political actors, for competing parties to tolerate one another. One issue of great importance in the context of institutionalizing political structures is internal democratic practices of the parties and cooperation among the parties. Apart from lack of a strong state and civil society, one of the main obstacles to democratic consolidation is an institutionally weak political system and political parties, where parties lack clear programmes, autonomous organization, strong linkages to society and social groups, and are unable to build strong networks and support base. This study argues that political parties have very positive impact on the democratic consolidation, hence the more political parties in Africa are democratic, the better the chances of consolidating the third-wave democracies across the continent. As Hofferbert noted, the structure, organization and performance of political parties are some of the most vital aspects of the road to democratic consolidation. For example, institutionalization of the parties in Ghana has led to the strengthening of the major political parties and contributed toward accelerating the country's democratic consolidation.

This study further argues that the democratic consolidation process is intrinsically interwoven with the strengthening of political parties and the promotion of internal party democracy in the third-wave democracies in Africa. Some of the processes that could foster consolidation are the move toward recurring patterns of political behaviour, which involves the internalization of common rules and procedures of political competition and action. Besides intra-party democracy, another major feature of consolidation is the need for inter-party cooperation and consensus to help stabilize the democratic political culture. Both ruling and opposition parties in the new democracies must be committed to preserving the democratic gains made during and after the transition to shield the democratic system against infringement of democratic values by anti-democratic forces. Parties must respect democratic principles and be loyal to the democratic system. Where parties are not fully committed to sustaining the democratic system, there is the tendency for abuse of power and electoral malpractices that could lead to non-democratic elements such as the military to derail the democratic process. For example, in Ghana, one of the major steps taken by the political parties to enhance inter- party cooperation is the establishment of the national party chairperson's caucus, in which the chairperson's of the political parties meet to discuss issues of mutual interest and settle their parties' differences. The growing efforts by political parties and pro- democracy civic groups toward consolidating Ghana's democracy, as well as the current support from the international donors to prevent military intervention and derailment of the democratic process attest to the brighter prospects of building the capacity of the political parties and consolidating democracy in Ghana.

Examining the Democratic Transition and Consolidation Theories

The diverse theoretical perspectives on democratic transition and consolidation show that in the last two decades, democratic transition and consolidation in Africa have attracted numerous studies, which mainly address the conditions for democratic transition and consolidation. The diverse views expressed by the transition theorists show that the third-wave democratic transitions and political reforms did not occur through one single variable, but a multiplicity of interwoven factors, which are internal and external in

nature. It would thus be inappropriate to argue that one single theory adequately explains the factors for the resurgence of the democratic transitions in the third-wave countries in Africa, because all the factors discussed by the above transition theories played significant roles in Ghana and other third-wave countries' transition processes. The theoretical framework also shows the critical role of civil society in democratic transition. Civil society occupies a central position in the third wave democratic transitions in the developing world. Civic groups greatly influenced the breakdown of the authoritarian regimes' hegemony over power in many developing countries and are helping in the consolidation of the third-wave democracies. These roles by civic groups also show that while in one context the function of civil society complements the role of the state, in another sense, it has an adversarial relationship with the state, which at times constitutes an important battleground in which the struggle for 'hegemony' over power is waged. This study argues that while civil society played key roles in the transition processes, political parties have been the major instruments of consolidation in the third-wave democracies.

My observations regarding the theoretical perspectives on democratic consolidation show that there are a number of disagreements regarding the viewpoints expressed by the various democratic theorists on the basic standards to be met before a fledgling democracy could be considered consolidated or on the path toward consolidation. The differing theoretical perspectives on the conditions necessary for democratic consolidation show a lack of consensus on the appropriate standards for consolidation. Whereas Linz and Stepan base their theory on both the behavioural and attitudinal variables, others like Diamond and Przeworski use single variables to explain their theories on consolidation. In Plasser's conceptualization, transition is about making sure that the behavioural and attitudinal adaptations of consolidation actually relate to the basic rules of democracy. This implies that if transition remains incomplete and some minimal criteria are not met, it will be difficult to achieve democratic consolidation without further changes in the basic rules. Linz and Stepan also argue that consolidated democracies need to have five interacting arenas to reinforce one another in order for such consolidation to exist. Whereas Plasser et al confirms Linz and Stepan's view that whatever is being consolidated must also conform to the minimal criteria of democracy, Schmitter has counter-argued that while the five factors identified by Linz and Stepan are important in democracy, they do not state clearly whether the creation and stabilization of these five factors are the only prerequisites for consolidation. Another issue with the theories is the difference in Schedler and Diamond's criteria for meeting the conditions for consolidation. Schedler highlights a number of conditions to be met to qualify a new democracy as moving on the path to consolidation. These are popular legitimation, the diffusion of democratic values, the neutralization of anti-system actors, civilian supremacy over the military, the elimination of authoritarian enclaves, party building and institutionalization, the organization of functional interests, the stabilization of electoral rules, the routinization of policies, the decentralization of state power, and the introduction of mechanisms of democratic values and judicial reform, as well as the alleviation of poverty and economic stabilization. Diamond also argues that strengthening state capacity, liberalizing and rationalizing economic structures, securing social and political order while maintaining basic freedoms and the rule of law, and improving horizontal accountability as well as controlling corruption go a long way to improve governance directly and help the process of democratic consolidation. This study argues that while some of these conditions may not be accomplished before a country's democratic system is set on the path of consolidation, as was the case in Ghana, they help accelerate the democratic consolidation process.

Additionally, while the main variables of democratic consolidation proposed by Burton, Gunther and Higley are the characteristic focus on the uniquely decisive role of elites in consolidation, other theorists such as Diamond equates consolidation with the attitudinal dimension, emphasizing the creation of legitimacy and distinguishing between democratic deepening on the behavioural level, and the process of consolidation. One problem with using legitimacy alone to determine consolidation is that even if legitimacy of a government is widely accepted, a small group can still pose a threat to the effort to sustain and consolidate democracy. Przeworski also builds his concept of consolidation exclusively on behaviour by questioning the explanatory relevance of normative convictions for the survival of democracy. He argued that democracy must generate substantive outcomes by offering all the relevant political forces real opportunities to improve their material welfare. In this regard, the basic tenets of democratic consolidation require democratic institutions to be fair and give all the relevant political forces a chance to win from time to time in the competition of interests and values. They must also be 'effective' and make even losing under democracy more attractive than a non-democratic alternative. In contrast to Diamond and Przeworski's views, Plasser et al counter-argued that Przeworski's argument failed to explain why some democracies collapsed due to serious economic crisis, while others did not; and although Diamond's "deepening" concept is closely related to consolidation, his view on democratic consolidation misses the crucial step between the recognition of the legitimacy of democracy in principle and its actual stabilization through democratic behaviour. Another area of disagreement among democratic theorists is the turnover test as a yardstick for consolidation. According to Pasquino, the mere fact that party elites have accepted, as a fundamental rule of the game, the process of alternation in power should be considered as an indicator of progress toward consolidation. While this view is based on the "one turn over rule," and is supported by theorists such as Przeworski, other theorists such as Huntington demonstrate this with the concept of the "two turn-over test". Furthermore, whereas theorists such as Diamond are of the view that legitimacy is the decisive variable and indispensable for democratic consolidation, others such as O'Donnell have questioned whether a lack of legitimacy is the same as a lack of consolidation and instability or whether it has a causal effect on consolidation. Some African democratic theorists such as Gyimah-Boadi also argued that African countries have not reached the threshold of democratic consolidation required in Huntington's minimalist formulation, that is, several peaceful electoral turnovers and alternation of power; and certainly none has reached the higher threshold of having all key political actors accept democracy as "the only game in town" in which a reversal is widely regarded as inconceivable. While this assertion may be valid to a certain extent with regard to some new democracies in Africa, this study argues that Ghana's

democracy is moving along the path of consolidation. Although there are still problems such as police and judicial corruption, nonetheless, major progress have been made in the way of institutionalizing the political system and democratic structures as well as harmonizing civil-military relations through various strategies by the state to influence all political actors and the society to accept the democratic political culture. Additionally, many of the issues that Ghana's democracy faces, such as minor election problems and inefficient electoral procedures, are not unique to one country, since such flaws are present in some Western democracies as well. For example, recent elections in the United States since 2000 have shown that similar problems hinder the practice of free and fair elections and electoral systems even in some developed countries.

It is apparent from the above discussion that a number of characteristic challenges confront democratic consolidation in new democracies, but the depth of these challenges varies across countries and regions. In the case of Ghana and many African countries that experienced long periods of military rule, neutralizing the power and influence of the military has greatly helped in the democratic consolidation process, but due to past experiences with military coups, the threat of military intervention has not completely been eradicated. Another issue is the lack of accountability in state institutions such as the police and judicial services to the constitutional provisions. In a situation where the state building challenge is compounded by significant ethnic divisions, as in many third-wave democracies in Africa, it becomes very necessary to construct democratic consolidation by implementing inclusive policies that give all citizens and groups political equality. As Mishler and Rose noted, for new democracies to be consolidated, their citizens must increasingly orient themselves toward the ideals and practices of democratic politics and it must achieve deep, broad, and unconditional support among the mass public as well as political elites. Institutionalizing political parties in Ghana could help build stable party systems and accelerate the country's democratic consolidation process. For example, Ghana's democratic consolidation has been facilitated by the emergence of relatively strong and effectively institutionalized political parties such as the NPP and NDC to serve as bulwark against a ruling government's encroachment of power. Regardless of all the issues discussed, in the African contest, preventing military intervention and establishing cordial civil-military relations is one of the key issues and a major challenge that face the consolidation of many third wave democracies in Africa. While the absence of organized groups that attempt to undermine democracy has been a crucial factor in democratic consolidation, especially in Ghana, the process of consolidating democracy in many third-wave democracies in Africa cannot be completed until the military becomes firmly subordinated to civilian control and solidly committed to the democratic system. Since regime sustainability over a long term is one of the criteria for consolidation, it is plausible to argue that Ghana's democracy is moving towards consolidation or well on its way to a successful consolidation and support for regime stability from the donors has persisted over the years. However, continued progress toward "full democratic consolidation" can further reinforce the resilience of the regime, and fortify it against destabilization in the future. It is apparent from the discussion of the democratic transition and consolidation theories that democracy cannot be thought of as consolidated until a democratic transition has been brought to a completion. As Linz and Stepan noted, a necessary but by no means sufficient condition for the completion of a democratic transition is the holding of free and contested elections based on broadly inclusive voter eligibility that meet the institutional requirements for elections. Normally, after a democratic transition is completed, before democracy can be set on the path of consolidation, certain conditions must be met such as people's attitudes must be re-oriented toward the promotion of the democratic political culture. As Plasser, Ulram and Waldrauch noted, since transition and consolidation usually overlap, decisions on the formal structure of core democratic institutions influence the behavioural and attitudinal components of consolidation, especially among elites. For example, many fledgling democracies such as Ghana continue to make changes to its institutional and legal frameworks in order to advance its democratic system toward consolidation.

Based on the views espoused by various democratic theorists and Ghana's recent democratic experience, this study argues that the process of consolidating democracy could be measured by the practice of free and fair elections, power alternation from an incumbent government to an opposition party and maintaining a stable political system through checks and balances as well as respect for rule of law and civil liberties. It also entails the maintenance of law and order in the society, the existence of strong political parties to actively participate in elections and parliamentary proceedings as well as how successfully and effectively the military and other anti-democratic forces are subjected to the new civilian government. While the theoretical framework on democratic transition and consolidation discussed above present characteristics that are relevant to the empirical evidence in the subsequent chapters of the study, placed in comparative perspective, each theory standing alone does not adequately explain all the variables of democratic transition and consolidation. In spite of the differences in the various theoretical perspectives on democratic transition and consolidation, together they contribute to our understanding of some of the factors that contributed to the third-wave democratic transitions and provide us with valuable knowledge on the prerequisites to be met by a new democracy in order to set it on the path of consolidation.

Party Development: A Conceptual Framework

Models and Concepts of Party Development

Party development rests on the concept of 'party organizational structure' and 'membership'. Different party development theorists have expressed diverse views on party development models. Four main party development models can be discussed in this section, namely, Duverger's 'Mass Party', Epstein's 'Electoral Party', Kirchheimer's 'Catch–All Party' and Katz and Mair's 'Cartel Party' models. In the mass party model, a party's organization is defined largely according to its relationship with civil society, and its organizational strength is measured primarily in terms of the size of its membership. In this model, party structures are also assessed mainly in terms of the modes of internal representation and accountability. Hence parties with large membership and internally democratic structures are able to organize better than those with small membership or that is not internally democratic. For example, in Ghana, the NPP and NDC parties that are able to organize nationwide have more members and supporters than the CPP or PNC, and the NPP that is more democratic internally is able to organize more effectively than the NDC. Some of the weaknesses of the mass party model is, it is characterized by a one-way, bottom-up control/representation system because party leaders rise from the

support of the people and are controlled by the people. This study however argues that this criticism is of less relevance to the effective organization of a party because that is what the promotion of accountable party structures, governmental institutions, internal party democracy and effective party organization is all about.

Alternative models of party development propounded by Leon Epstein, Otto Kirchheimer, and Angelo Panebianco have led to the decline of the mass party approach. In contrast to the mass party centered argument and the exclusive concern with the relationship between parties and civil society, Kirchheimer and Epstein's analysis of party organization in America and Western Europe produced an alternative view, based on the differentiation between electoral and non-electoral parties. Such a differentiation derives from approaching parties in terms of their activity. They argued that since parties provide a basis for electoral choice, structuring the vote involves a vast educational and campaigning apparatus. The validity of Kirchheimer and Epstein's views is that mobilizing voters for a party's cause in modern democracies for electoral victory is one of the important functions of political parties and party supporters, especially in many of the third wave democracies such as Ghana. In this regard, parties that are able to canvass for more support and votes are more likely to emerge as the winners and those that have lesser reach and appeal to the public end up losing in elections.

These developments, according to Kirchheimer, gave rise to the emergence of a new party model, the "catch-all" party. The "catch-all" party model advocated by Kirchheimer argues that the emergence of a new middle class with a homogenized mass culture and the development of the mass media have enhanced parties' capacity to reach a wide electorate, which affects all arenas of party organization. In the organization-to-

voter arena, the "catch-all" party set the scene for a new type of relations. The need to appeal to wide cross sections of the community meant that parties had to move away from their strict ideological-based policies to the center of the political spectrum in order to attract more voters besides their traditional sources of support from voters loyal to the party. For example, in Ghana, despite the differing ideologies of the parties, the desire to win more supporters and votes has made the parties move to the center of the ideological divide and to embrace the 'catch-all' model strategies. For this reason, all the major parties have adopted a mixture free market system and social development as their policy agenda in order to win more support and votes.

Katz and Mair have also devised a model on the basis of the relationship between parties and the state by disaggregating the party into three different categories, namely, the party in public office, the party on the ground and the party in central office. According to Katz and Mair, a variety of social, economic and political developments have facilitated the emergence of the cartel party model. They argued that wherever a cartel party is not certain of sustaining their electoral strength or winning enough support to be re-elected, the party leaders have tended to exploit state power and institutional manipulation in order to achieve their goals. For example, as shown in the next chapter on the background to Ghana's transition and the 1992 elections, in the initial stages of the transition, the NDC party exhibited cartel party characteristics by employing strategies such as hindering the operation of other parties and their members' activities, and restricting freedom of speech to shape voters' preferences.

The party development models discussed highlights the need for party leaders in Ghana to modify the parties' organization and electoral strategies in line with societal changes, and the need to accommodate and adjust their parties' organization to these changes. It also reinforces the view that leaders of the political parties' need to ensure that majority of members of the parties are fairly represented and involved in all aspect of the parties' organization. If parties are socially unrepresentative, members at the grassroots level will be less willing to fulfill their role as recruiters of supporters in the communities to generate electoral support for the parties, which could possibly alienate some potential voters of certain parties. Hence it is possible that lack of internal democratic procedures in a party's organization could lead to limited voter support. Another important feature of the party developmental models relates to their

tendency to explain organizational forms and changes in a historical context. That is, economic and socio-political developments are considered key determinants of organizational modes of activity and their transformations are often formulated on the basis of a pre-defined conception of democracy. In his discussion of party structure, organization and institutional frameworks, Richard Hofferbert argued that party development is conditioned by factors like institutional and constitutional design; hence the structure and performance of parties are key facets of the democratic polity. In this regard, the concepts of party institutionalization, party behaviour, organization and representation functions as well as democratization and the activities of democracy- oriented

CSOs constitute some of the indispensable aspects of party development.

Party Institutionalization and Party Development

Many studies on party development contend that party institutionalization is a major necessity for party development, which forms an important feature in the design of democratic institutions, especially in terms of representativeness and inclusiveness.

Writing on party development, Huntington defined 'institutionalization' as "the process by which organizations and procedures acquire value and stability". Low levels of institutionalization of the parties could result in a lack of competitiveness and reduced civic engagement in the parties. Parties, according to Panebiaco, can primarily be distinguished based on the degree of institutionalization they attain. As the way the party organization strengthens, institutionalization can be measured based on two levels. The premise for measuring a party's level of institutionalization is the level of interdependence and participation among its internal actors as well as its and representativeness and intra-party coherence. Two ideal types of political party institutionalization emerge from Panebiaco's conceptualization. That is, centralization of power by the party leadership leads to a low level of interdependence and lack of unity often characterizes a weakly institutionalized party. Also, a highly institutionalized party with a high degree of interdependence offers its members a relatively high level of cooperation and participation. For example, Ghana's parties can be categorized into different levels of institutionalization. In their discussion of party development, Joseph La Palombara and Myron Weiner argued that a party must have an organizational structure and make membership drive efforts, set up local units, seek electoral support from the general public and play a part in political recruitment, as well as be committed to the capture and maintenance of power, whether alone or in coalition with others. Rose and Mackie also suggested that to become institutionalized is to merit recognition as an established party, which requires parties to establish a cross-local organization to contest elections nationwide and consistently nominate candidates at successive elections. Analysis of institutionalization of political parties in Ghana is demonstrated in chapter six under party organization in the discussion of the NPP, NDC, CPP and PNC parties.

Party Organization and Representation Functions

Party organization constitutes another important feature of party development. Two broad types of party organization models can be identified namely, the exchange model and development model. Exchange models have their origins in Anthony Down's economic analysis of the vote-seeking behaviour of parties, his analysis focus on the trade-off between the freedom of action enjoyed by the party leadership and the constraints, which derived from maintaining a strong and active party membership. Exchange models are based on the theory of power as relational, asymmetrical and reciprocal, and as an exchange relationship or trade-off between party leaders and party members. As Moshe Maor noted, the exchange models are essentially related to a swap between the rewards party members get from the party leadership and the constraints the party leaders impose upon the rewards in return. Party leaders and members have mutual interest in mechanisms that allow party leaders to make credible compensation to the members by integrating them into the decision-making process to enhance intra-party democracy. Intra-party power relations in this sense manifest themselves in an unbalanced negotiation conceived as an unequal exchange in which the party leaders get more than the grassroots members, but are compelled to give something in return.

Strom's exchange model also focuses on the mechanism of exchange between party activists, who seek ways to control the party to ensure that they get what they have been promised by the leadership, and a leadership that wants to make certain that activists contribute what is required to solicit votes, such as vote canvassing and their active participation in campaign activities. The exchange model is based on the conception of political parties as office-seekers led by party leaders because they expect to benefit from their role. For example, as shown in party organization in chapter six of the study, whereas leaders of the various political parties in Ghana play dominant roles in the parties' organization, the grassroots supporters of the parties play subordinate roles in the parties' organization and in decision-making. Sharing decision-making powers with the members and enabling them to participate in party activities enhances their role in the party and their prospects for upward mobility as well as leadership accountability, so that the party can attract a broad spectrum of support in the society.

The representation role of political parties is also equally important in party development. As William Chandler and Allen Siaroff noted, "parties operate as the crucial intermediaries linking the state and society. The most basic function is that of representation involving the translation of public opinion to political leaders."Vickey Randall and Robin

Theobald summarize the role of political parties in party development in terms of representation and organization into four main functions as follows:

1. Political parties legitimize regimes by providing ideologies, leadership or opportunities for political participation, or a combination of the three;

2. They act as the medium for political recruitment, thus creating opportunities for upward social mobility;

3. Parties also provide opportunities for the formation of coalitions of powerful political interests to sustain government through interest aggregation, have major influences on policies in the process of designing programmes, supervise policy implementation, political socialization or mobilization of people to undertake self-help activities; and

4. They provide political stability in societies that are able to absorb increasing levels of political participation by the new social forces generated by modernization.

Other theorists such as Rod Hague, Harrop Martin and S. Breslin argued that apart from vote seeking and power maximization goals of a party, membership recruitment, interest aggregation and influencing government are among the major representation functions parties fulfill in a democratic system to promote party development. Party organization and representation thus constitute some of the integral aspects of party development.

Party Behaviour and Party Development

One important issue to address in this section on party development is party behaviour. That is, how political parties function, their organizational strategies, and what motivates party behavior. Two broad categories of explanations for party development fall within this framework of analysis. The first relates to the ideological aims of the party, which argues that it is the party's aims and objectives that represent its most characteristic features and are most influential in shaping its structure, organization development. The second view, which is termed the minimal definition, describes a party as an organized group and an association oriented toward political goals that attempts by its actions to maintain the status quo or to change the existing social, economic and political conditions by means of influencing the achievement or conquest of political power. As Maor noted, these views are clearly based on principles that a party is a group that pursues goals, and second, a party's ideology is the best indicator of its goals. The weakness of the first view is that it presupposes that all parties are goal- oriented groups and have clear-cut policies. As Panebianco rightly noted, it simplifies an issue that is problematic in the theory and practice of the party system. For example, since Ghana's democratic transition in 1992, two kinds of concerns have emerged over the organization and structures of the various political parties and their institutional frameworks. The first concern deals with the internal organization of political parties and their institutionalization. The second concern emerges from lack of intervention from the grassroots members and institutional frameworks within the parties, and civil society, especially at the grassroots level, which is due to the apparent large gap between the organizational incentives of the party leaders and the grassroots supporters. The leaders of the various political parties control power and resources and distribute patronage to the members at the lower levels. Apart from this, issues like unfulfilled promises, lack of elected representatives' involvement in community activities, lack of dynamic and competent leaders who are accountable to the electorate, as well as lack of strong institutions are some of the major problems highlighted by some party officials in all the political parties in Ghana during the study.

Arguing that the structure, organization, performance and behaviour of political parties are some of the most significant aspects of party development, David F. Roth and Frank L. Wilson also concluded that "parties in different political settings differ dramatically in the task they perform, their organization, their style of operation, and their relationships to the overall political unit". Whereas theorists such as William Cross argued that parties are responsible for aggregating citizen interests and articulating them in the political sphere, critics such as Patrick Dunleavy also argued that competition for power is the only mode of interaction between representatives of different social interests, thus failing to take into consideration other aspects of party behaviour such as negotiations, coalition building and alliances in policy-making. This study argues that party behaviour is assessed through a number of strategies. As an institutional process, political parties together with state institutions and civil society organizations play roles in the democratic process to promote participation, accountability and transparency in governance. Through the organization of political parties, members and party supporters are often guided by the codes of conduct that govern campaigning and election processes to prevent parties from intimidating voters from exercising their free choice. It also involves appropriate enfranchising of voters through a fair and efficient registration system. Through elected representatives, public officials and political institutions, parties meet communities' socio-economic needs in a fair and equitable manner, and serve as a bridge between civil society and government.

Analyzing the behaviour of parties in relation to their origins, David Easton discussed political party structure in relation to its development and behaviour. Maurice Duverger also outlined two models of party development, which can be internal and external in nature. He argued that parties with socialist background are based on non-

political grassroots organizations, while non-socialist parties are based on political grassroots organizations, which could also influence a party's behaviour. For example, whereas the NPP is based on political grassroots organizations and more democratic, the NDC has a socialist background and is less democratic. Its formation and organization was based on political organizations like the Workers Defence Committees (WDCs), Peoples' Defence Committees (PDCs), Committees for the Defence of the Revolution (CDRs) and the GPRTU. The differences in the organization and behavior of the two parties confirm Duverger and Easton's view that parties are profoundly influenced by their origins and ideologies. The central objective of party activities such as competing and seeking power, and controlling policy-making in the state, as well as aggregating societal interests, as key aspects of party organization and behaviour has been indisputable in the above theoretical views.

Democratization and Party Development

Democratization is another important feature for party development because it helps in the building and strengthening of the legal frameworks and institutional capacity of political parties and state institutions. Democratization thus presents some of the crucial tools and enabling conditions needed for addressing the challenges facing party development and democratic consolidation in many third-wave democracies such as Ghana's. Democratization involves a complete transition from authoritarianism to a multi-party system of government and the exclusion of the military from sharing power with the civilian government. It requires democratizing the state, and its legal and institutional frameworks through the promotion of principles of freedom, justice, equality, the rule of law, respecting the constitution, and the electoral system. It also entails strengthening the institutions of government and making them accountable to the people and by creating an enabling environment for the popular participation as well as the presence of a vociferous civil society to serve as a check on state power. Democratization also involves instilling the democratic political culture in all civil and political actors to accept the standards of democratic procedures, rules and principles. When political institutions are democratized, it helps to accelerate party development because the improvement in party structures and institutions rests on the promotion of intra-party democracy and broad-based participation by party members at the grassroots level in all aspects of decision-making. Since the democratic transition in Ghana, there has been consistent effort by the political parties, the government, civil society and international organizations that have a stake in the country's democratic development to democratize the institutions of the state through the strengthening of the legal and institutional frameworks, electoral reforms, freedom of speech, respect for civil liberties and increasing the participation of the people in decision-making processes. The effort by governmental and non-governmental bodies to democratize the state and instill the democratic political culture in the people shows the importance of democratization not only in party development, but also in democratic consolidation.

Democratizing political institutions also helps to promote democratic principles and political culture among party members at all levels of the party structure. Democratizing the party system and state institutions involve using diversified strategies because democracy is multidimensional in scope, in terms of its structural, cultural and institutional phenomenon. As a structural process, it involves an organizational arrangement that removes all structural constraints that inhibit the participation of minority and other groups in all aspects of the political parties and governance in any democratic society. Culturally, democracy transforms some of the values of traditional societies by adopting principles of responsible government such as the promotion of multi-party elections, tolerance of opposition, freedom of expression, rule of law, and democratization of the institutions of the state. Meeting these requirements of democratization could help in the development of the third-wave democracies' political parties and accelerate their democratic consolidation processes.

Civil society also plays a significant role in democratization and party development. Their role in democratic consolidation includes socialization through building trust, and promoting social capital and social relations among citizens for social and political development. Through demonstration, confrontation, negotiation and partnership civic groups are able to achieve a united front to work toward achieving societal demands on the state, and influence government to address issues that are of importance to the people. Hence, civil society forms part of the social infrastructure of society that makes the generation of trust possible, and makes it easier for trust relations to develop among the people to help strengthen democracy. As Putnam rightly noted, civil society promotes social trust and solidarity that greases the wheels of democracy. Civil society continues to influence government decisions in the socio-economic and political spheres in Ghana and other new democracies in Africa. Through civic groups' "watchdog" function they are able to ensure a certain degree of government and state institutions' accountability to the general public. For example, the activities of the media and other civic groups in Ghana help monitor public officials to be more circumspect of their actions by questioning their undemocratic behaviour and keeping them in check against abuse of power. Civic groups also play important advocacy roles in democratic development to promote issues that affect the interest of communities and the general public, and help to enhance citizens' socio-economic and political rights. Through partnership and negotiation, they influence state policies to address socio-economic issues. Civil society is thus seen as the main contributory factor that facilitates successful democratic governance, and party development, as well as improving institutional performance.

Analysis of the Party Development Theories

One major manifestation of the above theoretical perspectives is the fact that a number of factors such as party institutionalization, organization and behaviour influence party development in diverse ways. Parties are the means through which members are offered opportunities for mobility in the party and government at the national and local levels that would otherwise not be easily available to others who are not party members, and also facilitate competition for votes and power. There is no doubt that political parties play significant roles in every democratic society in terms of promoting the interests of their members, strengthening state/society relations and aggregating the interests of the people through policy making. Political parties also help in shaping public policy by generating information to the public, raising the electorate's political awareness, and promoting government accountability. Strengthening political parties to function effectively in these roles, and democratizing the political system and institutional structures of the state helps in strengthening the party system and invariably contributes to party development.

In taking the various theories on party development into cognizance, it could be argued that although not all-embracing, they offer an in-depth analysis of the role of political parties and political institutions in party development. Integrating Ghana's post-transition experiences in party development in terms of party institutionalization and internal organization with the literature on party development strengthens our discussion and

understanding of the party development theories because they help confirm which arguments apply to Ghana's transition and consolidation processes and which ones are not applicable to the country's democratic development. Thus the theoretical views on democratic transition and consolidation, and party development will be used to discuss the empirical evidence in the subsequent chapters by analyzing the information gathered from primary and secondary sources. These include interviews, questionnaires, direct observation and published materials relating to parties' structure, internal organization, and their role in elections, as well as their representation functions, in order to assess party development and its relationship to democratic consolidation.

Methodology

From September 2004 to June 2005, I conducted interviews with leaders of the political parties at the national, regional, district/constituency and unit/ward levels, some government officials such as Ministers, Members of Parliament (MP) and District Chief Executives (DCE), as well as some leaders of the civil society organizations. While there are many facets and issues in Ghana's democratic development, the study specifically focused on party development and the role of parties in Ghana's democratic development, which I believe makes a case for a new study in this area. The study relied mainly on the case study methodology with some attention to the cross-unit method of research design. For methodological purposes, a case study is best defined as an in-depth study of a single unit, where the researcher's aim is to explain features of a larger class of similar phenomena to shed light on a question pertaining to a broader class or unit. There are a number of advantages of using case study as the dominant research methodology over cross-unit analysis. The case study occupies an important position in

the discipline of political science and social science research in general. As John Gerring noted, when examining correlative relationships or proximate causal relationships, the case study format is apparently less problematic and is often highly informative and descriptive in orientation. One of the primary virtues of the case study method is the depth of analysis that it offers. It is necessary to point out that the case study method is more detailed than the cross-unit analysis. For example, while a cross-unit study might be satisfied to explain the occurrence of a democratic transition in a country, a case study of democratic transition in that same country might also strive to explain specific features of that event such as why it occurred, when it occurred, the way that it did, as well as factors that led to the event. Case studies commonly afford multiple observations of a single case, thus providing firmer evidence of the factual accuracy of a given proposition than would be possible in the analogous cross-unit study. The collection of original data is typically more difficult in cross-unit analysis than in case study analysis involving greater expense, difficulties in identifying and coding cases, and learning foreign languages. Theorists such as Gerring argue that the case study design blends with any social scientific theoretical framework including behaviouralism, rational choice, institutionalism, and interpretivism. The case study thus affords the researcher the opportunity to apply multiple observations of a single case in order to provide firmer evidence of the factual accuracy of a given proposition. What most clearly differentiates the case study from cross-unit study is its way of defining cases, not its analysis of these cases.

It is also important to note that single unit studies provide cases that are likely to be comparable to one another than multiple unit analysis. In a graphical structure, the case study occupies a tenuous ontological ground midway between ideographic and nomothetic extremes, which shows comparability of potential units and the utility of case study research design. The number of cases employed by a case study may be small or large (N), experimental or observational, synchronic or diachronic, and consequently, may be evaluated in a qualitative or quantitative fashion. The case study typically presents original research in some sort and using the case study method offer the researcher the opportunity to study a single unit in great depth that constitutes one of the primary virtues of the case study method. A case study of Ghana contributes to our understanding of democratic transition, consolidation and party development as a whole, since it examines the details of the concepts, which large-N literature may overlook.

In the same token, the study's treatment of several different parties, the role of parties in democratic transition and consolidation, and parties' internal organization shows a variation and allows for some pattern-matching or Millsean types of causal inference. For example, the study of Ghana's political parties and the process of its democratic transition and consolidation lead to generalizations about similar democratic developments in other third-wave democracies in Africa such as Nigeria and South Africa. As a result, it probably offers better evidence for an argument about the re-introduction of democracy and the development of the party system in Africa than for an argument about the developing world in general. Due to the similarities in the countries' cultural, political and socio-economic experiences, the situation in many African countries can be comparable to one another. In this regard, the study of Ghana's democratic transition and consolidation processes can be understood as a study of how a more general phenomenon in Africa occurred in one country setting. As Gerring argued, a case study is an in-depth study of a single unit or a relatively bounded phenomenon in which the researcher's aim is to explain features of a larger class of similar phenomena. Regardless of the usefulness of case study in social science research, there are some ambiguities that are weaknesses of the case study research design. Gerring discusses some of the ambiguities that hinder case study analyses, which are:

The problem of distinguishing different types of distinctive evidence; the blurry line between a unit that is intensively studied – the case study – and other adjacent units that may be brought into the analysis in a less structured manner; and when a single work combines single-unit and across unit analysis in a formal manner. Also, the argument that works generally share two empirical worlds; that the status of a work may change in the process of being analyzed by researchers; and the sort of argument that a case study is intended to prove or demonstrate.

It is important to note that both case study and cross unit methods have their strengths and weaknesses, and are all useful in research work. The two modes of analysis are interdependent. Cross-unit research may draw up a case study work and case study work may also include adjacent units. Hence both may be pursued, although not in equal measure but treated with equal diligence and recognition. The strongest conclusion by Gerring and other theorists is that single-unit and cross-unit research designs complement each other. In this regard, while case study is essential to social science research, it is important to employ a variety of methodologies in research. Having interview appointments with the officials of the various political parties, government officials and leaders of the CSOs in the research was generally not difficult. Prior to my departure from Canada to conduct the research, with the help of Internet sources, the Ghana telephone directory, and some political parties and government websites, I compiled a list of potential participants from among the political parties, public officials and CSOs. I contacted these groups of potential participants by electronic mail and telephone, informing them of my intention to interview them for my research project. Based on the positive responses I received from majority of the participants, I did not find it difficult to approach them in Ghana for the interview appointments. Additionally, I arranged before hand with the authorities at the University of Cape Coast in Ghana to affiliate with the Center for Development Studies (CDS). Based on this, a letter from the Vice-Chancellor of the university introducing me as a doctoral candidate from Queen's University and affiliated with the CDS also helped me a great deal in gaining easy access and the trust of many of the party leaders. I informed the identified participants by writing and/or by telephone, by email and personal contact to request their participation in the project, and to arrange for interview dates. Once the identified interviewees agreed to participate in the research, they were given letters of information and consent to read and sign before the interview. For the purpose of ethical considerations and since the subject under study is politically sensitive for open discussion, I sought the consent of the participants before the interviews. Party leaders, government officials and leaders of civic groups who were not comfortable with being identified were assured complete anonymity and have not been directly cited in this study. The study therefore identified all respondents who wished to remain anonymous throughout the chapters by code names to conceal their identities, while where the participants gave consent they were identified by their position or name. The codes indicate to the author the respondents' position, party or organization they belong to, location and date, as well as the serial number of the interview.

Interviews mostly took place at the national, regional and district offices of the political parties and other appropriate locations agreed upon by the participant(s). Before starting the actual interview process, I used a brief orientation session to explain to the participants the purpose of the research and what the information gathered in the study would be used for. This enabled the participants to familiarize themselves with the scope of information I needed from them. On the whole, the interviews went on smoothly and the reception was outstanding. Note-taking was the main interview approach used in the process of collecting relevant data for the study. My original intention was to conduct a survey of the participants and then follow it up with in-depth interviews of a smaller sub-sample of those surveyed. Due to my limited financial resources and the time limitations, coupled with the fact that many of the party leaders, MPs and Ministers had busy schedules, I noticed that such a strategy would not only inconvenience many of the participants, but also would take too much time and make it extremely difficult to accomplish my goals. In the course of the research, became evident after conducting a few interviews that the participants often unintentionally provided responses to questions that would have formed part of the comprehensive interviewing stage. I therefore

incorporated all my interview questions into one format and conducted in-depth interviews with the participants in a single appointment.

For the purpose of comparison, context and a wider scope of participants' views, and to have a broader reflection of representation of views in the study, the research was conducted in eight of the ten regions in Ghana and at least two districts from each of the selected regions. The reason for selecting eight regions was to give the research a broad coverage of the political parties and the Ghanaian society and also to ensure that the areas covered encompasses regions and constituencies where all the parties covered have representation. Also, due to the disparity in the support each party has in specific regions, to ensure that the data collected was representative, I ensured that participants from specific districts and regions where each of the major parties has strong support were included in the interviews. I further ensured that MPs of all the major political parties were interviewed based on the proportion of the number of their MPs in parliament. The participants were identified on the basis of the lists of leaders of the main political parties and major civic groups, which are available to the public. Approximately, two to five participants were drawn from each of the selected districts in the regions that were chosen for the study. On the whole, twenty questionnaires and eighty standard interviews with party leaders, government appointees and other public officials as well as twenty interviews with civil society officials were administered in the study. These involved specific questions to party leaders, organizers and paid party staff, MPs from the ruling party and opposition members of the four main political parties in Ghana – NPP, NDC, PNC and CPP, state officials, and civil society groups and organizations that have a stake in the promotion of democracy in Ghana. This helped to determine how inclusive and diverse the parties are, in terms of their ethnic and social composition, and internal hierarchy.

Various qualitative criteria can be used to assess party development and its relationship to democratic consolidation. These include, the level of participation in decision-making in the political parties and in public policy-making, the number of free and fair elections that have been successfully conducted, and how smooth and peaceful were the transition and power transfer processes to determine whether it passes the one turnover test suggested by some democratic theorists such as Przeworski. This study also argues that the main variable that connects the mass party, "catch-all" party and electoral party models of party development is their democratic conception, which distinguishes them from the cartel party model. Hence these party models are more appealing to the organization of Ghana's political parties and can be integrated into the Ghanaian case provided political parties in Ghana use the ideas expressed in these theories as yardstick and put them into practice in the parties' organization. Through the organizational strategies expressed by the "catch-all" party, the electoral party and mass party theories, parties in Ghana could gain more members and support from diverse groups across the country, such as the grassroots and middle-class supporters, as well as a combination of rural and urban-based supporters. Table 2. 1 below shows the regions and constituencies where interviews were conducted and some of the constituencies I observed the parties' campaign activities.

Table 2. 1. List of regions and constituencies covered and the number of party leaders interviewed

Parties	Regions	Selected Constituencies	Party Leaders Interviewed
NPP	Greater Accra,	Party Head Office, Accra, Tema East, Ga South, Ablekuma North, Ayawaso Central, Ablekuma South	5
	Central	Regional Party Office, Cape Coast, Assin North, Mfantsiman West, Agona East, Twifo/Heman/Lower Denkyira	5

Parties	Regions	Selected Constituencies	Party Leaders Interviewed
	Ashanti	Regional Party Office, Kumasi, Bantama, Subin, New Edubiase, Obuasi, Manhyia	5
	Eastern	Regional Party Office, Koforidua, Upper Manya	

		Krobo, Akim Oda, Suhum, Upper West Akim	4
	Brong Ahafo	Regional Party Office, Sunyani, Techiman North, Dormaa, Nkoranza, Berekum, Wenchi	4
	Western	Regional Party Office, Takoradi, Shama, Sekondi, Tarkwa-Nsuaem, Ahanta West, Mpohor-Wassa East	4
	Volta	Regional Party Office, Ho, South Tongu, Krachi, Ketu South, Hohoe North	4
	Northern	Regional Party Office, Tamale, Yendi, Salaga, Nanton, Bole, Wulensi	5
		NPP Total Interviews	36
NDC	Greater Accra,	Party Head Office, Accra, Tema East, Ga South, Ablekuma North, Ayawaso Central, Ayawaso East, Ablekuma South, Tema West, Ga North	5
	Ashanti	Regional Party Office, Kumasi, Bantama, Subin, New Edubiase, Obuasi, Manhyia	5
	Eastern	Regional Party Office, Koforidua, Upper Manya Krobo, Akim Oda, Suhum, Upper West Akim	4

Parties	Regions	Selected Constituencies	Party Leaders Interviewed
	Brong Ahafo	Regional Party Office, Sunyani, Techiman North, Dormaa, Nkoranza, Berekum, Wenchi West	4
	Central	Regional Party Office, Cape Coast, Assin North, Mfantsiman West, Agona East, Twifo/Heman/Lower Denkyira	5
	Volta	Regional Party Office, Ho, South Tongu, Krachi, Ketu South, Hohoe North	4
	Northern	Regional Party Office, Tamale, Yendi, Salaga, Nanton, Bole, Wulensi	5
	Western	Regional Party Office, Takoradi, Shama, Sekondi, Tarkwa-Nsuaem, Ahanta West, Mpohor-Wassa East	4
		NDC Total Interviews	36
CPP	Greater Accra,	Party Head Office, Tema East, Ga South, Ablekuma North, Ayawaso Central, Ayawaso East, Ablekuma South, Tema West, Ga North	3
	Central	Regional Party Office, Cape Coast, Assin North, Mfantsiman West, Agona East, Twifo/Heman/Lower Denkyira	2

Parties	Regions	Selected Constituencies	Party Leaders Interviewed
	Ashanti	Regional Party Office, Kumasi, Bantama, Subin, New Edubiase, Obuasi, Manhyia	2
	Western	Regional Party Office, Takoradi, Shama, Sekondi, Tarkwa-Nsuaem, Ahanta West, Mpohor-Wassa East	2
	Brong Ahafo	Regional Party Office, Sunyani, Techiman North, Dormaa, Nkoranza, Berekum, Wenchi West	2
	Eastern	Regional Party Office, Koforidua, Upper Manya Krobo, Akim Oda, Suhum, Upper West Akim	2
	Volta	Regional Party Office, Ho Central, South Tongu, Krachi, Ketu South, Hohoe North	2
	Northern	Regional Party Office, Tamale, Yendi, Salaga, Nanton, Bole, Wulensi	2
		CPP Total Interviews	17
PNC	Greater Accra,	Party Head Office, Accra	3
	Central	Regional Party Office, Cape Coast,	2

		Reional Party Office, Assin North, Mfantsiman West	
	Brong Ahafo	Regional Party Office, Sunyani, Techiman North, Dormaa, Nkoranza, Berekum, Wenchi West	2
	Ashanti	Regional Party Office, Kumasi,	2
	Northern	Regional Party Office, Tamale, Yendi, Salaga, Nanton, Bole, Wulensi	2
	PNC Total Interviews		11

Limitations of the Methodology

Despite the effectiveness of the methodology employed in the study, I wish to state that these methods have their own problems and weaknesses. It is necessary to point out that doing field research in any country poses some major challenges, which can be overwhelmingly frustrating when the setting for the research is in a developing country like Ghana, where logistical resources are scarce, technology is not well-developed in the

rural areas and record-keeping is poor. Due to the suppressive nature of past military governments' history, coupled with the resurgence of an inquisitive press in recent times, some people were reluctant to divulge information voluntarily for fear of being reprimanded by the party leaders, or feared that the information could be used against them by the press. I addressed this issue by assuring all the participants who requested to remain unidentified of their complete anonymity in the study. There is also the possibility that while some participants may have provided answers that they considered suitable to their views and their parties' position, it was also possible that some other respondents might have answered some questions in a way that they believed were expected and considered appropriate to the researcher. These problems were resolved by comparing the participants' responses with similar answers to the same question provided by other participants and ensuring that the sample of party leaders and public officials interviewed cut across ethnic, partisan, gender and social barriers. For example, about 40% of the participants were females. There was also the concern that some participants, especially some government officials and party leaders were not willing to openly express their views on some sensitive issues involving government policies and the internal organization of their parties.

Another weakness is the argument between qualitative and quantitative strategies, the subjective versus objective debate of oral testimony and the nature of memory and the extent to which an individual's testimony can be regarded as representative. For these reasons, while oral testimony is regarded as an effective tool for collecting information in research, it can also be misleading because there is the risk

of getting inaccurate or inconsistent information since a person may be reluctant to tell the researcher the unpleasant aspects of an issue that is not in the participant's or his party's interest, and may twist an issue or event to suit his/her party's interest or objectives. I addressed these potential problems however by basing the study on different research techniques and used several data sources. The advantages of using different techniques and sources in the research offered me the opportunity to crosscheck the information provided by the participants to confirm their responses and, above all, the other sources used helped to resolve the contradictions and weaknesses that might have cropped up from using one method. Another problem faced was that some high-level officials had busy schedules so there were occasional delays in the appointment. On some occasions, interviews were rescheduled, because of urgent matters arising from the participants' duties. I also addressed the problem of limitation of access to some archival records by using oral interviews with both present and past public officials and media reports to obtain the necessary information. In view of the weaknesses highlighted above, it would be an exaggeration to claim that the study covered all aspects of Ghana's party system and the institutional structures.

In spite of the problems posed in the process of the research, I wish to state that the volume of information collected through the interviews and data, and the different approaches used – documents, interviews, questionnaires and personal observation, – enabled me to gain insight into the participants' attitudes and values, and also helped me to obtain in-depth information on the parties, electoral systems, issues of representation and participation, and other issues that were examined in the study. Many of the party leaders were eager to participate in the research because they believe that getting involved could bring to light some of the internal and external problems facing the political parties and in doing so, help address them. Several participants also admitted that academic publications on Ghana's democracy have greatly contributed toward reforming the country's political system and opened up the country's democratic process to the international community. Since the majority of the participants were highly educated and familiar with research work, introducing myself with evidence that I am a research student convinced them of the objectivity of the study and the fact that I was not openly affiliated with any political party or the press helped gain the participants' trust.

The research gave me insight into the role and activities of the political parties and some of the major successes and challenges facing Ghana's democratic development in general. This study can be a fundamental basis for future research into Ghana's party development and democratic consolidation in the coming years, especially the changes being implemented by the parties, the government, the Electoral Commission and the civil society organizations to make the 2008 election an improvement over the ones held previously. The methodology chosen and techniques used in the data collection process are appropriate for the theoretical framework because combining qualitative and quantitative strategies, and conducting various interviews with party leaders coupled with my observation of the political parties' activities and campaigns facilitated the flow of the information in the study from the theoretical framework and research questions. In spite of its limitations, the methodology employed and the review of the literature helps our understanding of how some of the basic conditions outlined by the various theorists could create an enabling environment for democratic transition and consolidation; particularly through the role political parties and various civic groups have played in Ghana's democratic transition and consolidation processes.

Chapter Three

Ghana's Postcolonial History and the Road to the 1992 Democratic Transition

Introduction

The first part of the chapter briefly focuses on Ghana's postcolonial political experiences and the emergence of the PNDC regime to power in 1981. In the midst of the unstable political environment in Ghana after independence, in 1981, the PNDC assumed political power and maintained control of the state until the country's democratic transition in 1992. The second section discusses the role of the external donor organizations and countries in pressuring the PNDC regime to return the country's political system to multi-party democracy. The third part of the chapter also focuses on the background to the democratic transition, the origin and contribution of civic society in Ghana in their opposition to, and pressure on the PNDC regime, which resulted in the 1992 democratic transition. The section further discusses the historical background and development of Ghana's party system in terms of the roots of the party traditions and the ideological views that have influenced policies of the political parties, as well as the role played by some loyal members and pro-democracy movements that were supporters of the defunct political parties in the 1992 democratic transition. Although parties were banned under the PNDC rule, the contribution of the members of the defunct political parties to the 1992 transition was immense and complemented the role of the civic groups and external donors in securing the transition to multiparty democracy in1992, as well as facilitating free and fair elections in the 1996 election. Finally, the problems that were encountered by the political parties during the transition processes are also discussed.

From Authoritarianism to Multi-Party Democracy in Ghana

As noted earlier in the introductory chapter, until the 1992 democratic transition, Ghana's post independence history was plagued by political instability due to frequent military intervention in politics. The frequent changes in government, as discussed below, created a very unstable political environment in Ghana between 1966 and 1992. President Kwame Nkrumah's CPP government, which assumed power in Ghana after the country's independence in 1957, was transformed into a one party state system, which was overthrown in 1966 by the National Liberation Council (NLC) military regime. The NLC, in turn, ruled Ghana until 1969 when it handed over power to Prime Minister Kofi Abrefa Busia's Progress Party (PP) civilian government. Busia's government was short- lived, and was overthrown by Colonel Acheampong's National Redemption Council (NRC) military government in 1971, which later became the Supreme Military Council (SMC) I & II regimes, and was later led by General Akuffo.

In 1979, Flt. Lt. Jerry John Rawlings' Armed Forces Revolutionary Council (AFRC) government overthrew the SMC regime, which was followed by a period of oppressive rule. In 1979, there was a brief interlude of civilian rule under President Hilla Limann's People's National Party (PNP) government, but Limann was later overthrown by Rawlings' PNDC military regime on 31December 1981. The overthrow of Limann's government by Rawlings' PNDC government set in motion another chapter of militarism in the history of Ghana, and a period of "reign of terror" until the 1992 democratic transition. The return of Rawlings to power for the second time in December 1981 was greeted with a mixture of enthusiasm, skepticism and fear since many people were apprehensive about the prospect of another era of military rule. The PNDC declared that it intended to transfer power from the elites to the ordinary people to enable them to actively participate in the decision-making process. Hence the government used probity,

accountability and pursuit of social justice as its slogans, which were completely new concepts in Ghana's political culture. Nonetheless, immediately after the coup, all governmental power was vested in the PNDC regime. Like all the previous military coups that have taken place in Ghana, after the 1981 coup, the constitution was suspended, the Habeas Corpus Act was rendered invalid, the courts were undermined and a new form of "revolutionary justice" was introduced in Ghana. Unlike the previous military regimes, the PNDC did not abolish the Supreme Court established under the 1979 Constitution and allowed the formal courts to operate. However, to weaken the power of the traditional courts, the government set up parallel judicial systems known as the Peoples' Courts, Public Tribunals and the Citizens Vetting Committees (CVC), with wide range of powers over criminal and civil matters. The regular courts had no legal jurisdiction over the public tribunals and the Supreme Court's power over the public tribunals was limited to an advisory function. To make matters worse, the mainstream courts were banned from accepting any application for appeal in cases adjudicated by the public tribunals or issuing a writ of habeas corpus, mandamus, prohibition or other prerogative writs in respect of any action taken by a public tribunal. The forceful and violent subjugation of the judiciary by the PNDC regime came to a climax in the early 1980s when three judges of the superior court and a military officer were abducted, murdered and burnt by operatives of the PNDC regime. The government turned a deaf ear on the Bar Association's petition to set up an independent investigation into the murder of three high court judges in 1982, for which it argued it had evidence to implicate some key members of the PNDC, such as Rawlings, his wife, and Kojo Tsikata, who was heading the National Security. Apart from perceived corruption of public officials, one of the main flaws of the PNDC regime was its trampling of civil liberties and human rights. Whereas the PNDC was successful in mobilizing civil society to consolidate its power, it failed to meet their basic needs and recognize their basic rights. The PNDC centralized the public press and critics among the private press and the public were unlawfully imprisoned, tortured or secretly killed. The pro-socialist policies first adopted by the PNDC did not help the economy either, since the government's policies were also directed against the rich and the private sector and leading to loss of confidence in the economy and drastically affected local investments, which severely increased Ghana's economic woes in the early 1980s. As Fieldhouse noted, state intervention in the economy was probably counter-productive, mainly because the motivation behind policies was political, not economic. Facing imminent collapse of the economy, and realizing that the government's own policies were failing, the pro-socialist PNDC regime made an about face and turned to the IMF and the World Bank for assistance. The change from the PNDC's populist policies was evident in the statement by the PNDC Secretary for Finance and Economic Planning, Kwesi Botchwey, that "the government should prevent any relapse into the careless populism of the past that all but destroyed our national economy. "The regime abolished its populist policies and ideology to embrace free-market reforms in 1983, by implementing the economic recovery programme (ERP) and later the structural adjustment programmes (SAP).

External Pressures for Democratic Transition

Analysis of the role of external pressures that were brought to bear on the PNDC government to re-introduce a multi-party system of government and democratize the state shows the extent to which donor influence facilitated democratization in Ghana. While the donors have played many significant roles in the country's socio-economic and political development since independence, their scale and scope of influence in Ghana have expanded significantly since the 1980s. Due to the weakness of the economies, developing countries like Ghana have been more susceptible to external pressures to adopt democratic governments. Hence aid, sanctions, loans, and debt relief are among the key instruments available to the advocates of democracy like the World Bank and the advanced capitalist countries to persuade or coerce leaders in aid recipient countries, such as Ghana, to adopt democratic regimes.

Obviously, the IFIs and donor countries were some of the major driving forces behind Ghana's 1992 democratic transition and have continued to assist the country in its democratic consolidation, as well as in strengthening its political institutions. Some internationalist theorists such as Huntington and Fukuyama who support this view argued that pressure from external donors and changes in the international political economy led to the resurgence of democratic transitions in the third-wave democracies. For example, despite the view that Ghana was hailed as a 'success story or model pupil' in its macro-economic reforms in the 1980s, the IFIs recognized that the free-market reforms alone would not set the country on the path to recovery and sustainable development.

The World Bank argued that the constriction of political space in Ghana and other African countries has severely constrained socio-economic development; and called for the promotion of democracy as a solution for the development crises. In its November 1989 report, the World Bank highlighted problems with governance in Africa and emphasized the urgent need for marked improvement in that direction as a condition for aid. Hence in the late 1980s and 1990s, changes in the international political economy saw a change in policy direction of the International Financial Institutions (IFIs) such as the International Monetary Fund (IMF) and the World Bank, as well as some developed countries like the United States and Britain from supporting authoritarian regimes toward promoting multi-party democracy in the developing world. Consequently, the new policy prescriptions of the IFIs and developed countries in the recipient countries in the 1990s centered on the promotion of decentralization and multi-party democracy for increased participation in decision-making, sustainable economic growth and social development. The donors argued that satisfactory economic and social progress in Africa was dependent on improved political freedom and better governance because election is important for the promotion of democratic values. These conditions directly or indirectly became a vital prerequisite for receiving financial aid and as a panacea for achieving political stability and socio-economic development in the recipient countries. In the light of this shift in donors' policy framework, since the 1990s, international organizations have served as sources of empowerment for people in the developing world who are deprived of their political freedoms and social rights due to the dominance of authoritarian regimes.

For example, democracy and human rights were incorporated into some European Union (EU) agreements, such as the Lome Convention, and later, the Cotonou Partnership Agreement signed in June 2000 with countries in Africa, the Caribbean and the Pacific. The Euro-Mediterranean Partnership with North African countries was also signed in Barcelona in 1995 as a shared value and objective. The United States Agency for International Development (USAID), for example, emphasized that the allocation of funds to individual countries would depend on their progress toward democratization because "open societies that value individual rights, respect the rule of law, and have open and accountable governments, provide better opportunities for sustained economic growth than do closed systems, which stifle individual initiative."Other organizations such as Transparency International (TI), established in the 1990s, also argued that the lack of transparency and accountability has led to institutionalized corruption, and lack of restraint in government in the developing countries.

Through their determination to promote democracy and participation in Africa, donor countries and organizations have supported programs that are aimed at political empowerment, capacity building and socio-economic development. As noted by

Schmitz and Hutchful, some bilateral agencies such as the Canadian International Development Agency (CIDA) have promoted issues that are outside the realm of geopolitics and beneficial to people in developing countries by supporting civic groups and challenging public policy locally and internationally. For example, over twenty multilateral and bilateral development agencies are involved in the provision of development aid to Ghana, totaling US$650 million per annum, and by 1998, external donors had pumped a total of about US$8 billion into Ghana's economy. Organizations such as the Danish International Development Agency (DANIDA), the United Nations Children's Emergency Fund (UNICEF) and the USAID, have also greatly supported socio-economic and political policy analysis through some local CSOs like the Centre for Economic Policy Analysis (CEPA), the Institute of Economic Affairs (IEA), and the Centre for Democratic Development (CDD). CIDA, the USAID and the Canadian Parliamentary Centre (CPC) have supported capacity building initiatives and a variety of programs for parliamentarians in Ghana, and help some local non-governmental organizations (NGOs), such as the CDD, to organize conferences on democracy and constitutional review. Other organizations such as the USAID have also embarked on the Enhancing Civil Society Effectiveness at the Local Level (ECSELL) project, which has been renamed the Government Accountability Improves Trust (GAIT). This program is intended to empower civil society and promote downward accountability of District Authorities to the local people and CSOs, training of parliamentarians, upgrading of the ministries and agencies' technology systems and promoting more engagement of the local CSOs with the local government to meet their needs and hold local leaders accountable. The World Bank has also supported legal sector reforms to help create a friendly environment for private-sector development. In its effort to improve governance in African countries, the African Union has instituted the African Peer Review

Mechanism (APRM) to promote democracy in Africa and to assess how the newly developing democracies in Africa are promoting democratic principles and government accountability in the respective African Union member countries. Views expressed by the World Bank and the bilateral institutions on the need for democracy in Africa were also reinforced by the United Nations Economic Commission for Africa (UNECA), which argued that the lack of democracy is one of the primary causes of the crises in Africa. The re-introduction of multi-party democracy in Ghana and other developing countries in Africa, Asia, Latin America and Eastern Europe shows the extent that external actors have influenced the agenda of democratization and strengthening of political parties, which is evidenced in their effort to bring to light some issues of major importance to developing countries. In the case of Ghana, external pressure from the donor countries and organizations either influenced or coerced the then PNDC government to introduce multi-party democracy.

The shift toward democracy saw a change of the political system in Ghana and many developing countries in the early 1990s. Since external financial flows were crucial for the PNDC, donor dependence rendered the regime extremely susceptible to mounting external pressure and political conditionality to transform the authoritarian rule in Ghana to multi-party democracy. The dominance of influence of the foreign organizations and countries on the PNDC government shows that Ghana's democratic development was externally oriented and mainly developed "from above". Therefore, the initiatives of the loyal members and groups from the banned political parties and CSOs "from below", only complemented the external pressure through the political conditionality that were emphasized by the foreign donors and that set the pace for and accelerated the democratic process.

While the PNDC government refused to openly acknowledge the impact of external pressure on its decision to transform the political system in Ghana, policies and pronouncements of some leaders of the donor countries such as Douglas Hurd of Great Britian, and multi-lateral and bilateral organizations showed the extent of the influence on the change in policy direction by the international community on the government's domestic and foreign policy. The impact of donor influence on Ghana's democratic transition is evidenced in the fact that the government's formal announcement of a return to constitutional rule on May 10, 1991 coincided with the donors' conference held in Paris from May 14-15 1991. Thus the external pressure was based on the conditions that the donors' continued assistance to the government would depend on its ability to introduce democratic principles and implement polices that would promote good governance. For this reason, external pressure was instrumental in weakening the PNDC's strong hold on power and boosted the morale of the local pro-democracy movements that were agitating for a re-introduction of multi-party democracy in Ghana. Additionally, Rawlings' history and desire for power, and the PNDC's culture of suppression of dissent clearly suggests that, without the external pressure, the regime would not have loosened its tight grip on power so easily as it did. One major difference between the role played by the external agents and the local CSOs in the democratic transition was that whereas the external pressure was achieved through closed-door meetings, negotiations and coercion through diplomacy, the CSOs and groups loyal to the banned political parties were able to make inroads with the PNDC mainly through a mixture of negotiations, open confrontation, demonstrations and other forms of pressure.

Internal Agitation for Democratic Change The Origin and Role of Civil Society in Ghana's Democracy

Internal agitation for democratic change in Ghana was mainly based on the pressure from CSOs on the PNDC regime. The literature on civil society has grown significantly since its resurgence about three decades ago. A strong civil society enforces standards and improves the levels of accountability of both politicians and bureaucrats. CSOs played significant roles in the third-wave democratic transitions that occurred in the 1990s in many developing countries such as in Ghana, and continue to be actively involved in the effort to consolidate these new democracies. The origin and role of civil society organizations in Ghana dates back to the pre-independence era, mainly in the 1940s and the 1950s, and the period immediately preceding independence. The colonial era witnessed the rise of mass-based social movements consisting of students, professional associations, women, and trade unions in Ghana demanding the democratic transformation of the colonial state, popular participation and self-rule. The elite groups that led the independence struggle initially mobilized popular groups to challenge colonial domination. Soon after independence, the political leaders distanced themselves from the popular democratic demands and transformed the political structure to enable them to consolidate their newly acquired political power and control the resources in the state. Centralization of authority was an effective tool that was employed by the postcolonial state in Ghana to control the means of production and resources, and the desire for power consolidation led many of the postcolonial governments, such as the CPP government that ruled Ghana after independence, to co-opt, coerce and/or prevent CSOs from playing key roles in decision-making.

Whereas after independence, the political leaders sought to reduce the role and power of civil society through co-optation and coercion, the involvement of CSOs in the

independence struggle set the stage for them to agitate for political space in the postcolonial era. For example, the Anlo Youth Congress of the Volta Region led riots against Nkrumah's CPP government and demanded separation of the Volta Region from Ghana to enable the people of the region to join Togo as one nation. There were similar confrontations for political space between civic groups and the CPP in the Ashanti region. Similarly, the NUGS confrontations with Nkrumah's CPP government, the PP, NRC, and the SMC governments in the 1970s, and the more recent PNDC/NDC governments in the 1980s and 1990s were mainly due to the struggle for political space. Although this power struggles between the governments and the CSOs continued, the authoritarian regimes that dominated Ghana's political scene in the 1960s and 1970s managed to suppress the CSOs demands for democratic rule until the 1980s and 1990s, when there was a major resurgence of a vibrant civic terrain.

In many of the third-wave transition countries, such as Ghana, objections to military rule came from some well-organized local CSOs such as the Trade Unions Congress (TUC), the National Union of Ghana Students (NUGS), the Ghana Bar Association (GBA), the Catholic Bishops' Conference and CSOs formed by some loyal members of the then defunct political parties. The emergence of a relatively large non- state sector, consisting of professional associations, development-oriented and pro- democracy organizations, as well as various community groups, created political spaces for the already emerging strong and independent counter-hegemonic civil society in Ghana to challenge the state. These groups may be united by specific interests they share in common and interact with the state either in support of, or in opposition to the government as a way of expressing their demands and interests to the state. Thus the period of political instability and economic recession in the 1980s saw the emergence of various CSOs with different levels of engagement with the state.

This was manifested in the proliferation of local and international non- governmental organization (NGOs) such as social movements, professional associations, trade unions, student bodies, traditional authorities, and community-based organizations, which Bayart described as "an inclusive social phenomenon of actual existing civil societies. "As Ninsin and Drah noted, a major unintended and paradoxical effect of the ERP and the SAP implemented by the PNDC in Ghana, was the proliferation of voluntary associations at local and intermediate levels of society covering occupational, social service, community, religious and human rights interests. Many of the civic groups that operated in Ghana were independent of the state, established their own autonomous spheres of action, which were often in conflict with the PNDC regime and accumulated resources and capital needed to challenge the state. This led to a rapid expansion of a vibrant civic culture and remarkably increased the importance of the CSOs in the political terrain. It is thus reasonable to argue that the resurgence of the CSOs in Ghana in the 1980s and 1990s expanded their role in demanding political reforms, and engaging policymakers in developing and refining public policies from their formulation to implementation. One school of thought supported by theorists of the institutional view, such as Putnam, argued that civil society greases the wheels of democracy through trust, tolerance and an increase in associational life.

In recent decades, these roles played by CSOs have enjoyed vigorous support and revitalization in academic and policy circles by theorists who argue that democratic government is strengthened when there is a robust civil society to challenge the state. This view is strongly supported by organizations like the World Bank, the United States Agency for International Development (USAID) and the U. S. National Endowment for Democracy (NED). Civic groups are seen as institutions of social and political change and instruments for popular participation, political education and channels of communication with the government. The opportunity for civil society to agitate for accountability in government clearly shows the degree to which governments and political parties under Ghana's Fourth Republic have collaborated with the civic groups. This was not the case under the authoritarian PNDC regime's unchallenged power over state and society. The experience underscores what most analysts of civil society have noted as its potential to contribute to political reform and democratic development.

Many of the CSOs are involved in advocacy work, which has gained unprecedented attention in the political sphere in recent decades, especially after the introduction of adjustment policies by the PNDC. In Ghana, some factors that determined the effectiveness of the CSOs are their organizational skills, size, activities and influence in communities across the country, and the resources available to them. Their relations with the government over the years have been varied and complex since these groups may be affiliated with political parties, as was the case with the DWM, or may exist independent of any political party, like the CDD. For example, CSOs in Ghana served very useful purposes in the 1992 democratic transition process and greatly influenced the PNDC's decision to introduce multi-party democracy in Ghana, One general view that supports this argument is that civil society promotes democracy, because where strong and autonomous civic groups exist, they may undermine authoritarian rule and generate effective pressure for democratization. From this perspective, the proliferation of autonomous associations and social networks has been seen as a dynamic mechanism and a fundamental bulwark for the introduction and maintenance of democratic governance in Ghana and other third-wave democracies. Such urban-based pro-democracy civic groups as the ARPB, the GBA, Christian Council of Ghana, the Catholic Bishops Conference, the IEA, the CDD, the CEPA, the Ghana Legal Literacy and Resources Foundation, and the Ghana Committee on Human and People's Rights employed non-violent means of political agitation in pursuit of their demands for the re-introduction of multi-party democracy. The initiatives of the urban- based pro-democracy civic groups were complemented by the role of the private press. As Ninsin noted, these civic groups mobilized the public through press conferences, issued manifestos and communiqués setting out a list of democratic demands, sent memoranda and delegations to the government, sent pastoral letters to their congregations and memberships, openly denounced the legitimacy of the PNDC government, and used the private media to actively publicize their demands. Commenting on the role of civil society in democratic transition and consolidation, some theorists of the institutional view such as Linz and Stepan noted that civil society help start and push transitions to their completion. The involvement of civic groups in Ghana's democratic transition process appears to have led to an increasing atmosphere of tolerance and cooperation among

people from different ethnic backgrounds and political parties to collaborate for a common cause. For example, the membership of the MFJ that opposed PNDC rule was drawn from different ethnic groups and rival political parties like the Danquah-Busia and Nkrumah traditions.

From the period leading to the democratic transition and afterwards, CSOs have effectively played watchdog, advocacy and socialization functions in the Ghanaian society to help promote and strengthen the country's democratic development. For example, while political parties were banned under the PNDC regime, some members of the parties integrated into civic groups, such as the MFJ and acted as opposition in place of the political parties. Also, in the absence of party structures, some democracy-oriented civic groups such as the media, professional bodies, the Christian Council of Ghana, the Catholic Bishops Conference, and the NUGS among others, joined together to oppose the PNDC government and pressured the regime to re-introduce multiparty democracy in Ghana. As Saaka rightly noted, "in all of the periods of authoritarian rule in Ghana, the greatest confrontations the regimes encountered were with civic groups." In the period preceding the transition to multi-party rule and the 1992 elections, the National and Regional Houses of Chiefs also mounted programs to support the District Assembly elections and the opposition parties. Ghana's chieftaincy institution has taken some important steps towards incorporating positive elements of African traditions like popular participation and community involvement in Ghana's democratic development. For example, the Otumfuo Education Fund has established programs for social and political empowerment.

The pro-democracy groups reconstituted into different alliances and positioned themselves for a struggle against the PNDC and its supporting CSOs. Civic groups like the Coordinating Committee of Democratic Forces (CCDF) and the MFJ posed a greater challenge to the PNDC. The MFJ demanded the release of all political detainees, the granting of unconditional amnesty to all exiles, the drawing up of a constitutional timetable and the lifting of the ban on party politics. The MFJ and other pro-democracy CSOs also demanded the repeal of all repressive laws, such as the Preventive Custody Law (PNDC Law 4), the Habeas Corpus Amendment Law (PNDC Law 91), the Newspaper Licensing Law (PNDC Law 211), and sections of the Public Tribunal Law (PNDC Law 78), which dealt with the execution for political offences. These demands were achieved through demonstrations, negotiations and alliances with some leaders and members of the banned opposition parties to oppose authoritarian rule. Opposition from these groups and some leading members of the defunct political parties did put enormous pressure on the then PNDC regime to loosen its grip on the state. As Baffour-Agyeman noted, as the demand for more political liberalization gathered momentum, the PNDC could not help but try to create some political space to accommodate the increasing agitation for a return to democratic rule, first by introducing the decentralization program in 1988 and democratic rule in 1992. Despite the numerous problems that faced the CSOs and the undemocratic tactics used by the PNDC/NDC regime to suppress the CSOs agitation for democracy and government accountability, the latter increased their pressure on the government to democratize in the 1980s, which resulted in the 1988 District Assembly (DA) elections and the 1992 multi-party elections and transition.

Civil Society as a Destabilizing Force to Democracy in Ghana

Despite the invaluable role played by some CSOs in Ghana's democratic transition, other CSOs served as a destabilizing force to the pro-democracy movements in Ghana. In this regard, while discussing the positive functions of civic groups in Ghana's democratic development, it is necessary to highlight some of the undemocratic activities that some CSOs have pursued, and how they have supported authoritarian regimes to consolidate their power in Ghana. Although civil society has contributed immensely to the re-introduction of democracy in Ghana, some civic groups in Ghana have also produced opposite trends in the country's democratic development. An alternative school of thought from the institutional theorists view on civil society expressed by theorists such as Encarnacion, Robert Fatton and Abrahamsen argued that while advocates of civil society argue that it contributes to democratic development, it can also can be a destabilizing force to democracy. The destructive role of civic groups in destabilizing democracy is evident in the role that some groups played in attempting to destabilize Ghana's 1992 democratic transition. For example, for political and financial gains, some local NGOs such as the DWM and the GPRTU were used by or aligned with the authoritarian PNDC regime to suppress popular demands for democracy. Some critics such as Kofi Kumado, a Law Professor at the University of Ghana, denounced the governments' tight control and manipulation of some CSOs as an ideological tool by the NDC government.

The authoritarian governments often established or mobilized a pseudo alternative' civil society consisting of grassroots civic associations and quasi-political organizations whose members had been recruited from urban workers, the unemployed, the informal sector and/or people engaged in small-scale businesses in the private sector to counteract the anti-government forces. This strategy led to a pattern of marginalization of some CSOs such as the GBA, the ARPB and the NUGS by either giving them less representation or not being represented at all on important policy-making bodies such as the Consultative Assembly that drafted the 1992 Constitution.

The co-optation of others such as the DWM, the CDRs, the PDCs/WDCs, the GPRTU and the Verandah Boys and Girls Clubs, reached new heights in the PNDC era and during the period of agitation for democratic rule. The PNDC/NDC government used these pro-government CSOs, to weaken the pressure from pro-democracy civic groups' agitation for a transfer of power to a constitutionally elected government, and the large support from the government and sections of the public that these anti-democratic organizations enjoyed enabled them to impede the pro-democracy movements' agitation for change to democratic rule.

As Ninsin noted, seeing the DWM as an extension of the PNDC/NDC was sufficient to attract a massive following of lower class individuals and groups, especially in the rural areas, as a means of gaining access to the patronage networks that the movement controlled by virtue of its association with the government. For example, whereas many of the pro-democracy CSOs were cash-strapped, the government guaranteed a three million US dollars loan from the African Development Bank through the Agricultural Development Bank in Ghana for the DWM. The political structure encouraged patronage in the redistribution of resources to certain groups, which was generally considered unfair, especially in the disbursement of the Poverty Alleviation Fund. While this was done to strengthen the PNDC's monopoly of the political spaces, it also enabled Rawlings to consolidate his power against the increasing demands from the pro-democracy CSOs to democratize the system of government.

After the 1992 transition, under the NDC government, several members of the CDRs were incorporated into the ACDRs. Members of the newly reconstituted body often threatened the PNDC/NDC regime's political opponents, disrupted political and social rallies, and provided "hooligans" to wreck havoc on anti-Rawlings and anti- PNDC/NDC elements. For example, as a punishment for criticizing the PNDC/NDC, the government deployed pro-government hooligans to smear human excreta on the premises of the "Free-Press" newspaper, which was applauded by Kwamena Ahwoi, a former Minister in the NDC government, as a noble deed. With the help of the pro-government CSOs, the PNDC managed to subjugate some leaders of the pro-democracy movements and those who were adamant were targeted as "enemies of the government."

Other repressive methods adopted against civil society under the PNDC/NDC were the decree under PNDC Law 4, which allowed the regime to detain its critics without trial for indefinite periods and PNDC Law 91. This law restricted the application of the Habeas Corpus Act and was used extensively against some leaders of the pro- democracy CSOs. Another attempt to control civil society was the passage of a Religious Bodies Registration Law, which asserted the control of the state over the churches by introducing new registration regulations. In 1993, the NDC government also attempted to propose a bill that required local and foreign NGOs in Ghana to register with the National Council on Non-Governmental Organizations. This body was also empowered to de-register any organization at its own discretion. However, as a result of the vehement protest from the CSOs that the law infringed on the freedom of association, the bill was later aborted. Also, members of the Association of Ghanaian Contractors who were suspected of being supporters of the opposition parties were forced to renounce their party affiliation and join the PNDC/NDC or risk going out of business. For example, Rawlings is reported to have stated at an NDC rally in the Northern Region that, "since Alhaji Naabu had behaved himself, he would begin to receive some contracts."The strategy of using force and violence against anti-authoritarian organizations was not limited only to the PNDC/NDC government, but has been part and parcel of Ghana's post-independence history. For example, the overthrow of Hilla Limann's democratically elected PNP government in December 1981 was facilitated in diverse ways by the support of some CSOs such as the June Fourth Movement, the Kwame Nkrumah Revolutionary Guards, the National Democratic Movement and the NUGS. Also, the struggle over General Acheampong's NRC/SMC government sponsored Union Government (UNIGOV) proposal led to confrontation between government sponsored civic groups, such as the Society of Friends and the Peace and Solidarity Council, (SFPSC) against anti-UNIGOV groups as the People's Movement for Freedom and Justice (PMFJ) and Association of Recognized Professional Bodies (ARPB) that agitated for a return to constitutional rule in the 1970s. Nkrumah's CPP also established the Young Pioneer Movement and Workers Brigade to combat anti-government forces in the 1960s. Under the NRC/SMC and AFRC regimes, civic groups were targeted by the regimes through dismissals, and various forms of punishment were meted out to innocent groups and individuals. For example, in the AFRC era, the Makola Women's Association, an association of women traders, were punished by destroying the main market in Accra, and their attempt to protest this action was met with a repressive military crackdown in which several of the women were lined up naked and physically assaulted. These brutalities by the authoritarian regimes and their supporters against pro-democracy CSOs are some of the underlying factors that delayed the development of a stable democratic system in Ghana until the early 1990s.

Apart from government control, various challenges face CSOs in the discharge of their social responsibilities that also account for the delay in the development of democracy in Ghana. In Ghana and many of the third-wave democracies, the type of government in power and its commitment to democracy are complex elements that determine the environment in which CSOs function because the cooperation of the government is crucial in creating the enabling environment for CSO activities. Due to the central government's suspicion of CSOs as a threat to its overall power, there is minimal state support for CSOs that seek to remain autonomous from the state or pursue a political agenda to counter state hegemony. The local CSOs also lack funding and are more dependent on external support to boost their resource base, which shows a pattern of acute resource deficiency of civic organizations in Ghana. Due to limited personnel and expertise, many CSOs in Ghana are severely limited in their experience and capacity to carry out a comprehensive and participatory consultation exercise. For example, apart from a few CSOs such as the CEPA, the CDD and the IEA, many of the CSOs have no established record of expertise in any specific policy area. Despite the problems that hinder the smooth functioning of CSOs, this study supports the institutional theorists' view that civil society is one of the key factors in the promotion of democracy in Ghana and many developing countries.

Historical Perspectives on the Development of the Party System and Democracy in Ghana

The Roots of Ghana's Party System

The idea of democracy either under a parliamentary or presidential system of government is associated with political parties. In this study, the term political party is used with reference to both the party as a distinct political organization, and the party as an institution that embodies a specific political ideological tradition. Political parties in Ghana are backed by ideological and practical beliefs that sustain the continuity of a party's tradition. As noted earlier in this chapter, the roots of Ghana's party system can be traced to the emergence of the UGCC and the CPP political parties in the 1940s, prior to Ghana's independence in 1957. Due to the Eurocentric focus of theoretical studies on modern party systems, many Western theorists have paid little or no attention to the evolution of political parties and party systems in many developing countries like Ghana. In many ways, the development of the party system in African societies differs considerably from Western political party systems. Whereas the development of Western political party systems are bound up with the extension of popular suffrage and parliamentary prerogatives, African political parties can be seen as a product of colonial circumstances.

In Africa and particularly in Ghana, the development of the party system emerged from the development of nationalism, first under the Aboriginal Rights

Protection Society (ARPS) and later the United Gold Coast Convention (UGCC), to oppose colonial rule and the independence struggles in 1898, and the 1940s and 1950s respectively. As Maurice Duverger rightly noted, the emergence of Western parties was contingent on the emergence of parliamentary institutions, universal suffrage, ideological movements, unions, and churches as well as civil society and social movements, but African political parties were in some instances created instantaneously by a small group of political elites opposed to colonial rule and to contest elections in preparation for independence. Despite the differences in the emergence of party systems and the CPP's socialist ideology, there is no doubt that Ghana's party system has been inspired by the Western party systems, democracy and in some cases ideological orientation. For example, during the independence struggle in Ghana, some of the parties like the UGCC and the CPP that emerged after independence assimilated the Western political parties' traditions. Since the colonial era, many political parties have evolved in Ghana and parties have played key roles in the effort to sustain democracy in the country. The postcolonial political parties succeeded in cultivating nationalist sentiments and amassing the necessary human, financial and logistic resources to organize an aggressive pursuit of independence movements and propaganda campaigns in the process of competing for power. As Bill Freund noted, during the struggle for independence, African political parties provided an all purpose appeal to the people to gain the support and control over power. Also, the process through which political parties in Ghana compete for power or create political leverage to enhance their electoral prospects and attain power differs significantly, due to differences in their origins and ideological orientation.

Political Party Traditions and Ideologies

The party ideology is a set of philosophical views, which may be socialism, Pan-Africanism, liberal democracy or free-market principles that guided the policies of the original party of a particular tradition. Recent political party formations under the Fourth Republic have shown a close continuity with political parties that emerged prior to independence. Presently, three main political party traditions can be identified in Ghana, namely, the Danquah-Busia, Kwame Nkrumah, and Rawlings political traditions. As Jonah noted, unlike the party, the political tradition is a number of symbols, ideologies and political influences that are associated with the hero of a political party in Ghana's post-independence history. The beliefs that embody a party tradition also refer to the concrete achievements associated with the founders of the original party of the tradition in political and socio-economic development. As Safo Adu, a former leading member of the NPP noted, politics is history and past leaders cannot easily be dismissed because of the contributions they have made. It is the maintenance of tradition. The Danquah-Busia tradition can be traced to the UGCC, which was the first political party to emerge in Ghana (then the Gold Coast). Founded by Alfred Paa Grant and a group of politicians, collectively known as the "Big Six," the UGCC was very instrumental in opposing British colonial rule in the 1940s and 1950s. The Danquah-Busia tradition was continued under the banner of the Progress Party, which won the 1969 elections under the leadership of Kofi Abrefa Busia in Ghana's Second Republic. The Popular Front Party (PFP) led by Victor Owusu and the United National Convention

(UNC) led by William Ofori-Atta, which lost the 1979 elections to Limann's PNP in the Third Republic, also emerged from the Danquah-Busia tradition.

The present ruling NPP in Ghana is also a product of the Danquah-Busia tradition. The policies that are commonly pursued by governments under this tradition are free market policies and more recently neo-liberal fiscal restructuring, liberty of the individual, liberal democracy and rule of law. While there has been a major shift in all the parties' support base, recent elections outcomes show that the Danquah-Busia tradition has strong support mainly in the Ashanti, Brong Ahafo, Eastern, Western, and Central regions. This tradition has been seen to represent the dominant class of elite and professional groups and has its support base in the urban areas. Hence, most of the prominent supporters of this tradition since the 1980s were members of groups, such as the MFJ and the Ghana Bar Association. Despite the split in the Busia-Danquah tradition into the PFP and UNC, in the 1979 election, and apart from a few defections during the era of PNDC/NDC co-optation, the Danquah-Busia tradition stayed united and firmly opposed Rawlings' usurpation of political power, and fought relentlessly through non- violent means to unseat the PNDC/NDC regime in the 2000 presidential and parliamentary elections.

As the name implies, the Nkrumah political tradition emerged in 1948 under the leadership of Ghana's first president, Kwame Nkrumah, with the formation of the original CPP party, which was a breakaway party from the UGCC. It became a formidable, grassroots-based populist party in the period before and after Ghana's independence. The CPP led Ghana to independence in 1957 after defeating the UGCC and the other opposition parties in the 1951, 1954 and 1956 elections. Since the overthrow of

Nkrumah in 1966, over the past four decades the Nkrumah political tradition has fragmented into various parties like the National Alliance of Liberals (NAL) party and the Peoples National Party (PNP) that assumed power in 1979 in Ghana's Third Republic under President Hilla Limann. The current CPP, the PNC and the EGLE parties also trace their roots to the Nkrumah CPP traditions. In contrast to the Danquah-Busia tradition, the Nkrumah political tradition has been characterized by mass defections to the PNDC/NDC and disintegration into a number of weak political parties like the PNC, the revived CPP, the Great Consolidated Popular Party (GCPP), and the Every Ghanaian Living Everywhere (EGLE) Party.

The Nkrumah tradition is influenced by a socialist political ideology and development policies, which were implemented in Ghana in the 1960s. This tradition has historically been identified with socialism, Pan-Africanism, anti-imperialism and active state involvement in the economy. Thus, socialist/populist policies were the benchmark of the Nkrumah tradition until the emergence of the Rawlings tradition. Parties that trace their roots to the CPP base their campaign platform on Nkrumah's aggressive social policy in the 1960s. The Nkrumah tradition has shifted considerably and lost a great deal of grounds to Rawlings' NDC party and other Nkrumahist parties such as the PNC, especially in the Volta and Northern regions. Recent election trends show that the party has strong support mainly in the Western, Greater Accra, and Central regions. It has often been seen to represent the grassroots of the lower classes. For example, the CPP was popularly called "the verandah boys party," with its support base in some parts of the poorer urban and rural areas.

Some contemporary political parties in Africa such as the NDC in Ghana originated from military rule. The more recent

Rawlings populist tradition emerged in the period following the 31December 1981 coup led by Jerry John Rawlings that overthrew the democratically elected PNP government. The 1990s saw the emergence of a third party tradition, the Rawlings PNDC/NDC political tradition, which has the NDC party as its base. In the period preceding Ghana's transition to democratic rule, after eleven years of military rule, the authoritarian PNDC regime was transformed into the NDC political party to challenge the two dominant political traditions in Ghana. The Rawlings political tradition is therefore a collection of members from both the Nkrumah and Danquah-Busia traditions, as well as voters who are not firmly aligned with any political party. It has strong regional support mainly in the Volta and Northern regions, and the party's grassroots support base is particularly strong in the rural areas. However, from the 1990s, power over decision-making has gradually been centralized from the grassroots populist organizations, such as the PDCs and WDCs to the elites within the party, and particularly, in the hands of Rawlings himself.

Due to Rawlings' charisma and the party's patronage to some civic groups, the NDC gained nationwide support in most of the regions during the 1980s and 1990s, which partly accounted for its successes in the 1992 and 1996 elections. Initially, the policies that the PNDC/NDC tradition pursued in the early 1980s were socialist/populist oriented, but due to external pressures from the IMF and the World Bank, as well as the developed countries like the United States, the government changed from its populist policies to pursue stringent neo-liberal macro-economic fiscal policies, first under the ERP, which was later transformed into the SAP. From 1988 onwards, when the PAMSCAD initiative was introduced, the government adopted a centrist approach and implemented more aggressive populist social policies alongside free market policies. The NDC prides itself on its centrist ideology, basing its policies on a mixture of populist and neo-liberal policies. Apart from a few defections after the 2000 and 2004 election defeats, as well as a stream of secessions by some leading members to form the National Reform

Party (NRP) and the Democratic Freedom Party (DFP), the Rawlings' political tradition has to face a more acute test if the party losses the 2008 election.

An examination of the above party traditions and their influence on contemporary parties in Ghana show that the successful re-incarnation of the Danquah- Busia tradition into a strong political party, and the Nkrumah tradition into fragmented parties are evidence of the fact that the multi-party culture in Ghana continues to develop from its roots, despite years of banning of political parties' activities by the PNDC regime. Apart from the political activities of the parties, what has kept the party political tradition going in Ghana is a complex network of personal friendships and mutual support in the form of funerals, birthday parties and other social activities. What critics have termed "funeral politics" is a popular strategy employed by the various party traditions, especially in times of military rule, to maintain their existence. Continuity of party political tradition has become very important among Ghanaian politicians who accept it as legitimate and desirable, and has highly influenced their political calculations and affiliations. As President Kufour noted, "the Danquah-Busia and Nkrumah traditions are both time-tested and honourable. They have attracted to their respective folds sons and daughters of the nation whose over-riding concern is seeking by their respective means what they consider to be the nation's highest good. "Parties often base their policies on their party traditions. For example, the NPP uses the Danquah/Busia tradition's belief in respect for civil liberties, support for the rule of law and Busia's local government and rural development policies as the party's basic principles; the CPP, PNC and other Nkrumah tradition parties use Nkrumah's aggressive social policies of the 1960s to campaign on their parties' platform for the revival of social welfare and state-directed development; and the NDC party sees Rawlings as the symbol of unity for their party and campaign on his development policies as the party's main objective.

The UP and CPP traced their roots to the UGCC tradition. Both Danquah and Nkrumah were key members of the UGCC, but later Nkrumah broke away to form the CPP due to differences in opinion on Ghana's independence from British rule. One main difference between the main political parties studied is that to a large extent, their origin and approach to promoting democracy differ in many respects. While the NPP emerged from the United Party or Danquah/Busia political tradition, which has been in existence since independence and survived the storms of numerous coups and political instability in Ghana from the 1960s to early 1990s, the NDC party is an offspring of the PNDC military regime and a more recently fashioned party. Whereas the NPP's economic ideology is based on free-market principles, and has basically focused on the promotion of the rule of law and civil liberties since independence, the PNDC/NDC has less concern for the rule of law and civil liberties, and with its shift to the center in the 1980s prides itself on promoting social development. In framing a party's manifesto under the present macro-economic environment in Ghana, utmost care is taken by the party leaders to design it in such a way that it covers a wide spectrum of society and their diverging interests, and tries to balance this with the divergent views within the party about the issues or policies a party intends to pursue.

Political Parties and the 1992 Democratic Transition

Despite the ban on political parties under the PNDC rule, many members of the banned political parties maintained their networks and allegiance to their respective political party traditions and formed pro-democracy organizations such as the MFJ to oppose the PNDC authoritarian rule and complemented the pressure by the donor

agencies and countries as well as the CSOs. While theorists of the combined confrontation and negotiation view such as Andreas Schedler attribute the third-wave transitions to the initiatives of political parties, this study argues that although political parties have been instrumental in the process of consolidating many of the third-wave democracies, in Ghana, their role in the democratic transition processes was limited to the activities of the some loyal members and pro-democracy CSOs. But for the effort of the donors and CSOs, it might have been impossible for the members of the banned parties alone to successfully to pressure the PNDC for a return to multi-party democracy. Immediately after the ban on political parties was lifted, some of the party-oriented pro- democracy groups revived their old party traditions or establish new parties such as the Danquah-Busia and Nkrumah traditions to compete in the 1992 election. Some of the members of the pro-democracy movements became leading members of the opposition parties that sprang up to oppose Rawlings' PNDC regime, and later, NDC party.

Conclusion

It is apparent from the above discussion of PNDC rule that, although the regime promised to bring accountability, economic growth, and promote participation and social justice in Ghana, by the time of the transition in 1992, all these goals have not been attained. The PNDC's imposition of a "culture of silence" kept opponents of the regime from speaking against the atrocities that were committed against targeted groups within the society. People who were vocal against the regime were unlawfully arrested and detained, and/or killed without recourse to the law. Evidence of the failure of the PNDC to manage the economy is seen in its change from socialist to capitalist policies, and its over-reliance on external funding, which led to intense external pressure from the donors on the regime to democratize the state. The period leading to, and after the 1992 transition saw a dramatic change in the domestic policy environment from government hostility towards civil society and the opposition parties to an atmosphere of tolerance and accommodation. The change in relations was due to the constitutional provisions that guaranteed the fundamental rights and freedoms of individuals and groups within the Ghanaian polity, which was in contrast to the relationship that existed between the PNDC and the civic groups during the early years of the PNDC rule. There is ample evidence from the role of the IFIs and developed countries to

prove that the internal impetus for democratic reforms was buttressed by changes in the international political economy and the increasing need for foreign assistance in the 1980s, which enabled the donor agencies and countries to pressure the recipient countries to accept the political conditionality. As Bratton and van de Walle noted, "multifaceted forces, which may be structural or contingent, external or internal, may create openings in authoritarian rule. "For example, in Ghana, donor dependence rendered the PNDC government extremely vulnerable to mounting pressure from the external donors to reform its political institutions and democratize. These developments, incidentally, coincided with the resurgence of CSOs in the 1980s and led to increasing internal resentment of authoritarian rule. Hence, the external pressure served as a catalyst to the internal pressure from the parties and, mainly, civic groups.

The role of the CSOs in Ghana's democratic development has been discussed to show how civic groups have influenced and continue to promote democratic development in Ghana and the developing world. Public and CSOs resentment to the centralization of power and oppressive methods employed by the PNDC, and the dishonesty and self- enrichment of the political leaders at the people's expense, which Bayart has termed "politics of the belly" were vigorously resented by the Ghanaian public, and led to 1992 democratic transition. The reincarnation of old party traditions into modern parties such as the NPP and CPP, and the establishment of a new one NDC shows how vigorously, competitive and strong Ghana's party system is, and the importance of the roots of the party traditions to contemporary political parties in Ghana. Pressure from the loyal members and groups of the banned political parties such as the MFJ, also played significant roles in restoring Ghana to a democratic political system. It is important to note that the political party traditions can also be counter-productive to the development of a strong and unified opposition party to challenge an overbearing incumbent government in elections. For example, despite their disdain for the PNDC authoritarian regime, the political traditions blocked vital political alliances between the NPP and CPP and prevented the formation of larger, more viable and highly competitive political coalitions and a united front to defeat the NDC in the 1992 polls. The establishment of a democratic system of government in Ghana has increased participation in the public sphere and helped to overcome the long-standing tradition of authoritarianism. While the re-introduction of multi-party democracy in Ghana occurred due to three main factors; namely, the role of the external pressures, civic society organizations and members of the defunct political parties, the role played by the respective actors varies considerably.

Chapter Four

Political Parties and Democratic Transition: The 1992 and 1996 Elections under the Fourth Republic

Introduction

The first part of the chapter examines the modalities for the 1992 transition and some basic conditions guiding elections in Ghana. The second part of the chapter thus discusses the 1992 election and the problems that were encountered by the political parties during the election, as well as the boycott of the parliamentary elections by the opposition parties to protest what they alleged to be widespread election malpractices on the part of the then incumbent PNDC/NDC government. Since political parties and elections function mutually in modern democracies to promote democratic development, it is important to discuss the role of parties in securing and promoting free and fair elections, and democracy in Ghana. The third section also discusses changes that were implemented by the political parties and the EC prior to the 1996 election to put Ghana's democracy back on track after the 1992 parliamentary election boycott. The opposition parties' boycott of the elections and their demands for political reforms led to some major innovations prior to the 1996 election, which had positive impacts on the election outcome.

In assessing the significance of the 1992 and 1996 elections, I will pose a number of questions. How free and fair were the multi-party elections that were used to determine the legitimacy of the NDC government and its elected officials? How accessible were the government controlled public print and electronic media, and other means of communication to all the political parties? How free were the other parties and their supporters from government intimidation? What proportion of the electorate had a fair opportunity to exercise their voting rights? And how free and fair were procedures for the

registration of candidates and parties or how inclusive and accessible for all citizens were the registration and voting procedures? Examining these questions critically would help address some of the problems that the parties encountered in the 1992 election. The chapter also discusses some of the changes that were made prior to the 1996 election.

The Long Journey to the Evolution of Multi-Party Democracy in Ghana

The 1992 democratic transition is a by-product of the 1988 decentralization programme launched by the PNDC to promote its idea of a "participatory democratic system" in Ghana. The long road to democratic transition and elections in Ghana began in 1984 when the National Commission on Democracy (NCD) was set up in 1988, with Justice Daniel F. Annan as its chairman, and entrusted with the authority to organize meetings, seminars and debates to solicit views from the Ghanaian public on the system of government to be re-introduced in the country. The NCD was charged with the task of formulating what the government termed a "true democracy," as opposed to the notion of a "grassroots democracy" promoted during the first phase of the PNDC rule, which did not lead to the empowerment of the majority of the people who were not in favour of military rule. At the end of the debates and seminars, to the government's astonishment, the commission's final report clearly indicated that the overwhelming majority of Ghanaians preferred the re-introduction of multi-party system of government.

The outcome of the NCD report led to the launching of the "Blue Book" in 1987 that contained the proposals for the establishment of the District Assemblies (DA) in the then 110 districts, which unveiled a further stage in the evolving democratic process and set the date for the DA elections in 1988 and implement the first phase of the DA elections between December 1988 and February 1989. The NCD Report was eventually followed by the drafting of the 1992 Constitution by the Consultative Assembly setting out the guidelines for forming political parties and for conducting, organizing and standing for presidential and parliamentary elections in Ghana. In May 1991, the PNDC government put together a Committee of Experts to formulate constitutional proposals under PNDC Law 252 on the proposed constitution and to assist the Consultative Assembly (CA), which was established under the PNDC Law 253 of 1991, to formulate the draft Constitution and provide technical know-how for the CA.

In the process of drafting the Constitution, the CA was to take into account the NCD Report, the abrogated 1957, 1960, 1969, and the 1979 Constitutions and aspects of other national Constitutions that could have a positive impact on Ghana's 1992 Constitution. The 1992 transition timetable was designed as follows: a national referendum about whether to change to multi-party democracy or its notion of populist democracy occurred on 28 April 1992, the lifting of the ban on politics from May 18, 1992, the holding of presidential and parliamentary elections on 3rd November and 8th December 1992 respectively, and the inauguration of the Fourth Republic on 7th January 1993. These political developments led to Ghana's 1992 presidential and parliamentary elections. It is important to note that negotiations between leaders of the banned political parties, the international donor community and the PNDC leadership as well as the outcome of the NCD's Report and the success of the DA elections paved the way for the re-introduction of multi-party democracy in Ghana in 1992.

Hence theorists of the negotiated transition view such as Przeworski, Eisenstadt, Haggard and Kaufman attribute most third-wave transitions to the agency of the elites in the incumbent authoritarian regimes and the opposition parties. When the PNDC announced that the ban on political parties was lifted, the euphoria that greeted the announcement showed that the majority of Ghanaians considered the return to multi-party democracy long overdue. As noted above, what the PNDC started as partial democratic reforms under the decentralization program in 1988 DA elections became a real competitive democratic process by 1992 and Ghana's long-standing political paralysis was finally broken.

The Modalities for the 1992 Democratic Transition and Elections in Ghana

The Constitution established the democratic principles in the legal and institutional framework on which the election procedures, rules and regulations were based, and stipulated some rules and regulations guiding political parties, candidates and the electorate on the conduct of and participation in elections. Ghana has a mixture of the majoritarian and plurality electoral systems. In Ghana, presidential and parliamentary elections are held on December 7of the election year - every four years. Ghana's electoral system has the following basic characteristics:

1. Universal adult suffrage for citizens who are 18 years or older;
2. Official registration of the political parties and voters, a non-compulsory registration or voting policy and secret ballot;
3. A non-partisan District Assembly (DA) and lower local government unit elections;
4. Presidential election based on the pluralist system in which the winner is required

to receive at least 51% of the valid votes cast to win, or a run-off election would be held within 21 days, if none of the presidential candidates is able to obtain the required majority of the valid votes;

1. Parliamentary and local elections are based on the first-past-the post system whereby the winners are those candidates that receive more votes than any other opponent does, regardless of the percentage of votes won;
2. No minimum voter turn-out is required for presidential and parliamentary elections;
3. The administration of all national and local elections is under the jurisdiction of the Electoral Commission (EC);and

A person may stand for election either as a political party candidate or as an independent candidate. To be on the ballot as a presidential candidate, one must be at least 40 years of age, must be supported by two registered voters from each of the 110 districts (totaling 220 supporters). A presidential candidate must name his/her running mate or vice presidential candidate at the time of filling nominations with the INEC at the national head office. The vice president must also meet the same qualifications required of a presidential candidate.

The 1992 Election and its Aftermath

The lifting of the ban on political parties in 1992 saw the resurgence of a number of political parties of different size and ideological character. In this way, what used to be the dominant party traditions – the NPP representing the Danquah-Busia UP tradition and Nkrumah's CPP parties – like the PNC, the revived CPP, the GCPP, and the EGLE Party re-surfaced to compete with the Rawlings' NDC party in the 1992 elections. The period leading to Ghana's 1992 multi-party elections saw the emergence of alliances among the political parties, which can be categorized into three main groups. The first was the "Progressive Alliance," which was led by President Rawlings, consisted mainly of the supporters of the PNDC who formed the NDC, and some of the breakaway Nkrumahist parties, such as the National Convention Party (NCP) - whose flag bearer,

K. N Arkaah became Rawlings' Vice Presidential candidate, and the EGLE party to contest the 1992 elections. Leaders of the "Progressive Alliance" argued that it was the only political group that could ensure political and economic stability in the country. The second major party, the NPP was a resurgence of the liberal democratic ideology and represented the Danquah/Busia party tradition. This party tradition was popular during Ghana's independence struggle and in the postcolonial era, and now among formerly independent voters who were fervently opposed to PNDC rule or those who had suffered one form of injustice or another either under the PNDC or one of the previous military regimes. The NPP was led by Adu Boahen, who became popular through his courageous and ardent criticism of the PNDC regime during the heat of the revolution for its human rights abuses and the "culture of silence" imposed on Ghanaians in the 1980s.

Contrary to the view of the NDC-led "Progressive Alliance," the "Democratic Alliance" consisting of the NPP and its allies, argued that only a change of government could avoid a continuity of the PNDC authoritarian regime and ensure the re-emergence of a full-fledged multi-party democracy that ensures the promotion of civil liberties and political rights. The third group of political parties was the remnants of the Nkrumahist groups. These Nkrumahist tradition parties broke up into small parties during the eleven years of the PNDC rule. Either through co-optation with incentives or coercion, many of their members joined the PNDC and later the NDC. These parties were the People's National Convention (PNC), led by Hilla Limann, former President in the Peoples National Party (PNP) government during the third republic that was overthrown by Rawlings in 1981; the Peoples Heritage Party (PHP) led by E. A. Erskine; and the National Independence Party (NIP) led by Kwabena Darko, a businessman. In all, five presidential candidates contested the presidential elections and five parties competed for the 200 parliamentary seats made available in the legislature in the 1992 elections. The enthusiasm and vibrant competitive atmosphere created by the activities of the various parties confirm arguments put forward by some African democratic theorists such as Boafo-Arthur and Aryee that political parties are key instruments for promoting democracy and as an important link between the government and the people as well as mobilizers of people for participation in elections, and for aggregating the their interests. This point is further buttressed by Bermeo and Schedler's view that regardless of the level of their role in the transition process, political parties are critical agents of democratic transition and consolidation. In the period leading to the 1992 elections, there was a surge in political rallies and campaigns several months prior to the election date and all the political parties campaigned fervently to win support among the electorate. Though such rallies were peaceful, there were some incidents of confrontation between the supporters of the NDC and those belonging to the main opposition party, the NPP, which normally occurred after the rallies. In spite of the PNDC/NDC government's strategies to rig the election, the opposition parties, especially the NPP was very vigilant and documented many of the electoral irregularities, which the party compiled into its famous "Stolen verdict". The INEC election report indicated that the total number of registered voters for the 1992 elections was estimated to be 8,229,902. The total turnout of voters was about 50%, but

the number of valid votes cast was around 48%, which indicated substantial spoilage by way of rejected ballot papers, due to mistakes in voting procedures and election irregularities. Table 4. 1 below shows the percentage of seats won by the parties and their candidates.

Table 4. 1: 1992 Presidential and Parliamentary Election Results

Presidential Candidates	Percentage of votes won	Political Parties	Parliamentary Seats

	Presidential Candidates		
Jerry John Rawlings (NDC)	58.4%	NDC	189
Albert Adu-Boahen (NPP)	30.4%	NPP	0
Hilla Limann (PNC)	6.7%	NCP	8
Kwabena Darko (NIP)	2.8%	EGLE	1
Emmanuel Erskine (PHP)	1.7%	Independents	2

As indicated in the table above, Rawlings emerged the winner of the presidential election with 58.4% of the votes cast, and became the first president of Ghana under the Fourth Republic. His closest competitor and the NPP's presidential candidate, Adu-Boahen also won 30.4% of the votes. In the parliamentary elections, only parties and candidates belonging to the Progressive Alliance – NDC, NCP, and the EGLE party participated. The distribution of the seats won were as follows: NDC had 189 seats; NCP won 8 seats; EGLE party won 1 seat; and there were 2 Independents (See Table 4:1 above for election results). In practical terms, the NCP and EGLE parties were not in opposition since they were part of the progressive alliance. While the 1992 election was marred by allegations of electoral malpractices by supporters of the ruling party, it set the pace for subsequent elections that have taken place since the country's democratic transition, and created the enabling environment for reforming the country's legal and institutional frameworks, and electoral system. This confirms Huntington and Dahl's view that elections play an important role in a country's democratic transition and consolidation.

The 1992 Election's Disconcerting Outcome and the Issue of NDC Legitimacy

One of the main criticisms of the 1992 election is that in the period leading to the elections, the PNDC solely designed, implemented and controlled the transition processes without consultation with the opposition parties. The pro-democracy CSOs and the opposition parties that emerged, after the ban on parties was lifted, criticized the composition of the Committee of Experts and the Consultative Assembly on grounds that the PNDC packed its sympathizers into these Committees to use them as its rubber stamp. For example, the CA inserted "Transitional Provisions" in the 1992 Constitution, which sought to insulate Rawlings and other members of the PNDC, as well as its appointees from prosecution by any court or tribunal in Ghana for any act or omission during the administration of the PNDC. The PNDC regime also dictated the terms, conditions and the timetable for the transition to democracy.

The absence of a level playing field in the elections in which the PNDC/NDC was a player, referee and linesman enabled the PNDC/NDC to manipulate the process to enhance the electoral prospects of Rawlings and the NDC party. This virtually guaranteed the NDC's success and the opposition's failure. As Katz and Mair noted in their discussion of cartel party model, not certain of sustaining its electoral strength or winning enough support to be re-elected the PNDC//NDC party leaders exploited state power and institutional manipulation in order to achieve electoral success in the 1992 election. For this reason, the Alliance of Democratic Forces (ADF), which was an amalgamation of some pro-democracy movements consisting mainly of members of the Nkrumahist and Danquah-Busia traditions, condemned the manner in which the PNDC regime single- handedly managed the transitional processes and challenged the PNDC to convene a national conference and prepare a genuinely national program for the transition. For example, the PNDC appointed the INEC without consulting the ADF. The PNDC played an active role in the 1992 transition and steered it to its advantage. The PNDC government's role in the 1992 election rightly provides evidence for the argument made. O'Donnell argued that in the process of the transition to democratic rule, some authoritarian regimes used their political power advantage to control the transition process in order to maintain their power. Despite the vigorous protests from the opposition parties, and the ADF, the

PNDC directed the INEC to use the 1988 voters' register for the presidential and parliamentary elections of 1992 with the flimsy excuse that the country lacked the financial and material resources and time to carry out a fresh nation-wide registration exercise. This action disenfranchised many voters who could not register prior to the 1998 DA elections. Due to the lack of sufficient preparations by the parties and the electorate, and the tendency of the PNDC/NDC to manipulate the 1992 elections to its advantage at the expense of the opposition parties, various forms of electoral fraud, such as vote rigging, double voting, voting by minors, and stuffing of ballot boxes with fake ballots tainted the genuineness of the entire electoral process. As Aubynn noted, in some instances, the NDC bought or collected identification cards from certain individuals who were suspected of being opposition supporters in some constituencies in the rural areas under the pretext of offering the voters jobs and loans. The conditions under which the 1992 elections were organized did not set a good pre cedent for Ghana's new democracy, because there were several cases of electoral fraud mostly by supporters of the incumbent government.

Electoral offences are defined in the People's Law, 1992 (PNDCL 284). They include offences relating to nomination papers and the ballot; unauthorized voting; offences committed by election officers; impersonation; bribery; threats to voters; and unethical influence. Despite these provisions, the ruling government took advantage of its incumbency and committed most of the listed offences. The restrictions imposed by the PNDC government on the opposition parties in the form of preventing them from having representation at the polling stations, preventing them from witnessing the counting of ballots and restricting opposition campaign meetings did not create a level playing field for all the parties. Also, using militia men to intimidate the supporters of the opposition parties, "buying off" the opposition parties' supporters through the distribution of patronage and lack of understanding of the electoral process by many voters, led to the waning of the opposition parties' confidence in the 1992 elections. Reports from the opposition parties, the media and other pro-democracy bodies stated that the 1992 transition and election were marred by various electoral malpractices orchestrated by the ruling government and its supporters that severely compromised the democratic process.

Regardless of the constitutional provisions that guaranteed the independence of the EC, the problems associated with all the three elections held since 1992 show the vulnerability and inadequacy of the initiatives of political parties and the EC to control the electoral process for fairness and transparency. For example, in the 1992 elections, President Rawlings campaigned for several months before lifting the ban on political campaigns. Even after the ban on political parties was lifted on May 18, 1992, it was difficult for the opposition parties to get police permits for rallies. The police also confounded the opposition parties by delaying grants of permits to hold rallies, as well as filling of ballot boxes with already thumb printed ballots by supporters of the PNDC/NDC. These activities made the notion of free and fair elections a sham. The opposition parties also complained that the NDC dominated the state-owned media and influenced the way that it disseminated news. The NDC candidates gained the advantage of having state resources such as money, logistics and access to the state media at their disposal for political campaigns, while the cash-strapped opposition parties had to struggle to raise funds from members to fund their campaigns. The lack of fairness in political campaigns and the irregularities in the electoral process show how some parties in Ghana manipulated elections to achieve their goals in the initial stages of the transition, regardless of the constitutional provisions.

While the NDC had a definite financial advantage, the opposition parties who were already financially weak, were further constrained by a constitutional clause that limited individual contributions to the parties and were further placed in a disadvantaged position in terms of restrictions imposed by the NDC that prevented them from freely putting their message across to the voters. As the National Vice Chairman and Acting General Secretary of the NPP noted, "whereas the PNDC/NDC party had unlimited access to public media, and state financial and logistical resources, the opposition parties were cash strapped and restricted in their campaigns and advertising because the government negatively targeted the businesses of their financiers. He further noted that the opposition parties the incumbent PNDC government also employed such tactics as using invalid electoral rules and threats to voters by the government controlled security forces that were present at the voting centers across the country. "One of the key problems that affected the fairness and transparency of the 1992

elections and impeded the country's efforts to build a viable electoral system in Ghana was the feud over the opposition's challenge to the voter's register as an appropriate list of qualified voters in the country. Some opposition party leaders claimed that the voter registration lists were outdated, thus disenfranchising large numbers of the electorate, especially the youth who might have voted for change; and also the voters' list was inflated, opening the way to double voting in some polling stations, especially in the Volta region, which is the NDC's stronghold. Some of the NPP and PNC opposition party leaders interviewed claimed that the NDC intentionally refused to update the voter registration list to disenfranchise many of their supportersThe overblown number of registered voters and the election malpractices raised some suspicions by the opposition parties and brought vehement protest from the other parties, who claimed that the PNDC government had falsified the voters register with "ghost names" to enable it rig the elections. In a situation where large numbers of people were disenfranchised, some candidates who would otherwise not have won the elections got elected so the government became less representative.

Despite the protests from the opposition parties, Rawlings refused to open up the voting lists to those who had not registered for the earlier referendum on district assemblies, and the partially updated register in 1991 meant that hundreds of thousands of PNDC/NDC opponents were left without a chance to participate in the elections. As one leader of the CPP noted, in the 1992 elections, the playing field was far from level, because the elections were also marred by a bloated voters' register and a biased and partisan INEC appointed by Rawlings that enabled the ruling PNDC/NDC government to manipulate the presidential elections to its advantage. Evidence of widespread electoral irregularities by the NDC in the 1992 election has been confirmed by Owusu Agyekum, the Minority leader for the 1992 parliament and a leading member of the then NCP and Rawlings Progressive Alliance, who admitted in *The Crusading Guide* newspaper of 30November – December 62004 that Rawlings and the NDC cheated in the 1992 election. He also noted that although the NCP leaders bitterly complained to the leadership of the NDC about the latter's covert manipulation of the 1992 parliamentary elections in favour of NDC candidates, their grievances were not addressed. Another issue of concern was inconsistencies in determining what should be regarded as damaged ballots and the improper sealing of the ballot boxes, which enabled some NDC activists and government appointed DCEs to stuff some of the ballot boxes with fake NDC ballots. For example, in Kumasi, a PNDC District Secretary was allowed to use her car to collect ballot boxes to a central collation center without the supervision of the agents of the other parties. This raised genuine suspicion that the PNDC was using its grip on power to rig the 1992 elections. The undue influence exerted by some polling agents also contributed to making the elections unfair. The parties' effort to educate their supporters was based on explaining how, where, when and why they should cast their votes for the party. Also, as a result of lack of unity among the political parties, the PNC led by Hilla Limann, despite its small number of supporters, refused to join any alliance in the period leading to the 1996 election. Also, the Alliance for Change (AFC), which was formed by the opposition political parties from the Danquah-Busia NPP and Nkrumah's CPP traditions in April 1995, to challenge the NDC in the 1996 elections, successfully organized the *kume preko* demonstration in reaction to the Value Added Tax (VAT), but broke up before the 1996 election was held. The 1992 presidential election was followed by a stream of protests by the opposition parties citing incidents of election irregularities. In Ghana, one of the main areas in which the opposition parties contributed to democratic transition as noted by some theorists of the combined confrontation and negotiation view such as Schedler is its role in electoral reforms after the 1992 election. The opposition parties vigorously disputed the results of the presidential elections of November 1992 and boycotted the parliamentary poll in protest. In a press conference held in Accra after the opposition boycott of the 1992 elections, the NPP presidential candidate, Adu Boahen issued a joint statement on behalf of the opposition parties –NPP, PNC, PCP and CPP - and reported on what was referred to as the "stolen verdict," which included hundreds of detailed allegations of irregularities in one hundred of the country's two hundred constituencies. The 'Stolen Verdict,' which was published by the NPP and other opposition parties, denounced the 1992 election as the most controversial in the country's history, because it was fraudulently conducted with a fraudulent outcome. It is well documented in the "Stolen Verdict" and other research on the 1992 elections that it was characterized by serious voter irregularities. As Nugent confirmed, in the 1992 and 1996 elections, it is reasonable to believe that members of the ruling party did interfere with the polls, along with complaints of violence and harassment of voters, especially the NDC's stronghold in the Volta region. Many election observers reported witnessing situations where the electoral officials issued ballots to voters and attempted to influence the voters' choice under the pretext of educating them on how to mark the ballot. This shows that the political conditions under which the opposition parties competed in the elections breached the rules of democratic competition and deeply flawed the 1992 transition and elections. As one NPP Regional vice-chairman noted, one problem that gave rise to the widespread election malpractices was that there was little or no civic group participation in election monitoring. The majority of election monitors were government security agents, and there were a few international elections monitors to monitor the ballots in all the constituencies. It is possible that the irregularities and unfair practices that took place long before the voting day influenced the 1992 electoral outcome. The opposition NPP presidential candidate, Adu Boahen also showed the press what was alleged to be thirty- two fraudulent ballot papers found on a rubbish dump in Kumasi. He further claimed that twenty-nine out of the thirty-two ballot papers were thumb-printed in favour of the NDC and bore the INEC stamp number 5363, which suggested to the opposition that a staff member or group of employees at the INEC were deeply involved in a conspiracy to rig the elections for the NDC and that Rawlings won the elections through fraudulent manipulations and systematic rigging of the ballots. INEC, which was established under the PNDC Law 271, was charged with the primary responsibility of registering the political parties, and the administration, regulation, control of the 1992 elections. The opposition parties regarded INEC as a body that supported the PNDC's election machinations. For example, on the issue of revising the voters' register, some members of INEC openly supported the government's position. Additionally, when the electorate is afraid to exercise their voting rights or are coerced to vote a particular line, their electoral preferences are restricted. The General Secretary of Western Regional branch of the NDC admitted that "the 1992 election was not perfect, but attributed the problems to lack of experience on the part of the parties, the INEC, the election monitors and lack of understanding of the voting processes on the part of the electorate". The NDC MPs dominated the *de facto* one party 1992 parliament and fully exploited its majority advantage. As a former NPP MP noted, the absence of a viable opposition party in parliament turned it into the government's rubber stamp to affirm every bill that was sent to parliament without any in-depth analysis or debate. This

enabled the NDC to push through some unpopular legislation that favoured the party and its leaders, but not necessarily the public interest. Another problem that faced Ghana's 1992 democratic transition and the NDC government was the issue of legitimacy. The widespread election rigging in the presidential elections and the eventual rejection of the election results by the opposition parties created a legitimacy deficit for the NDC party and had adverse effects on the development of the party system and a sustainable democracy in Ghana. As Lodge noted, problems of legitimacy may arise if a government loses the confidence and support of the people. Some other tests of legitimacy include levels of voter participation, the commitment of all the parties to participate in the elections, and their willingness to accept the election results. Due to the opposition boycott of the parliamentary elections, the 1992 elections did not meet this test of legitimacy. As noted by some democratic transition theorists such as Linz and Lipset, a democratic transition is complete when a civilian democratic administration assumes control over political power and the military because Ghana's transition ended with the P/NDC staying in power. This meant that Ghana's transition process was not completed after the 1992 election. Evidence of this was the intervention of the donor countries for cooperation among the parties and the long negotiations that took place even long after the transition, as well as the changes that were implemented before the 1996 election to put the countries democratic system back on track. In the light of these allegations of electoral fraud, the opposition parties stated categorically that unless some significant changes were made to the electoral processes, they would not participate in future elections conducted at the national and local levels.

These conditions included among others: an interim government to supervise the transition and electoral processes; compiling of a new voters' register; issuing of voter ID cards; and the establishment of a new and substantive EC whose membership would include representatives of all the political parties. Due to the allegations of violence and widespread electoral fraud, Ghana's democracy and political stability as well as the confidence of the international donor community that had supported the transition process was shaken. As a result of the intervention of religious bodies, and the international community, the period after the boycott of the 1992 elections led to negotiations between the ruling and opposition parties. The NPP entered into dialogue with the NDC government. The party's attempt to negotiate with the ruling party divided the NPP into pro-dialogue and anti-dialogue members and alienated the NPP from the other opposition parties. The PNDC/NDC was also compelled by international pressure to negotiate with the opposition parties to eliminate the controversy surrounding the transition process and presidential election. The PNDC/NDC also needed to erase the legitimacy deficit image that plagued the government to make the *de facto* one party parliament acceptable to the international community, the political parties, civic groups and the general public. This compelled the NDC to make compromises and give some concessions to the opposition parties. As a former NPP MP noted, the negotiations and compromises made by the NDC was done at the party's interest because it helped to eliminate some of the legitimacy deficit that plagued the PNDC/NDC government prior to the transition to convince the international donors that the party is democratic. Despite all the problems encountered in the transition and election processes, the 1992 election was a stepping stone for the success of the 1996 elections and major breakthrough for the development of democracy in Ghana since for the first time in about twenty years, majority of Ghanaians had the opportunity to actively participate in political campaigns and multi-party elections in general. Some of the changes made after the 1992 elections will be discussed in the next section to show how the failures of the 1992 elections were addressed in order to improve the 1996 elections.

The 1996 Election and the Electoral Reforms

One of the areas where political parties in Ghana have contributed toward democratic transition and consolidation processes was spearheading reforms in the country's electoral system. This role reaffirms the views expressed by some theorists of the combined confrontation and negotiation school of thought such as Schedler and Bermeo that political parties were instrumental in the third-wave democratic transitions. For example, the successes of Ghana's democratic transition before and after the 1992 election was due to a combination of negotiations and successive confrontations between the supporters of the opposition parties against the PNDC/NDC government. Streamlining Ghana's electoral system by the parties helped to strengthen the country's democracy and rekindle people's interest in the democratic system. In *Democracy and Elections in Africa*, Staffan Lindberg highlighted the importance of elections and electoral systems in developing and sustaining democracy in Africa. The success of the 1996 presidential and parliamentary elections confirmed the progress that was made within the four years of constitutional rule. A number of far-reaching reforms, including the establishment of an autonomous EC, the formation of the Inter-party

Advisory Committee, and the establishment of the National Media Commission were implemented. There was also increased role for the print and electronic press and the active participation of civil society groups in election monitoring. These reforms and initiatives were achieved as a result of negotiations, compromises and cooperation between the EC, the ruling NDC party, the opposition parties, some CSOs, and the support of some donor countries and organizations that have a stake in the success of Ghana's democracy.

The Establishment of an Independent Electoral Commission (EC)

One of the primary steps taken to put Ghana's democratic system back on track after the 1992 election fiasco was the establishment of an independent Electoral Commission. The Electoral Commission (EC) was first introduced in the 1969 Constitution and headed by a sole Commissioner, and maintained in the 1979 Constitution. However, the EC was abolished by the PNDC military regime after the overthrow of the PNP in 1981. In the initial stages of the transition, the PNDC established the INEC as an electoral body to oversee the 1992 elections. However, due to the controversy that surrounded the 1992 elections, in 1993, the political parties together with the Inter Party Advisory Committee pressured the government to establish an EC independent of the government. Its seven-member body includes the Chairman, two deputies and four members are appointed by the president and approved by parliament after going through a vetting process. To ensure its autonomy, the position and power of the chairperson and his two deputies are enshrined in the Constitution and the president cannot sack them without parliamentary approval.

The autonomy and independence of the EC is safeguarded under the 1992 Constitution. Article 46 states that in performing its functions, the Commission "shall not be subject to the direction or control of any person or authority," its chair and members

have permanent tenure of office and have the same conditions of service as justices of the Superior Courts, and its expenditures are charged directly on the country's Consolidated Fund. As the Chairman of the NPP noted, the establishment of the EC was a necessary step and a major factor in the rebuilding of the opposition parties' trust in the independence of the country's electoral institutions. The EC occupies a unique place in the country's democratic development in the performance of its constitutional functions in a fair and open manner. It has undertaken a number of significant innovative and effective electoral reforms since its inception and has wide-ranging functions and powers set out in Article 45 of the 1992 Constitution. It has successfully conducted three consecutive presidential and parliamentary elections, as well as local level district assembly elections.

Against the background of the alleged electoral malpractices in the 1992 elections, the EC, in collaboration with the IPAC introduced some unique electoral reforms to promote transparency and a level playing field for all the political parties. These included:

Compilation of a new voters' register with the collaboration and active participation of the political parties and IPAC. Representation of the People's Law (Law 284) empowers the EC to register all eligible voters, assign them polling stations and to compile the voters' register, which qualifies people to vote in all elections. The EC also has power to revise the register at periods as determined by law. The political parties were given copies of the provisional and final voters register to enable them to confirm the authenticity of the list.

1. District Registration Review Committees were established to resolve all disagreements relating to the registration process and to ensure the compilation of a viable voters register. The DRRC consists of representatives of all the political parties in the District; the commanding officer of the Ghana Police in the District; the District Director of Education; a representative of all chiefs of the District; and the DEO of the EC.

2. To eliminate "ghost names" and voting malpractices, the EC trained and dispatched party agents to monitor the re-registration exercise for the local and national elections at the respective constituencies;

3. The EC has the statutory responsibility of setting election dates and making election regulations within the framework of the Constitution. In this case, the date for the presidential and parliamentary elections was

permanently fixed on the 7of December of every election year;

4. The number of polling stations was increased from 18,000 to 20,000 to facilitate the election process and reduce inconvenience to voters and reduce election irregularities. The EC was also empowered to demarcate and periodically revise electoral boundaries for national and local elections and organized education programs to enlighten the public on the electoral processes;

5. Transparent ballot boxes were introduced at all the 20,000 polling stations to prevent ballot boxes from being pre-stuffed with fraudulent thumb-printed ballots by agents and supporters of the ruling party before being sent to the polling stations;

6. The introduction of cardboard voting screens to prevent voters from dumping concealed ballots in the ballot box;

Voter identity cards with photographs bearing the name, sex age and a serial number were issued to voters throughout the regional capitals and some rural constituencies, while thumbprint ID cards were initially issued to voters in the rural areas where photo-ID cards could not be issued. This exercise was later extended to all parts of the country.

1. New voting forms were introduced and some old ones were redesigned to promote transparency and simplify the conduct of elections. The process of reporting election results was simplified through the introduction of new forms of communication, such as fax, telephone and e-mails; and

2. The EC has the mandate to conduct and supervise all public elections and referenda; and conduct elections for officers of certain statutory bodies, including: the Trades Union Congress, the Veterans Association of Ghana, the Ghana Medical and Dental Association, the House of Chiefs, and the District Assemblies.

3. The EC was also entrusted with the registration of political parties; and

Entrusted with the appointment of permanent and temporary election staff in consultation with the Public Service Commission.

The Constitution requires that the EC be represented in each of the ten administrative regions and 138 districts in Ghana, which are headed by Regional Directors and DEOs respectively. Besides its permanent staff at the national, regional and local levels, the EC engages the services of temporary staff during elections such as Returning Officers who are assisted by two deputies and have the primary responsibility of administering the elections in each of the 230 constituencies under the direction and supervision of the DEOs. There is also a Presiding Officer for each polling station who has full control of the personnel and proceedings at the polling stations. Four Polling Assistants assist each Presiding Officer in each constituency. The EC also works in collaboration with the political parties by allowing the parties to appoint party agents who are representatives from the various political parties contesting the elections to work with the Presiding Officers in the constituencies. As the deputy chairman noted, the EC is involved in a number of programs, such as the training of personnel and exchange of staff with other countries in the sub-region to serve as election monitors and learn from other country's experience. Election candidates are also allowed to appoint one agent to represent them at each polling station in the constituency to observe the entire proceedings on the candidate's behalf. For a free and fair election to take place, prior to the 1996 elections, the EC organized periodic exhibition of the voters register to ensure that all registered voters were confirmed on the voters' list and "ghost names" were removed from the register. The final exhibition of the register was done on 28April to

7May 1996 at all the 20,000 registration centers. The exhibition of the register afforded the voters the opportunity to make sure their names were on the ballot, correct their personal data, identify their voting centers, and object to unqualified persons on the register, such as minors, aliens, and those who have died since the initial registration exercise.

The Formation of the Inter Party Advisory Committee

One major innovation before the 1996 elections that emerged from the opposition parties' objections to the 1992 presidential election results and strengthened consensus building was the establishment of the Inter Party Advisory Committee (IPAC) in March 1994. The formation of IPAC was one of the major victories of the opposition parties after the 1992 election and very significant because the institution continue to play a crucial role in Ghana's party system and democratic development in general. IPAC's membership includes the chairman of the EC as the head of the body and other staff from the EC, as well as representatives of the political parties. Its main functions were to assist the EC to meet the needs of the political parties such as election dispute resolution. The inter-party conflict management body formed by the EC and the political parties, with the support of the donor countries and organizations was very instrumental in resolving the political impasse in Ghana's 1992 transition. The representatives of the donors attended Advisory Committee meetings as observers together with the leaders of the political parties and the EC. One of the key issues that could undermine the basis of consensus in a political system and thereby constrain the sustainability of the political parties cooperation is the inability of the leaders of the political parties to reach compromises on ground rules of political contestation as occurred during and immediately after the 1992 democratic transition. Since Ghana's democratic transition, IPAC has served as effective machinery for resolving party grievances and election disputes. The dialogue brokered by the political parties and IPAC was a necessary step toward stabilizing and strengthening Ghana's fledgling democratic experiment, and shows that mutual agreements and the existence of conflict management mechanisms is important for the sustainability of inter-party cooperation. Some of the major decisions reached prior to the 1996 election were the holding of the presidential and parliamentary elections on the same day and the use of transparent ballot boxes with numbered seals. IPAC was decentralized to the regional and district levels to deal with problems that might crop up during local and national level elections. This body became an important mechanism for dialogue, consultation and consensus building to ensure peace and stability before, during and after the 1996 elections and subsequent general elections. Since its inception, IPAC was very influential in the political reforms that took place after the 1992 election fiasco to put Ghana's democracy back on track, and has made significant progress in reforming Ghana's electoral system. Before the 1996 elections, IPAC successfully requested the issuing of voter identification cards and other significant electoral reforms, which were all implemented, despite the NDC government's stiff opposition to the reforms. Political parties draw their

sustainability from a vibrant electoral process that is fair to all, and that was the crux of the political disagreements between the main contending parties. As Boafo-Arthur noted, since the long-term sustainability of the political system and the institutions within the system depends on a transparent electoral system, party leaders and the donor community saw the need for pursuing mutual consensus by the parties to assure the sustainability of the democratic system. Apart from enhancing public confidence in the electoral system, it helped to reduce vote rigging and invariably, the number of complaints from losing parties. All these measures helped to sustain consensus among the parties, electoral reforms and the revitalizing Ghana's democratic system. The inter-party dialogue spearheaded by the EC and IPAC led to reconciliation of the major parties and helped in designing the modalities for changes made prior to the 1996 election.

Although the initial efforts at reconciliation by IPAC proved futile, due to the unwillingness of some of the parties to cooperate and compromise and partly due to the refusal of some party leaders who regarded the negotiation as a sell-off and refused to join the process in the initial stages. Nonetheless, dialogue became the IPAC and EC initiative, and the foundation for further attempts at consensus building as well as the fashioning of a robust electoral system within which contesting parties drew their strength and vitality. Through the initiative of IPAC, the parties have established the chairpersons' caucus, in which the chairpersons of the parties meet to discuss issues of mutual interest and resolve inter-party conflicts, which has further enhanced the parties' level of cooperation and tolerance. IPAC has also been instrumental in promoting peace and harmony among the political parties since the power alternation, as it helped negotiate the power transfer from the NDC to the NPP government in 2001. IPAC continue to play key role in settling disputes among the parties and in the newly constituted Chairpersons' Conference.

Introduction of Election Monitoring by some Civic Groups

Another novel feature that was introduced with the support of the political parties prior to the 1996 election and further strengthened before the 1996 election was election monitoring by CSOs, which was a new concept to Ghana at that time. In their study of political transition, O'Donnell, Schmitter and Whitehead discussed the crucial role of civil society in building pressure for democratic transition in many African and Latin American countries and the defeat of some incumbent authoritarian regimes. The emergence of election monitoring bodies as Ghana Alert and the NEDEO, which consisted of about twenty-three prominent national organizations, including the Christian Council, the Catholic Secretariat, the Federation of Muslim Councils, the Ghana National Association of Teachers, the National Union of Ghana Students, the Ghana Journalist Association, the Ghana Trade Unions Congress, the Ghana Committee on Human and People's Rights, and the Ghana Association of Women Entrepreneurs helped to mobilize most of the human and logistic election-monitoring resources in the country. In all, NEDEO and Ghana Alert trained 4,200 election-monitoring personnel in all the regions and deployed them to all the 200 constituencies across the country and about 3100 polling stations. These organizations also engaged in the training and deployment of the election monitors, and supplied the monitoring staff with transportation and communication equipment. The IEA trained fifty people drawn from all ten regions of the country and from various civic groups and deployed them as election monitors to some key constituencies. It also provided technical support and initiated a program that trained and deployed personnel to thirty-five key constituencies to observe and report on the pre- election environment long before the elections day. The Catholic Secretariat also provided a nationwide wireless communication network to facilitate the elections. The significant role that the political parties and CSOs, such as NEDEO, played in the 1996 elections showed the increasing collaboration of the parties and CSOs in promoting free and fair elections through election monitoring and other related activities. Some institutional theorists such as Putnam highlighted the critical role of civil society in building pressure for democratic transition in many third-wave countries and greasing the wheels of democracy to facilitate smooth and peaceful transitions. Unlike the 1992 election when the PNDC/NDC government and its agents took control of the election administration processes, the involvement of the CSOs in election monitoring in the 1996 election helped to reform the process of elections in Ghana and to reduce the electoral rigging practices of the incumbent NDC government. To complement the initiatives of the local groups, external observers like the African American Institute, the Carter Center, and the Commonwealth Secretariat were heavily involved in Ghana's 1996 election. This was in sharp contrast with, and a significant improvement over the 1992 election when only about 200 domestic election monitors, dominated by pro-government CSOs, such as the ACDRs and state security agencies controlled by the executive, served as election monitoring personnel. The election monitoring activities of the IEA, NEDEO and Ghana Alert were funded through the generous donations from the National Endowment for Democracy (NED), CIDA, Canadian Parliamentary Center, the National

Democratic Institute (NDI), the German Party Foundations, the Westminster Foundation, the Hans Siedel Foundation, the USAID and other foreign sources. The NEDEO program shows how civil society is increasingly taking advantage of the democratic opening to play key roles alongside the political parties in Ghana's democratic project.

Establishment of the National Media Commission and Role of the Media

The enactment of the 1992 Constitution created the enabling environment for the emergence of a vibrant media. The private independent newspapers and radio stations could publish news without fear. The Constitution made provisions for the establishment of the National Media Commission (NMC), with a view to ensuring the independence of the media and monitoring of their performance. While the PNDC managed to suppress the upsurge of a vibrant private press from the 1980s to 1992 through various strategies, such as arrest and detention without trail; closing of media houses and harassment of publishers; after the 1992 transition to constitutional rule, the press became more vocal. In the NMC Act of 1993, parliament gave the Commission the power to make regulations about its complaints procedure and any other matter that may require the efficient discharge of the media's functions. As Putnam rightly put it, a strong civil society forms an essential foundation for the transition and consolidation of fledgling democracies. With the establishment of the NMC, the press had a medium of a single

mouthpiece through which it challenged the NDC government on infringement of the people's rights, independence and freedom. The 1992 Constitution has a number of provisions that support the media's role in the country's democratic project. The Constitution guarantees under Article 162 that there shall be no censorship in Ghana and that any law that seeks to negate these provisions shall be null and void. With regard to strengthening the media, sections (4) and (5) under Article 162 of the 1992 Constitution state that editors and publishers of newspapers and other institutions of the mass media shall not be penalized or harassed for their editorial opinions and views, or the content of their publication, and provides for the freedom and independence of the media, a ban on censorship, and recognition of the media's watchdog role to uphold the accountability of the government. "All agencies of the mass media shall, at all times, be free to uphold the principles, provisions and objectives of this constitution, and shall uphold the responsibility and accountability of the government to the people of Ghana. "Article 55 Section 11 of the Constitution specifies that the state shall provide fair opportunity to all political parties to present their programs to the public by ensuring equal access to the state-owned media. Section 12 of the same Article also states that all presidential candidates shall be given the same amount of time and space on the state-owned media to present their programs to the people. Article 163 also stipulates that all state-owned media shall afford fair opportunities and facilitate the presentation of divergent views and dissenting opinions. The Constitution further stipulates that there shall be no obstacles in the way of any person who seeks to establish a newspaper, journal or other media publication for mass communication or information. This include the prohibition of any form of impediments to the establishment of private press or media; the passing of laws requiring licenses as a condition for establishing or operating any of the recognized media for mass communication or information; subjection to government control and interference with editors and publishers of newspapers and other institutions of the mass media; or the harassment of such persons for their editorial opinions and views on the content of their publication. The constitution also states that these wide-ranging freedoms shall be exercised in accordance with laws in the interest of national security, public order, public morality, and for protecting the reputations, rights and freedoms of other persons; and all state-owned media are required by law to afford fair opportunities and facilities for the presentation of divergent views and dissenting opinions. The enforcement of these provisions by the NMC in the period leading to the 1996 elections created an atmosphere of free speech and enabled the press to publicize allegations of corruption against some government officials, which were investigated by the CHRAJ in 1996, leading to adverse findings against some high-ranking public figures. Article 167 of the Constitution also explicitly defines the NMC's regulatory power, which gives the Commission the authority to make certain regulations to monitor the activities of the media in the following ways:

1. To promote and ensure the freedom and independence of the media for mass communication or information;

2. To take all appropriate measures to ensure the establishment and maintenance of the highest journalistic standards in the mass media, including the investigation, mediation and settlement of complaints made against or by the press or other mass media;

3. To insulate the state-owned media from government control; and

To make regulations by constitutional instrument for the registration of newspapers and other publications, except that the regulations shall not provide for the exercise of any direction or control over the professional functions of a person engaged in the production of newspapers or other means of mass communication. The Newspaper Registration Regulation required that all publishers register with the Commission after paying a stipulated fee; that newspapers file quarterly updates and renewed their registration annually.

The yardstick by which broadcasting standards were set to regulate broadcasting in Ghana addresses a number of issues including objectivity and fairness, national identity in programming, accuracy, decency, language, authenticity, morality and social values. These rules also deal with children and religious programs, quiz programs, news and current affairs programs, advertisements and political broadcasts. The penalty for non-compliance of these rules could result in harsh punishments, such as fines and even jail terms. While some media practitioners complain that these rules are too rigid and are constrained by socio-cultural norms and traditions of the society, content regulation, as a feature for upholding broadcasting standards is not unique to Ghana alone. Several countries have similar bodies such as the Canadian Radio and Television Commission (CRTC) to check media excesses. The guidelines placed on the Ghanaian media are considered necessary for ensuring that their publications conform to the society's cultural traditions, while at the same time serving as a useful guide to the government, elected officials and the political parties in promoting democratic principles in Ghana. Regardless of the rules that bind the print and electronic public and private media, they play essential roles in the development of the party system and Ghana's democracy.

The importance of the media in Ghana cannot be overemphasized. Without it, candidates are not able to reach out to every voter across the country. The press is the crucial avenue for the dissemination of information to create mass awareness for the public. People form their opinions about parties and candidates based on what they see, hear or read about an issue that greatly influences their votes. Despite the freedom

granted the media by the NPP government and the important role they continue to play in Ghana's democratic consolidation, the media continue to face major logistic and financial challenges. The high production cost of newsprint limits circulation of the private press. The lack of professionalism in the activities of some media outlets and weak investigative skills of some journalists also undermines the work of the media. The important role of the media in Ghana's democracy also requires media practitioners to be objective, fair, and transparent. In carrying out their duties, they should strike an ideal balance between fair criticism and media sensationalism. Obviously, the reforms that were introduced prior to the 1996 presidential and parliamentary elections were instrumental in reducing the numerous election malpractices that plagued the 1992 elections and created the enabling environment for the 1996 elections to take place in an orderly fashion without any major complaints or violence.

The Outcome of the 1996 Election: Pre and Post Election Problems

As a result of the major changes made in Ghana's electoral systems, the 1996 presidential and parliamentary elections were held in a peaceful atmosphere without any opposition boycott. Voter turnout for the election was 78. 2 % of all eligible voters. As Table 4. 2 below indicates, the ruling NDC party candidate, Rawlings, won the presidential elections in the first round of the ballot. The distribution of the 200 parliamentary seats after the election was as follows: the ruling NDC had 133 parliamentary seats; the leading opposition NPP had 61 seats; PCP got 5 parliamentary seats; PNC obtained 1 seat; 1 vacant seat; and there was no independent MP in the 1996 parliament. The success of the 1996 elections also demonstrated public support for Ghana's democracy. In one of the CDD Afrobarometer polls on different issues on Ghana's democracy, 71. 1% of the respondents said that they discussed politics with other people. Also, 93. 6% of respondents said they were registered as voters, while 88. 6% reported voting in the 1996 general elections and 76. 5% believed democracy is preferable to any other form of government. However, just 54. 4% said that they were pleased with the way that democracy actually works in Ghana. Unlike in the 1992 parliament, which was a *de facto* one party parliament, the presence of the opposition parties in parliament led to effective debating of issues. The 1996 elections therefore served as a major stepping-stone in the effort toward putting Ghana's democracy back on track and set it on the path of consolidation. Table 4. 2 below shows the percentage of votes received by the parties and their candidates.

Table 4. 2: 1996 Presidential and Parliamentary Election Results

Presidential Candidates	Percentage of votes won by Presidential Candidates	Political Parties	Parliamentary Seats
J. J. Rawlings	57. 4%	NDC	133

(NDC)			
J. A. Kufour (NPP)	39.6%	NPP	60
Edward Mahama (PNC)	3.0%	PCP	5
N/A	N/A	PNC	1
		Vacant seat	1

While there were improvements in the 1996 election, it was also marred by serious problems. Despite all the precautionary measures and money that was spent on the elections, the extensive preparations that were made toward the administration of the election, and the lessons from the 1992 election, the 1996 election was not as free and fair as expected. In the early stages of Ghana's democracy, the media were subjected to a variety of harsh treatments by the government. The period prior to, during and after the 1996 elections saw the harassment and unlawful arrest of some media personnel by the NDC government. As one journalist noted, one major obstacle that posed a real threat to free press was provision for criminal libel, which originated from Section 185 (d) of the Criminal Code of 1960 and was maintained in the 1992 Constitution. Notwithstanding the use of the criminal libel law by the NDC regime in the 1990s, and the number of difficulties faced by the media, journalist remained steadfast in their work. The media was also vulnerable to other forms of government interference. For example, the NDC instituted difficult registration bottlenecks, such as the refusal of the government to permit the supply of essential materials, and withholding of vital government information and party advertisements that were likely to promote the anti-government press' sales. The opposition parties argued that the factor that was heavily weighted against

them in their campaigns, but greatly favoured the ruling NDC party was its control over the state-owned print and electronic media. The state-owned media had a broader coverage than the small privately-owned media houses and the imbalance in access to the media. Regardless of the changes that were instituted by the NMC, the NDC government continued to influence, coerce and manipulate the state-owned media to its advantage. For example, in the period leading to the 1996 elections, the NPP complained that the GBC, which was at the time better resourced in terms of financial, material and human resources and had a broader audience across the country than the privately owned print

and electronic press, refused to advertise its programs to counter some negative advertisements made by the ruling NDC against the NPP's presidential candidate. The NPP also claimed that the management of the Graphic Communications Group Ltd. refused to carry its counter-advertisement in response to an NDC ad, which portrayed their party symbol, the elephant, as destructive. Opposition parties also alleged that the management of the state-owned media refused to accept or publish opposition party advertisements.

In 1993, the NPP took the GBC to court with the claim that the GBC covered and broadcasted a forum held by the ruling NDC government on the budget presented before parliament that fiscal year, but it failed to give coverage to a public forum the NPP organized to present its position on the government's budget. As a result of the imbalance in the media's exposure of the parties, the NPP issued a writ demanding that the Supreme Court interpret and enforce the provisions of Article 55 (11) of the 1992 Constitution and give an order enjoining the GBC to afford all parties fair and equal opportunity to present their views on the budget. In the case, the court unanimously upheld all the claims by the NPP for a fair opportunity from the state-owned media. The court ruled that "equal access" as stipulated in the 1992 Constitution meant that equal time and space must be allotted to each political party to have the opportunity to present its political, economic and social programs to the electorate for the purpose of persuading them to vote for the party in both the parliamentary and presidential elections under identical terms and conditions prescribed by the Constitution for gaining entry into the state-owned media. While some members of the ruling NDC party claimed that the private media was hostile toward their party, the opposition parties also complained that the state-owned media's one-sided reporting favoured the ruling NDC party. Other complaints against the

media in 1992 and 1996 were that they failed to discuss issues about the parties and elections, and did not focus their attention on voter education, as well as the performance of the media, especially the state-owned media in reporting on the campaigns and elections, lacked professionalism, fairness and objectivity.

Regardless of the innovations that were achieved by IPAC and the EC, the ruling NDC party managed to delay and in most cases disrupt the reforms that were being implemented. For example, in 1994, NPP presidential candidate in the 1992 election, Adu-Boahen, accused President Rawlings of foot dragging for his refusal to sign a contract that would enable the EC to obtain funding to compile a new voters' register, procure transparent boxes, provide identification cards for all Ghanaians of voting age and train personnel to assist in the conduct of elections. The opposition also complained about abuse of incumbency by the ruling party through the use of state financial and logistical resources to the detriment of the opposition parties, which were already severely cash strapped. As a result of these disagreements between the ruling and opposition parties, and pressure from IPAC on the government to cooperate in the reforms, the NDC pulled out of IPAC. Some parliamentary candidates also complained that the Election Returning Officers deliberately or accidentally exchanged the scores with those of the competing candidates, thereby making them lose the election. Some ballot boxes never got to the collation centers and so the results of the affected polling stations were not tabulated. In some NDC strongholds, there were allegations that some polling officials who were bribed by the PNDC dumped an unspecified number of ballots already thumb-printed for the ruling party into the ballot boxes to increase their votes.

One other major complaint against the 1996 presidential and parliamentary elections was the perception that the voters' register had about 9. 3 million registered voters during the fresh registration of voters in October 1995. The opposition parties argued that considering Ghana's census figures prevailing at the time, there was no way that the voter population could reach that number and therefore queried the figure. The justification for this allegation was that whereas in 1996, there was a 78% voter turn out, representing 9. 3 million votes cast in the first round of the presidential poll, in the 2000 elections, due to additional measures instituted by the EC and the political parties to check electoral fraud, the number dropped to 62%, which represented 6. 5 million votes cast. Apart from lack of financial and logistical resources, the opposition parties' campaign activities were crippled by the government's control over the public media, which at that time covered a wider spectrum of the population than the private press. Another issue was conflict among party supporters. For example, in October 1996, there were violent clashes between NDC and NPP supporters in Tamale in the Northern region, Kumasi in the Ashanti Region and Sunyani in the Brong Ahafo Region as well as in Kibi in the Eastern Region in which at least 20 people were severely beaten and seriously wounded. Another problem that tainted the success of the 1996 elections was the government's interference with the CSOs election monitoring activities. Despite the flourishing environment and involvement of CSOs in the elections, the pro-democracy and anti-NDC civic groups continued to face severe obstacles and hostility from the NDC government. Some leading members of NEDEO interviewed admitted that in the 1996

elections, the NDC government used a number of strategies through the state security agencies and paramilitary bodies to disrupt their election monitoring activities. Since this was the first time a group of independent CSOs had been actively involved in a nation- wide election monitoring, their activities were regarded as a form of sabotage against the ruling party. Most of the CSOs and election monitoring agents were branded as anti- government elements and were targeted for various forms of reprisals and censorship. To a greater extent, the NDC government used pro-government CSOs such as the DWM to counter the activities of the pro-democracy movements. This confirms Abrahamsen and Encarnacion's view that civil society can obstruct and/or destabilize democratic development. Judging from the PNDC/NDC origins, one could justifiably conclude that the NDC government was not accustomed to opposition from the parties and CSOs, and saw the active involvement of the CSOs and party operatives in election monitoring as a threat to its power and legitimacy. Irrespective of the problems that were encountered by the press and CSOs, there is little doubt, however, that their roles and the election reforms led to the general success of the 1996 election and gave impetus to Ghana's historic 2000 election and the power alternation that followed.

Conclusion

Members and pro-democracy groups loyal to the banned political parties played significant roles in the process of negotiating the 1992 transition, which complemented the role of the CSOs and external donors in securing multi-party democracy in Ghana. Analysis of the 1992 and 1996 elections shows the problems that faced Ghana's democratic transition processes, such as the registration of voters, organization of elections and election monitoring. In all these, the opposition parties continued to

challenge the P/NDC government's control and manipulation of power even after the 1996 election, which contributed to further changes and the success of the opposition NPP in the 2000 elections. It is apparent that the EC has been increasingly effective in its role as the election administering body in the country and ensuring that the political parties abide by the rules guiding elections to promote free and fair elections in Ghana. Political parties in Ghana have also been very instrumental in the country's democratic consolidation process through the activities of IPAC and the party chairperson's caucus. The formation of IPAC promoted cooperation among the opposition parties in the 1996 and 2000 elections. As a first of its kind in thirteen years, the 1992 election offered a majority of Ghanaians the opportunity to actively participate in political campaigns in various ways and exercise their voting rights in the 1992 election after several years of disenfranchisement by various military regimes.

The study argues that while Ghana's 1992 elections worked to enhance consensus among the opposition parties through the formation of the IPAC, it did not remove some fundamental impediments that would have leveled the playing field for all the parties and could have offered the opposition parties better prospects of defeating the incumbent regime. The private press in particular has significantly influenced the conduct of free and fair elections in Ghana and the development of the country's democracy since the 1992 transition. In analyzing the role of the civic groups in election monitoring and promoting free and fair elections in Ghana, it can be concluded as well that the election monitoring activities of these local and international organizations greatly strengthened Ghana's electoral system, especially the voting processes and enhanced the freeness and fairness of elections since the 1996 election. The next chapter continues with a discussion of the political parties' role in strengthening Ghana's post-transition electoral systems and the country's democratic consolidation process through their activities in the 2000 and 2004 elections.

Chapter Five

Political Parties and Democratic Consolidation: The 2000 and 2004 Elections

Introduction

The first part of the chapter discusses the 2000 election to show the extent to which the political parties have helped in strengthening Ghana's post-transition democracy and promoted electoral reforms as well as contributed toward the country's democratic consolidation process. This section also focuses on the changes that were implemented to promote free and fair elections in 2000, and facilitated the peaceful and successful power alternation from the incumbent NDC party to the NPP. The second part of the chapter focuses on the 2004 election and the improvements that were made by the EC in collaboration with the political parties and CSOs that resulted in the more orderly and successful election in 2004. In looking at the role of elections in the process of developing Ghana's democracy, the chapter examines some of the factors that contributed to the successes in the 2000 and 2004 elections, and some of the problems that continue to hinder Ghana's electoral system. The discussion in this section thus focuses on a series of questions. To what extent has Ghana's election procedures been reformed? How has the electoral reforms helped to promote free and fair elections in Ghana? And how has political parties in Ghana contributed toward the consolidation of democracy? Answering these questions can help in our assessment of how parties' have contributed toward Ghana's democratic consolidation process.

The 2000 Election and the Question of Continuity or Change: Ghana's Democracy at the Crossroads

The Emergence of the NPP Government: Getting the Politics Right

Political parties in Ghana played significant roles in negotiating further changes to the country's electoral system, through street demonstrations and monitoring of elections that led to free, fair and transparent elections in 2000. Ghana's democratic transition culminated in the 2000 election that brought the NPP to power. Hence the year 2000 saw a dramatic shift in Ghana's political landscape and in its post-independence political history. Ghana's Fourth Republic and democratic experiment, which began in 1992 after ten years of PNDC rule, entered its third phase on 7December 2000 when Ghanaians went to the polls to elect a new president and a new 200-member parliament. Before the elections, seven political parties filed nominations, which included the NDC/EGLE alliance with John Atta-Mills as its presidential candidate, the CPP led by George Hagan, the PNC with Edward Mahama as its flag-bearer and Democratic Peoples Party (DPP) led by William Ofori-Atta, as well as the United Ghana Movement led by Wireko Brobbey. The NPP was led by John Agyekum Kuffour as its flag-bearer, the GCPP under the leadership of Dan Lartey and the NRP, which is a breakaway party from the NDC, with Augustine "Goosie" Tandoh as its presidential candidate. The main campaign issues in the 2000 election focused on the question of continuity or change - whether the NDC should be maintained or change the government by voting for an opposition party, in this case the NPP.

The presidential and parliamentary elections took place on the 7of December 2000 and the presidential run-off was held on December 28, 2000. The percentage of

voter turnout for the 2000 presidential elections at the national level was 61. 7%, representing 6,605,084 out of about 10. 7 million registered voters who actually voted on the elections day. In the presidential run-off, held on December 28, slightly fewer voters (59. 65%) cast valid ballots, in which President Kufour (NPP) defeated Mills (NDC) 57% to 43% to claim the presidency. Compared with turnout levels in the 1996 general elections, when 77. 01% of registered voters cast valid ballots, the figures for 2000 presidential elections were considerably lower, which was partly due to voter apathy and the result of the measures instituted to check election malpractices in the 2000 election. The election outcome was the climax of the discontent arising from the NDC's vertical authoritarian decision-making style, hegemonic dominance of power, dashed public expectation of economic prosperity and social development. Also, the NDC government's gross civil and human rights abuses, the perceived corruption of public officials and the impact of the austerity adjustment policies were evident in the people's 'protest vote', which swept the incumbent regime from power.

The success of the opposition NPP in the presidential and parliamentary elections ended the PNDC/NDC government's long reign, and ushered in a new political era on 7January 2001. The power transfer and with Rawlings out of the scene, erased any traces of the military influence on Ghana's democratic system and set it on the path of consolidation. Linz and Stepan's argue that a democratic transition is completed only when the executive, legislative and judicial powers under the new democratic government are not constrained by law to share power with the military or is rid of any

traits of military influence. The NDC presidential candidate's concession and the smooth transition of power from one elected government to another show that the 2000 election was the freest, fairest and most transparent than the 1992 and 1996 elections. The presence of a large contingent of foreign and local election monitors in the elections unanimously declared the 2000 elections as "free and fair." For example, the registering of unregistered voters and re-opening of the voters register showed that unlike the 1992 and 1996 elections, people were not unduly disenfranchised. Linz and Stepan argued that a necessary but by no means sufficient condition for the completion of a democratic transition is the holding of free and contested elections based on broadly inclusive voter eligibility that satisfies electoral institutional conditions. The overall view of the observers was that the conduct of the election was transparent and the outcome was peaceful and boosted public support for multi-party democracy in Ghana. Table 5.1 below shows the votes won by the parties and candidates, and the distribution of the parliamentary seats after the 2000 elections was as follows: the NPP had 100 seats, the NDC got 92 seats, the PNC had three seats, the CPP got one seat, and there were four independent MPs. NDC lost thirty-eight seats to the NPP in the 2000 elections. None of the presidential candidates initially won a majority of the vote to win the presidency. Table 5.1 below shows the 2000 presidential and parliamentary results and the distribution of votes for the respective parties that contested the election.

Table 5. 1: The 2000 Presidential and Parliamentary Election Results

Party Candidates	Percentage of votes won by Presidential Candidates	Political Parties	Parliamentary Seats
J. A. Kufour (NPP)	57. 4%	NPP	99
J. Atta-Mills (NDC)	42. 6%	NDC	92
		PNC	3
		CPP	1
		Independents	4

The public excitement that accompanied the 2000 presidential and parliamentary elections also show that a majority of Ghanaians saw it as both an opportunity and a challenge to strengthening Ghana's infant democracy. There was also a great deal of public awareness of the electoral process and excitement about the prospects of changing the government through a peaceful process. A CDD poll conducted in 2002 shows an overwhelming majority, 87% of Ghanaians, expressed the opinion that the best means of choosing their national leaders is through open, competitive, elections and a resounding majority, 83%, rejected military rule, 82% rejected personal dictatorship, 79% rejected a one party state and 69%

rejected traditional rule. Additionally, external funding for the 2000 election was increased significantly. For example, the EC received about US$8. 4 million in donor funding from the U. K. Department for International Development (DFID), DANIDA, CIDA, EU and USAID, and UNDP Elections Trust Fund contributed a further US$1. 7 million to the EC. Despite Rawlings' agitation for a recount, the NDC's presidential candidate, Atta-Mills, peacefully accepted the election results and his

party's electoral defeat without any challenge or confrontation. Regarding the conditions for democratic consolidation, Linz and Stepan argued that for democracy to be consolidated, all political actors must accept the laws, procedures and institutions of democracy as the only viable and legitimate frameworks for seeking and exercising political power to govern the society, and aggregating the people's interests. In this way, democratic institutions, rules and procedures become the yardstick for measuring the extent to which democratic principles are ingrained in the society. As Diamond noted, democratic consolidation is a process of completing regime change or cementing the transition. Thus the power transfer in 2001 and the politically stable atmosphere coupled with the relative absence of major ethnic conflict created an enabling environment to set the country's democracy on the path of consolidation. While the 1996 election put Ghana's democracy back on track, the opposition parties' success in the 2000 election set it on the road toward consolidation. To this end, Ayee argued that a consolidated democracy occurs when the ruling government meets all the procedural criteria of democracy, and in which all political parties abide by the democratic principles and accept the established political institutions, and when an opposition party defeats an incumbent government after the transition. A major benchmark of democratic consolidation was met in the 2000 elections and the country reached an important milestone in its political history when the incumbent NDC government was defeated in the presidential and parliamentary elections, and a peaceful transfer of power from the ruling NDC party to the opposition NPP took place under the presidency of John Agyekum Kufour. This was of historical importance because it was the first time ever in the country's history that a democratically elected government had

fully served its two consecutive four-year terms and was replaced by a government from an opposition party through the ballot box. With the alternation of power, although Ghana's democracy has not met Pasquino and Huntington's "two turn-over test," it meets Liphart and Przeworski's "one turn over rule," which requires that in a consolidated democracy, the party that assumes power in the initial elections at the time of transition to democracy, loses a subsequent election and turns over power to the opposition party that wins the election. This showed that Ghana crossed the democratic consolidation threshold after the 2000 elections continues to head in the direction of strengthening its democratic consolidation process. This trend is made possible mainly through the initiatives and cooperation of political parties and CSOs as well as the support of the international donor community.

The 2004 Election: Continuing the Trend toward Democratic Consolidation

The success of the 2004 election was another landmark achievement in Ghana's democratic development, and shows that there has been a consistent pattern of improvements in the electoral process since the 1992 transition that ushered in Ghana's democratic process. Although the success of the 2000 election stimulated people's interest in the 2004 election and contributed to its advancement in terms of transparency and fairness, the 2004 election was a significant improvement over the 2000 election. Political parties that contested the 2004 election greatly contributed to its success through their cooperation on issues, tolerance of one another, and the promotion of peaceful campaigns and inclusive elections. As Linz and Stepan noted, a necessary but by no

means sufficient condition for the completion of a democratic transition is the holding of free and contested elections based on broadly inclusive voter eligibility that meet the institutional requirements for elections. The month of October witnessed resurgence in the political parties' campaign activities, and gathered momentum in November till the Election Day on December 7, 2004. There were a number of rallies and campaigns by all the political parties that contested the 2004 elections to introduce presidential and parliamentary candidates to the electorate in the regions and districts/constituencies across the country.

Political rallies were well attended, party supporters and sympathizers at these rallies numbered from hundreds to thousands, depending on whether the rally was being held in a rural or urban setting. Through the rallies and campaign activities, the parties solicited support for their respective candidates and promoted their development agendas. As Hofferbert noted in his analysis of democratic consolidation, the structure, organization and performance of political parties are some of the most vital aspects of the road to democratic consolidation. For cultural reasons, no candidate is turned away from a town or village, and the chiefs and the people in the community give all election candidates a warm welcome. However, the reception may vary from one candidate to another depending on which party the chief and people are affiliated with. In one case directly observed, despite the animosity that existed between a paramount chief and an MP, the chief gracefully accepted the drinks and customary gifts that were offered by the MP as a symbol of seeking permission to hold a rally in the community under the chief's jurisdiction.

The success of the 2004 election is evident in the 85. 1% voter turnout and the number of CODEO members who agreed on the transparency of the election processes. The Electoral Observation Committee of the Religious Bodies consisting of the Ghana Catholic Bishops' Conference and the Christian Council of Ghana also gave a thumbs-up to Election 2004 indicating the election was free, fair and devoid of any major acts of intimidation that could have undermined the entire democratic process and its outcome. CODEO noted that despite some minor incidents, voting in the 2004 elections was generally smooth across all parts of the country. One of the major factors that contributed to the peaceful election in 2004 was the institutionalization of the parties and electoral system, which enhance trust and cooperation among competing parties. Plasser, Ulram, and Waldrauch emphasize the central role of the institutionalization of parties and state institutions. The institutions and internal organization of the democratic government that assumes power could serve as valuable elements of continuity after the transition and pave the way for democratic consolidation. As Diamond noted, by defining clear and workable rules of the game to which contending political actors can credibly commit themselves, and by establishing more dependable structures for mediating political conflicts and concerns, parties operate in a friendly environment. As Table 5. 2 below specifies, in the presidential election, the ruling NPP candidate, President John A. Kufour had 53. 3%, the main opposition NDC party candidate, John Atta-Mills 43. 8%, the

PNC candidate, Edward Mahama 1.93%, and the CPP candidate, George Aggudey received 1%. The parliamentary elections results were as follows: NPP had 128 seats; NDC received 94 seats; CPP got 3; PNC had 4; 1 independent MP; and 3 constituencies were disputed and resolved afterwards. Table 5.2 shows the 2004 election results and the percentage of votes won by the parties.

Table 5. 2: 2004 Presidential and Parliamentary Election Results

Party Candidates	Percentage of votes won by presidential candidates	Political Parties	Parliamentary Seats
Kufour - NPP	53.3%	NPP	128
Atta-Mills - NDC	44.64%	NDC	94
Edward Mahama - PNC	1.93%	PNC	4
George Aggudey - CPP	1%	CPP	3
		Independent	1

The CODEO observers acknowledged that on average, there were five polling station officials and five political party agents at each polling station. The observers found the overall conduct of the election processes satisfactory since 94% of the monitoring observers reported that the procedures for election set-ups were followed. The report also noted that 93% were satisfied with the voting procedure and nearly 96% indicated that the procedures for counting and declaring election results were followed. Moreover, 95% of the observers reported that the party agents signed the statement of results and 96% noted they were satisfied with the vote counting exercises. In addition, 94% of collation center observers indicated that security personnel were present, 96% said election observers were also present at the collation centers, 88% of the observers noted that the constituency results sheets were signed and dated by the party/candidate agents and the election officials and 87% said the electoral processes worked acceptably. Also, a French election observer, Etienne Manuard, who is an Attache to the French Embassy in Accra not only described the election as peaceful, but also noted that Ghana's way of voting is very rational and economical compared to the many Western countries.

Reasons for the Success of the 2000 and 2004 Elections

The 2000 parliamentary and presidential elections were of major significance for the development of democracy in Ghana. With the power alternation that took place through the ascension of the NPP to ruling government status, and the NDC to the opposition bench, Ghana made an important step toward democratic consolidation. The emergence of the NPP from political opposition in the 1992 and 1996 elections to assume power in 2000 and win the 2004 election is an indication that the power alternation that took place in the 2000 elections could recur with the NDC or an alliance of the Nkrumahist parties assuming power in the future, provided the other opposition parties are able to unite under one umbrella to challenge the NPP and NDC domination of political power in the country. For example, in the course of my interviews, many party leaders and government officials indicated emphatically that they would like to see a three party system in Ghana rather than a dual party system. The success of the 2000 and 2004 presidential and parliamentary elections can be attributed to the following factors:

Political Parties' Role in Electoral Reforms and Democratic Consolidation

Political parties are major institutions of democracy without which democratic consolidation could not be achieved. The importance of political parties in the 2004 election and in Ghana's democratic consolidation is evident in the role they played together with the media and election monitoring CSOs in promoting free and fair elections in Ghana. Through IPAC, political parties have been cooperating on a number of issues, which has inadvertently led to increased trust relations among the party leaders. It is also apparent from the above discussion that the emergence of the NPP to power has led to increased freedoms and respect for civil liberties and the rule of law, which represent vital inroads in Ghana's democratic consolidation. Diamond shares the view that one of the important institutional arenas for democratic consolidation is the party system. Political parties remain essential tools for representing political constituencies and interests, aggregating demands and preferences, recruiting and socializing new candidates for public office, organizing the electoral competition for power, designing policy alternatives, setting the policy-making agenda, forming effective governments and integrating people into the democratic political culture. Furthermore, unlike governments in the First, Second and Third republics, the ruling party has managed to subordinate the military to civilian control, which is gradually faded any chances of military intervention. Also, the institutionalization of the political system and parties in Ghana has been crucial for the country's democratic consolidation, since strengthening the formal representative and institutional structures of government, as well as the party structure and organization of the political parties accelerate democratic consolidation. As Linz and Stepan noted in their discussion of the role of political party institutionalization in democratic consolidation, institutionalized party systems that are loyal to the democratic process thus enhances democratic governance and legitimacy by facilitating legislative support for government policies; by channeling demands and conflicts through established procedures; by asserting civilian control over the military and other anti-democratic forces, and by making the democratic

process more inclusive, accessible, representative, and effective. The role of the parties in IPAC in conflict management has also helped to facilitate the country's democratic consolidation.

The End of NDC's Political Advantages, Secession of the National Reform Party and Power Struggles within the NDC Party

With the more charismatic and manipulative Rawlings leaving the scene after serving his two terms in office, the tables were turned in favour of the NPP and led to a new power dynamic in Ghana's political parties. As a leading member of the NPP puts it, by 2000, the NPP strategies had been reorganized. The party learned from its political and campaign blunders and corrected many of them, such as holding party primaries to elect its presidential and parliamentary candidates so close to the election period, which gave the winning presidential and parliamentary candidates little time to campaign. The secession of a group of party leaders to form the National Reform Party further weakened the NDC. Due to the lack of internal democracy in the NDC, some aggrieved members seceded from the party to form the NRP, which partly affected the electoral fortunes of the party in the 2000 elections. In the 1996 elections, there were some cases in which candidates who were not favoured by Rawlings and his wife were rejected and so were not allowed to contest the primaries. This led to a great deal of discontent within the party, especially among the MPs who were in the 1992 parliament, but lost in the 1996 primaries, as well as some members of the regional and national leadership and the party's grassroots supporters. Prior to the 2000 elections, the selection of John Atta-Mills as the presidential candidate was done by appointment in Rawlings' Swedru Declaration in June 1999 when he single-handedly chose his Vice President as the party's presidential

candidate, as was the case of Rawlings himself in the 1992 and 1996 elections, without any challenger. This action led to the explosion of tensions and sparked a major feud within the party.

Although this declaration met with stiff opposition from both the party's top hierarchy and some of its grassroots members, the decision was not reversed because of Rawlings' claim to ownership of the party, which led to the rift between him and some key members of the party. As noted above, no matter how strategic this move was, it led to the rebellion and secession of a group from the party to form the NRP to compete against the NDC in the 2000 elections. Since then, the party has been saddled with defections, internal power struggles, rebellions and disintegration as the former chairman of the party and a group of members loyal to him seceded and to form the Democratic Freedom Party. As a leading member of the NDC admitted, some of the members of the NRP knew of the strategies that were used by the NDC to win the 1992 and 1996 elections and revealed these secrets to the other opposition parties. The secession of the NRP also led to loss of some of the supporters of the NDC across the country, since some of the party's supporters either voted for the NRP, NPP or the other opposition parties. This led to the NDC's loss of the much-needed votes to win in both the presidential and parliament elections. It also marked the beginning of agitation for internal reforms within the NDC and the numerous internal conflicts that continue to plague the party, which has further led to the secession of the former chairman, Obed Asamoah, and some key figures to form the Democratic Freedom Party (DFP). All these events have led to the continued disintegration of the united front with which the NDC contested the 1992 and 1996 elections.

Electoral Reforms Implemented by the Electoral Commission and the Inter-Party Advisory Committee

The changes that have been implemented since the 1992 election have defined the structural and strategic elements of Ghana's electoral successes and its democratic development. The electoral administrative measures implemented prior to the 1996 election, and the procedures employed in the 2000 and 2004 elections made these elections a success. For example, whereas in 1995, the EC issued ID cards to registered voters in only the ten regional capitals and ten rural constituencies, in the 2000 and 2004 elections, ID cards were issued to voters in all the constituencies across the country. This step promoted efficiency in the elections and checked electoral fraud, such as double voting, voting by minors or with "ghost names. Since the re-introduction of democracy in 1992, Ghana has built institutions and procedures that have helped to eliminate many of the other forms of electoral fraud. The restructuring exercise undertaken by the EC in collaboration with the political parties and CSOs prior to the 2000 and 2004 elections led to several significant improvements in Ghana's election administration processes. In the 2000 and 2004 elections, the counting of votes took place at each polling station and the public witnessed the process.

Immediately at the end of voting, the Presiding Officer, in the presence of the candidates' agents, opened the ballot boxes and emptied the contents onto a table. The ballots were separated, based on the candidates or parties, counted and recorded on the Declaration of Results form. The DEO then submits the results to the Regional Office of the EC, who, in turn, forward them to the national office. All these reforms undermined the electoral rigging practices, such as stuffing of ballot boxes, changing the election results, destruction of opposition parties' ballots, double voting, tampering with election results and candidates "self-certifying" their own electoral victories. Unlike in previous elections, in pursuance of its constitutional mandate, the EC re-opened the voters' register from 6to 15May 2000 to register all Ghanaians of legal voting age - who had turned 18 years - and enable those who for various reasons were not registered at that time to register. Since the conduct of a transparent, free and fair election is fundamentally vital to an emerging democratic society like Ghana, the EC displayed the provisional voters register nationwide to enable all registered voters to crosscheck their names, photographs and other pertinent information required for voting, and any inconsistencies were rectified. One innovative feature of this was that the register was exhibited for the second time from 30June to 9July 2000, at all the 20,113 registration and polling centers across the country for the 2000 election. The changes made by the EC and steps taken to strengthen government institutions helped to streamline Ghana's electoral system. A number of NPP leaders interviewed noted that the establishment of a substantive EC not

only made it independent of the NDC government manipulation, but also gave impetus to the success of the 2000 elections.

Change in Public Perception of the Political Parties and Active Participation of the Public in the 2000 and 2004 Elections

In contrast to the 1992 and 1996 elections, the 2000 and 2004 elections were marked by active public participation. Many people have had a better understanding of the electoral processes and democratic systems more clearly and participated actively in all aspects of the electoral process from campaigns to radio discussions. Mishler and Rose argue that democratic consolidation requires citizens' increased orientation toward the ideals and practices of democratic politics. Evidence of the public interest in the

election is, a survey conducted by the *Statesman* newspaper showed that 87% of Ghanaians wanted a debate involving all the presidential candidates of the political parties prior to the 2004 elections to furnish them with the opportunity to assess the policies and personalities of the presidential aspirants. For example, the 83% voter turnout and the closeness of the 2000 elections show how people showed interest in the 2000 elections. As one party leader puts it, the keen public interest in the 2000 election shows that what was required to win the election was far more than just patronage and/or having access to the media and state resources.

The level of participation was equally impressive since people freely called in to radio stations to discuss political issues and express their views without fear of any repercussions from the government. The outcome of the 2002 CDD survey on democracy and economic development in Ghana shows that there is generally strong support by the public for democracy in Ghana. Democracy is the preferred system of government for an overwhelming majority of Ghanaians, since 82% of respondents in the polls expressed a favourable inclination toward democracy. In the same poll, 76% regard Ghana's current political system to be fully democratic with only minor problems, as against 24% of Ghanaians who thought democracy in Ghana is highly imperfect with major problems. Whereas in the CDD poll in 1999, 55% of respondents expressed satisfaction with democracy, after the change of government, in 2002, 72% said they were satisfied with the way democracy works in Ghana.

Other bodies like the NCCE that are involved in public education encouraged public participation in the 2000 and 2004 elections. For example, in the period leading to the 2000 and 2004 elections, the NCCE organized a number of public forums to educate the electorate on the need to promote peace and unity by the leaders of the various political parties. Prior to the 2004 elections, in the Cape Coast area, the NCCE organized civic education campaigns in a number of tertiary institutions, forums for political parties and a street procession in November termed "Peace March 2004" for all the political parties. The increasing participation of the public in all aspects of the democratic process enhanced the quality of public discussion and enlightened many people who were hitherto either not interested in politics or ignorant about public policy. In the 2000 and 2004 elections, there were major shifts in the political terrain as many NDC sympathizers and independent voters shifted their support and voted for the NPP for various reasons.

The Role of Election Monitoring Groups

Another major factor that led to the success of the 2000 and 2004 elections was the continued active role of the CSOs in Ghana's elections, from registration of voters to election monitoring on the day of the elections, which has contributed to Ghana's democratic consolidation process. Diamond, Putnam, and Whitehead discussed the central importance of civil society as a driving force behind democratic consolidation in their respective works. Nonpartisan election monitoring efforts have been critical in deterring fraud, enhancing voter confidence, and affirming the legitimacy of election results. With their successful participation in the administration of the 1996 elections, CSOs such as the IEA, CDD, and the CODEO have enhanced election monitoring in Ghana. The most dominant of the election monitoring CSOs is CODEO, which was formed in May 2000 to replace NEDEO. CODEO consisted of about thirty-four religious, professional, labor and independent non-governmental organizations committed to the promotion of democracy, peace and stability in Ghana. In general, CODEO played significant roles in the 2000 and 2004 elections.

The overall objective of the coalition was to deepen civil society participation and involvement in the 2000 elections to help reduce election related conflicts, enhance electoral transparency and lend legitimacy and credibility to electoral outcomes. These objectives were achieved through two main activities, namely, pre-election monitoring and election-day observation activities. Some party officials interviewed admitted that the introduction of election monitoring in Ghana through the parties and CSOs partnership in election administration has helped to streamline several electoral processes and was a major factor for the success of the 2000 elections. CODEO's success in the monitoring of the 2000 and 2004 elections shows that having non-partisan observers to help in election administration is essential for enhancing transparency and credibility of electoral outcomes as well as maintaining public confidence in the election process, which are crucial for the promotion of political stability and socio-economic development. With the support of the USAID and other international donors, CODEO in collaboration with the CDD, undertook a pre-election monitoring and Election Day observation exercises in the period leading to the general elections, between 1June to 6December 2004, to promote public participation and check against any possible electoral malpractices.

The CODEO initiative involved the compilation of the voters' register; civic education for voters; monitoring party congresses, primaries, rallies and campaigns; monitoring the political atmosphere in some constituencies; resolving electoral complaints lodged by parties; noting the abuse of incumbency; and promoting the activities of agencies that are vital to Ghana's electoral processes. The presence of CODEO's election observers led to a peaceful atmosphere at the polling stations, since their presence alone encouraged discipline in the contesting candidates, party agents, and EC officials. The exercise also helped to draw attention to some areas that required the EC and party leaders' intervention. The CODEO project helped to broaden public participation in the election activities by intensifying public interest to increase voter turnout in the elections, and promote public confidence in the 2004 election and the democratic process in general.

Increased public participation also helped to prevent election fraud and some electoral disputes that may have arose in some constituencies and led to broad public acceptance of the election outcome. The participation of the public in the election not only as party members, candidates and voters, but also as interested and concerned observers whose intention is to promote free and fair elections greatly enhanced the transparency and legitimacy of the 2004 election. As Putnam noted, the emergence of a rich civic culture is indispensable for democratic consolidation. CODEO's activities were divided among three committees to support the election monitoring initiative. The Recruitment, Training and Deployment Committee was responsible for compiling a list of potential observers from member organizations at the national, regional and district levels, planning and coordinating the recruitment and training of observers, trainers and supervisors, and planning Election Day activities. The Logistics and Resource Committee advised the Advisory Board on the logistical needs for CODEO's operations, secured the EC's approval for the observers and retrieved field

returns from CODEO observers. The Drafting and Reporting Committee was charged with reviewing training manuals and observer guidelines, checking lists and incident report forms, and drafting interim and final reports on the CODEO election observation project. CODEO's election monitoring activities were two fold, namely Pre-Election Monitoring and Election Day Observation. These covered the compilation of the voters register, including photo-taking exercise, voter education, monitoring party congresses, party primaries, and campaigns, and encouraging gender participation. CODEO's training of election observers was designed into three stages. The first phase of the CODEO initiative was the training of forty-three observers at the national level, the second stage involved the training of 479 election observers for all the ten regional centers and the third phase of the training involved about 6000 observers at sixty-four training centers across the country. In all, during the 2004 election, CODEO trained and dispatched 7,360 election monitors to the 230 constituencies across the country. This number was a significant improvement over the number of election monitors who were dispatched by NEDEO and CODEO to monitor the 1996 and 2000 elections respectively. Cooperation among various civic groups that cut across religious, gender, party affiliation and ethnic boundaries bolstered the effectiveness of CODEO's election monitoring activities and enhanced the transparency and legitimacy of the electoral outcome. The CODEO project greatly helped to promote free, fair, transparent and peaceful elections and public confidence in the electoral processes by deterring, preventing and detecting electoral fraud as well as helping to prevent and/or manage electoral conflicts among some opposing party supporters. For example, the attitudinal dimension of democratic consolidation stresses the importance of socialization, trust and cooperation in democratic consolidation. In this regard, civil society alongside political parties serves as a major driving force behind Ghana's democratic consolidation. This point reiterates Plasser's view in the literature review that trust has an integrated effect on democratic consolidation because it widens the scope of action and serves as an incentive for political parties to cooperate. Aside from the CODEO and CDD initiative, the role of some religious bodies also greatly contributed to the success of the 2004 election. The Ghana Catholic Bishops' Conference and the CCG trained and deployed about 3,500 observers for the 2004 elections with financial support from the Catholic Relief Services and other religious non-governmental organizations. The wide-ranging roles that the CSOs played in the 2000 and the 2004 elections showed the increasing political space that they have assumed in Ghana's democratic development. There was also increasing collaboration between CSOs and the political parties in the 2000 and 2004 elections administration to promote more peaceful, freer and fairer elections. As it happened in the 1996 elections, the initiatives of the local CSOs were complemented by an increasing number of external election monitoring groups. Among others, the Carter Center, the Commonwealth Secretariat, African American Institute, the African Union and the International Foundation for Electoral Systems, the CPC, NDI, the USAID and the NED were all heavily involved in the 2000 and 2004 elections. Some foreign observers from other West African countries, such as the Catholic Bishops in Nigeria and Liberia also joined their Ghanaian counterparts in the election monitoring effort. The effort of the external election monitors was a major improvement over their role in the 1992 and 1996 elections, since they provided enormous financial, logistical support and training to facilitate the work of the local CSOs. Nonetheless, the importance of the local election monitoring CSOs is evidenced in the fact that the activities of the external election monitoring groups were mainly centered in the capital city and were active mostly on the day of the election.

The Role of the Media

The predominant role of the media in the pre-election and election coverage of the party campaigns and rallies also led to the success of the last two elections. The 2000 and 2004 elections were, so far, the two most hotly contested and received a great deal of media attention. Both the public and private print and electronic press covered the election campaigns with great interest. In playing these roles as the voice of the people and champion of their cause in the political domain, the press was eminently placed to draw the attention of the people to their civic responsibilities, under the constitutional provisions. Due to the state-owned media's favourable reporting of the ruling party in the 1992 and 1996 elections, in 1999, the issue of objective and fair coverage of the activities of all the political parties by the state-owned media was brought to the attention of parliament for debate. As a result, the NMC was charged with investigating the issue. The School of Communication Studies at the University of Ghana was also contracted to undertake a study entitled "Fair Coverage of Political Parties by the State-owned Media of Ghana. " The outcome of this study showed a clear indication that the NDC was favoured over the opposition parties. According to the report, the NDC received 44. 5% of print, 55. 8% of radio and 37. 3% of television attention; the main opposition NPP followed a distant second with 22. 7%, 21. 5% and 15. 2% for print, radio and television respectively; and the other minor opposition parties had more marginal coverage. This study led to protest from the opposition parties to the GBC and the Supreme Court to bridge the gap in media coverage of the parties. In this case, the ruling NDC and the opposition NPP, in particular, had fair airtime in the public and private press for their numerous press conferences to put across their platform to the voters.

Based on this report, the NMC introduced new measures that streamlined the operations of state and privately owned media's coverage of the political parties during election campaigns and to protect the media against government interference. For example, when in 2001, the then Minister of Information, Jake Obetsebi-Lamptey, summoned Chief Executives of the print and electronic media to a meeting to discuss standards of media content, the NMC vehemently opposed this action and issued a strongly worded statement protesting the action of the Minister since it claimed that the Minister's action contravenes the 1992 Constitution, which gives the NMC the sole power to regulate and censor the media for publications, and leads to government interference in the media. As a result of the widespread criticism of the public media from the parties, some CSOs such as the IEA and the Media Foundation for West Africa (MFWA) organized programs to create awareness in the media. The IEA organized the "Media in Society" programs, the MFWA organized seminars and public lectures to educate both the private and public media. The CDD also organized similar seminars and workshops to arouse the awareness of the media in terms of their roles and obligations toward strengthening Ghana's democracy.

In the period leading to the 2000 elections, the Freedom Forum, the GJA and GBC, as part of a two-day Africa Media Forum initiative titled "Press, Power and Politics," jointly organized a national forum, based on a ninety minutes discussion live and invited the presidential candidates to answer questions from a panel of journalists and the public on Ghana's democracy. These seminars and public forums helped to enhance the awareness of the media personnel on the need to cover activities of all the political parties in a fair, objective and transparent manner. For example, the IEA used its Speakers' Breakfast Forum to bring together all the media stakeholders such as the NMC, the GJA and the Private Newspaper Publishers Association of Ghana (PRINPAG) as an information session by the media to address how they intend to contribute toward a peaceful transition from one government to another in elections. On many issues, the NMC worked in collaboration with PRINPAG to promote the professionalism and independence of the press.

Unlike in the 1992 and 1996 elections in which the NDC government managed to frighten the media with various forms of harassment, arrests and detention, in the 2000 and 2004 election campaigns, the media were able to stand up against the ruling party. For example, the GBC refused to adhere to the NDC's request to withdraw an NPP advert that specifically targeted the NDC by profiling a young girl recounting the economic hardships brought on the people by NDC policies. The media also helped raise the electorate's standard of knowledge and awareness on parties' policies. In the period leading to the 2000 elections, the GBC, in collaboration with private FM radio stations hosted a program headlined "The Voters Right" to discuss issues of the rights and responsibilities of the Ghanaian voter. Other media houses discussed issues and party manifestos, and aired various political and civic education programs such as "Platform" on Radio Gold, "Agenda 2000" on Choice FM and "Decision 2000" on Joy FM to educate the public on their voting rights and voting procedures. The CDD, with the support of the Open Society Initiative of West Africa (OSIWA) and the USAID, organized a forum for aspiring parliamentary candidates in their various constituencies in

the Brong Ahafo Region. The GJA also launched a media-political party dialogue program to create the platform for media and political parties to discuss issues and to help the electorate make informed decisions. Reports of lapses ranging from the late start of voting, shortage of voting materials, unruly conduct by armed security personnel, and confrontations among ruling and opposition party activists were broadcast on the radio stations to alert the EC and the public of the problems and areas that were affected. For example, in the Ablekuma North constituency in Accra, the media alerted the EC about destroyed election materials, which enabled the EC to promptly dispatch new voting materials to the polling station to avoid disenfranchisement of voters in the constituency. One area where the media improved its performance remarkably during the elections was political advertising. In an IEA poll, 73. 6% noted there was improvement and 53% agreed the improvement was considerable. While there is no doubt that the state-owned media gave predominant coverage and access to the ruling NDC during the 2000 election, the gap in coverage of the ruling party and main opposition party was not as wide as in the 1992 and 1996 elections because the private media were more critical of the ruling party.

The active role played by the private print and electronic media balanced the deficit in the public media's coverage of the parties, which led to almost equal amount of time and space and fair opportunities to the parties and stimulated public interest in the 2000 and 2004 elections to make it more competitive than the 1992 and 1996 elections. On the whole, there was little disparity in the coverage of the parties by the private print and electronic media at the local and national levels in the 2000 elections. The significant role of the media in the 2000 election was evident in the January 2001 statement published in the *Daily Graphic* newspaper, signed by the national chairman of the NPP, thanking the media for its role in making the elections peaceful and a success. The NMC also issued a statement commending the media for their thorough and incisive coverage of the processes leading to and during the 2000 elections, which helped to ensure free and peaceful elections. The media in Ghana has thus served increasingly as an authentic instrument of communication between the political parties, the government and the people, as well as a protector of the rights of citizens from state encroachment.

Some Problems that Hinder Elections in Ghana

Election Irregularities and Conflicts among Party Supporters

Despite the important role that political parties play in democracy, some parties have not been ideal arenas for promoting free and fair elections. Regardless of the improvements in the 2000 and 2004 elections, some major difficulties remain with Ghana's elections due to election irregularities, which made the 2000 elections' outcome in some regions and constituencies highly questionable. Some voters and election observers alleged that there were massive voting irregularities in the Volta Region, which is described as the NDC's "World Bank. " For example, despite the fact that the Ho West constituency used photo identification in the 1996 election, in the presence of two NPP polling agents at two polling stations in Dededo, the presiding officers permitted over 100 voters to cast their votes using thumbprint identification and another 100 voters were allowed to vote without any form of identification. Information from the CODEO further revealed serious problems in the Volta Region, especially during the run-off. This confirmed the opposition parties' and independent election observers' allegations that the officials in the Volta Region collaborated with some NDC leaders to perpetrate numerous electoral irregularities in the 1992, 1996, 2000 and 2004 elections. A survey by the CDD in collaboration with the NDI, as part of the African Political Party Finance Initiative conducted between May 20 and 28, 2004 established that about 80% of the number who admitted having received an incentive to vote said it influenced their voting behaviour. Some of the most common cases of voting malpractices that occurred in the 2004 election were intimidation and harassment of voters and improper voting procedures. The 1992, 1996, 2000 and 2004 elections were characterized by sporadic violence in some constituencies, particularly, in the Northern Region between members of the ruling and opposition parties. In communities where there were pronounced local disputes, some politicians tried to win votes by supporting one group against the other. For example, on December 8, 2000, the resulting bloodshed in Bawku in the Upper East Region left more than fifty people dead, hundreds of homes and businesses destroyed, and thousands of people displaced. There were reports of clashes between the NDC and NPP supporters in some constituencies as occurred in Cape Coast in the Central Region, Yendi and Kumbungu in the Northern Region. In Ashiaman, Bongo, Pusiga-Pulmokom and the Cape Coast constituencies, there were various conflicts between NPP and NDC supporters. Also in Ahafo-Ano and Buem constituencies, reported incidents of NPP and NDC supporters defacing and tearing down the opponent party's posters generated tension between the two parties in the constituencies. Some party members destroyed the banners of the other parties, although those who were caught or reported were arrested and prosecuted in a court of law. Ghana's elections are also characterized by intimidation and threat of voters by supporters of the political parties. The polarized relations and enmity that often exist between party members during and after elections is one of the destructive characteristics of the party system in Ghana.

Abuse of Incumbency Advantages by Ruling Parties

Another major problem hindering Ghana's elections and democratic development, which the political parties have not addressed effectively, is systemic abuse of incumbency through arbitrary use of state resources for party or personal gains at the expense of the opposition parties by a ruling party, public officials and party members standing for elected public office. Abuse of incumbency takes many forms, including politicizing access to public facilities and funds, using government vehicles and facilities for political rallies/campaigns, turning official events into campaign rallies, privatizing public amenities for partisan purposes, and the actions of some past NDC and present NPP DCEs in abusing the laws guiding their office as a non-partisan position. Abuse of incumbency also occurs in the form of the use of institutional resources, such as employing logistical and financial resources for electoral campaigns rather than official duties; budgetary allocation abuse, which also occurred by using public funds for politically motivated projects during elections for which the money is not intended; and state media resource abuse, through biased information and advertising for the purpose of influencing the electorate to support a party.

National Democratic Congress

The NDC's ability to exploit incumbency and to appropriate state resources was a key factor in Rawlings and the party's electoral victories in both the 1992 and 1996 elections. Generally, the government's political views, its staff, policies and ideological

traits were not very much changed from its authoritarian past. In this regard, the electoral playing field was not level for all of the parties because the ruling party monopolized state resources, including state print and electronic media, whilst the opposition parties mainly relied on limited individual contributions. For example, while the 1992 elections served as a major stepping-stone toward democratic development, it did not remove some fundamental impediments that would have leveled the playing field for all the parties, and could have offered the opposition parties better prospects of defeating the incumbent regime. The NDC excessively exploited a number of incumbency advantages through development project delivery and direct bribery through the distribution of gifts. Financial resources are very important for party organization in terms of the party's appeal to voters, its national appeal and its ability to carry out programmes and campaigns to solicit membership.

In this regard, some supporters of the NDC used state financial and material resources for electoral campaigns, abused voting and counting procedures, and stuffed ballot boxes. This gave the NDC candidates the undue advantage of having access to state resources for political campaigns in the form of finance, logistics and access to the state media, while the cash-strapped opposition parties had to raise funds from individual sympathizers to fund their campaigns. As Debrah noted, many NDC District Chief Executives ensured that beneficiaries of the poverty alleviation fund were card bearing NDC members. As one party chairman noted, not only did the DCE's prevent the opposition MPs from using their share of the local government unit budget under the 'District Assembly Common Fund' to pursue any development in their constituencies, but also ensured that anti-NDC rural voters/communities were discriminated against and blacklisted in the distribution of state resources. The 1996 elections were also not as free and fair as was expected. Despite all the precautionary measures and money that was spent and the extensive preparations that were made, the elections were again marred by serious lapses. The ability to exploit incumbency and to appropriate state resources was a key factor in the NDC's electoral victories in both the 1992 and 1996 elections. The elections only served to entrench PNDC/NDC rule because the opposition parties, civic groups and other key democratic institutions that were constitutionally mandated to counter the advantages of the ruling party were severely constrained by numerous impediments, while some pro-government CSOs were empowered financially and politically to boost the electoral fortunes of the NDC party. For example, in 1993, the Chamber of Independent Business Associations (CIBA) received 150 million cedis from the government as a grant. Prior to the 1996 elections, the Bank of Ghana was made to provide CIBA with foreign exchange with which it imported 330 shipping containers of assorted goods to be distributed as gifts to voters in order to influence their votes. In return, in 1996, the organization not only became an active wing of the NDC campaign machinery, but also, together with other pro-government organizations, made cash donations to the campaign of the NDC from profits made through contracts and business transactions carried out for the government. The resulting discrepancy in financial and logistic resources made available to the ruling and opposition parties did not promote free and fair elections. This practice of annexing civic groups for political gains greatly promoted clientelism, corruption and patronage in Ghana's political system.

In addition, being the incumbent party in power, the NDC government supplied free fuel to transport owners through the GPRTU in exchange for members of the body using their vehicles to convey NDC supporters free of charge to party rallies and polling stations and help the party in its campaign during elections. Kickbacks were forcibly collected from contractors to finance the NDC party. Through countless dubious tactics, members of the Association of Ghanaian Contractors who were suspected of being supporters of the opposition parties, especially the NPP, such as Bugri Naabu, a leading contractor in the Northern region, were forced to renounce their party affiliation and join the NDC. Rawlings is reported to have stated and boasted at an NDC rally that since Bugri Naabu had behaved himself, he would begin to receive some contracts. In many instances, the CDR cadres were accused of terrorizing the opposition parties during elections. Another form of abuse of incumbency was that ruling parties took unfair advantage of the state-owned media at the expense of the other parties. Widespread abuse of incumbency under the NDC government, such as the use of state resources to support the ruling party's activities occurred in the in the 1992, 1996 and 2000 elections, when the ruling NDC monopolized virtually every political space. The limitations placed on the opposition parties in fundraising and the NDC governments' persistent abuse of incumbency posed a great challenge to the opposition parties' electoral competitiveness in the 1992 and 1996 elections.

New Patriotic Party

Like its predecessor NDC government, the NPP also enjoyed a tremendous advantage in the state-owned media coverage. Whereas in the 1992, 1996 and 2000 elections, the NPP and the other opposition parties vehemently opposed the PNDC/NDC for taking undue advantage of the state's logistical and financial resources at the opposition parties' and the public's expense, in the 2004 elections, the ruling NPP also allegedly inherited and used those incumbency advantages, although not to the same extent as the NDC. While the NPP, as the ruling government, did not prevent the other parties from having access to the state-owned media and some logistic facilities, such as vehicles to the opposition parties during elections, which was started during the NDC era, some leading members of the opposition parties, especially the NDC, argued that apart from the vehicles that were allocated to the parties, some of the NPP party's public officials additionally benefited from the use of state vehicles for campaigns, which gave the party and some of its candidates an undue advantage over the opposition parties. Some leaders of opposition parties also complained about the government's delay in the release of campaign vehicles and other state-funded logistical support to the opposition parties, since they claimed it was purposely intended to stifle their campaign activites. Besides, there were also a number of complaints from the opposition parties on the timing for the opening of the voters' register. It was alleged that in October 2004, an NPP DCE in the Eastern Region used his political power to influence the removal of an NDC parliamentary aspirant from his position as tutor in a public school. In the Northern Region, a DCE whose office is supposedly non-partisan is reported to have used an official vehicle to transport party supporters to a campaign rally for an NPP parliamentary candidate. In Ashanti Region, a DCE was spotted using his personal Nissan Patrol carrying NPP party items to a campaign rally. In Brong Ahafo, a DCE invited the NPP parliamentary candidate to the launching of the District Health Insurance Scheme, but denied the opposition candidates the right to attend on the grounds that the event was by invitation only. Also in the Central region, a DCE openly campaigned for the NPP and urged the crowd to return the NPP MP to power. In the Ashanti region, a large sum of money from the District Assembly's coffers was given to the NPP executives by the DCE to convey party members to a durbar grounds to see the President. Also, in November

2004, at a ceremony to mark the National Farmers Day Celebration in the Krachi East and West constituencies in the Volta Region, and in the Biakoye constituency, some DCEs allegedly encouraged the people to vote massively for the NPP to help promote development in the area. The CDD has cited abuse of incumbency through public officials' use of state resources for partisan purposes as a major obstacle to Ghana's democratic development. In a study by the CDD, sponsored by the Westminster Foundation for Democracy (WFD) of the United Kingdom, to monitor the ruling party's abuse of incumbency prior to the 2004 elections, the CDD noted that some DCEs were using state resources to campaign for the NPP. It was alleged by some NDC members that the Kumasi Metropolitan Assembly (KMA) allowed the NPP to erect signboards inside two main roundabouts at Asafo in Kumasi. Also, in Nabdam, a Skill Training and Employment Workshop turned into a pro-NPP program and in Okaikoi South, a sitting MP inaugurated publicly funded streetlights and commissioned an NPP branch office at the same event. He also accused public officials of using events that were intended to be non-partisan to convince voters to vote for the incumbent party. Another way in which leaders/officials in the ruling party allegedly abused their incumbency advantages is using official visits for political campaign tours.

It is important to establish a clear line between official/state visits and partisan campaigns to prevent the exploitation of incumbency for electoral advantage. Mixing of political campaign tours and official/state visits by incumbent party officials and political leaders was widely reported in the monitored constituencies. There were several instances where visits were designated as "official", although the President and the Vice President introduced their party's parliamentary candidates, solicited the support of voters, made partisan political speeches and included campaign messages in their speeches. For instance in November 2004, on a visit to the Jaman South constituency of Brong Ahafo Region, the President was alleged to have asked the people to vote for the NPP parliamentary candidates in the district after he had cut the sod for the construction of a post office in the district. Some traditional leaders were also reported to have openly expressed their support for the ruling party. Failure to draw the line between official/state visits and partisan campaign visits by incumbent officials creates the potential to grossly abuse incumbency.

Shortage of Election Logistics and the Issue of the Bloated Voters' Register

While the first phase of the voter registration exercise in the 2004 election was reported to be fairly successful, there were accounts of lack of logistical resources in the Volta, Greater Accra, Northern and Ashanti Regions. For example, it was reported by the CODEO election monitors that there were shortages of materials in some polling stations in Ayawaso Central, Krachi East and West, Ejisu-Juabeng and Bawku West. These shortages were due to the EC's inability to supply registration officials with adequate logistics and provide adequate vehicles to transport voting materials and personnel. The effectiveness of the photo taking exercises in the voter registration were also marred by low participation, which indicates that there was inadequate civic education to prepare the public for this exercise. One issue that attracted national interest in the 2000 elections was whether or not voters could use thumbprint voter identification cards. The Supreme Court ruled that both the photo and thumbprint identifications could be used in the voting process. The issue of a bloated voters' register, a controversy surrounding the 1992 and 1996 elections, also re-surfaced in the 2000 elections, after the release of Provisional Census figures in August 2000 by the Statistical Service Department, which indicated that people aged 18 years and above constitute about 50% of the 18.4 million total national population. The opposition parties argued that the register was bloated because the 10.7 million registered voters on the register would indicate that the register was inflated by about 1.5 million if the census figure was correct. With this position, they managed to convince the EC to re-examine the register and through this some spurious names were detected and removed during the exhibition exercise. Despite this initiative, the Chairman of the EC admitted that there could still be more bogus names that could not be easily identified on the list. Conclusion

Apart from the role of political parties in Ghana's democratic consolidation process, analysis of the 2000 and 2004 elections also show considerable improvement in Ghana's electoral system in the registration of voters, voting procedures and counting of ballots, party organization and campaign strategies as well as election monitoring by civic groups and the role of the media. One issue that continues to draw hamper Ghana's democracy is the abuse of incumbency. This has been a major source of confrontation

between the political parties since the 1992 democratic transition, and continues to create tensions between a ruling party and the opposition parties in every election year. Whereas parties and their candidates "grease the electorates' palm" to gain their support and votes, the majority of the electorate in Ghana also believe that "pulling the right strings and knocking on the right doors" by supporting a winning party could offer them benefits in the form of jobs, material gains and other favours for themselves and their communities, which they believe serves as a trade-off for their votes. While the 1992 democratic transition set the Fourth Republic on the path to promote government legitimacy and accountability, the 2000 elections set the country's political system on a path to democratic consolidation. In looking at the changes that have been implemented since the 1992 elections, it becomes apparent that while Ghana's electoral system is not perfect, as in many democracies around the world, there has been significant improvements have taken place. This can be attributed to the cardinal role played by the political parties, the EC and civil society in identifying the problems faced by candidates and the political parties in elections and finding workable solutions to them. Contrary to the situation in 1992 and 1996, the conduct of the media in covering the nominations, campaigns and general elections was laudable and paramount in making the 2000 and 2004 elections more transparent, freer and fairer than the 1992 and 1996 elections.

It is important to note that the up-coming 2008 presidential and parliamentary elections will probably be more interesting than the previous elections held in the past for the following reasons: Like the NDC, the NPP has been in power for two terms and the 2008 election is another transition election after the 2000 power alternation. Another

reason is the internal power struggles in both the NDC and NPP. With regard to the NDC, there is on-going confrontation between the party's founder, Rawlings and his wife on the one hand, and the party's presidential candidate, Atta-Mills on the other hand on the issue of who should be Mills' vice-presidential candidate. Whereas Rawlings and his wife favoured Betty Iddrisu Mahama, the Mills camp supported John Mahama, who was openly criticized by Rawlings and his wife, but won the nomination. While the situation in the NDC has created a major rift between the Rawlings's and some leading party members, the NPP has its own internal problems to deal with. A few months following the party's 2008 presidential primaries in December 2007, Alan Kyerematen, one of the NPP presidential candidates, defeated by Nana Akuffo Addo, announced his resignation from the party in April 2008.

While Kyerematen cited issues of mistreatment of his supporters by some party members as his main reason for resigning from the party, the perception of some critics is that he intends to run as an independent presidential candidate or join the democratic Reform Party as its presidential candidate. This situation is disturbing for the NPP because it could cause the party some of the much needed votes it would need to win the 2008 presidential election. In retrospect, the PFP, a Danquah-Busia tradition party lost the 1979 presidential and parliamentary election to Limman's PNP, an Nkrumahist party due to William Ofori-Atta's break-away from the Danquah-Busia tradition to establish the UNC party. In the midst of these developments and the apparent confusion in the two leading political parties, the CPP led by Paa Kwesi Nduom, is allegedly gaining momentum in its support base, and there is speculation that the party is negotiating with the PNC to enter into an alliance for the 2008 election. If the changing dynamics and current trends in the major parties continue to unfold in this manner, the 2008 election would be more competitive, exciting and possibly lead to some major upsets in the election.

Chapter Six

Political Parties' Administration in Ghana

Introduction

The literature on political parties in this section focuses on the organization and structural features of the party system, participation and representation, as well as the parties' procedures for promoting internal democracy and candidate selection processes. The first section of the chapter discusses some of the fundamental conditions for the formation and regulation of political parties in Ghana. The second section focuses on political parties' structure and internal organization at the national and local levels, their membership recruitment strategies, candidate selection processes and the issue of internal democracy, as well as parties' fund raising practices to show how the present system promotes a level playing field for all the parties. Over the last five decades since Ghana's independence and during the last two decades of the country's democratic transition, the contemporary literature on Ghana's party system has given little attention to party structures and institutional frameworks. It is thus essential to discuss internal party organization and ideological underpinnings, which serve as key for understanding the political parties' behaviour and goals in this study. The chapter also examines the level of representation for social groups and grassroots members in the parties, and how they are encouraged to participate in decision-making.

Some Basic Conditions Guiding the Formation of a Political Party

One of the main provisions of Ghana's political parties' Law is that the name, emblem, colour, motto, or other symbols must not have ethnic, regional or religious connotation, nor give the appearance that its activities are confined only to a part of the society. With these conditions defining the establishment of parties, after the lifting of the

ban on political parties by the PNDC in 1992, leaders of the defunct parties organized their supporters to revitalize their previous party traditions or form new political parties and established new party offices across the country to participate in the 1992 elections. The 1992 Constitution makes provisions and guidelines for the formation of a political party. Article 55 of the 1992 Constitution guarantees the right to form political parties and the state's responsibility to provide fair and equal opportunity for all political parties to present their programs to the public by ensuring equal access to the state-owned media. Articles 55 and 56, together with the Political Parties Law, PNDCL 281, provide the legal and institutional frameworks for the formation, operation and regulation of political parties in Ghana as follows:

- ✓ Every citizen of Ghana of voting age has the right to form or join a political party;
- ✓ A political party must be registered with the EC in order to have legal status to operate;

- ✓ At least one of the founding members should be resident and registered as a voter in one of the 138 districts;

- ✓ It must have branches in all the 10 regions of Ghana and should, in addition, be organized in not less than two-thirds of the districts in each region;

- ✓ All political parties are to be given equal opportunities to present their programs to the public through the state-owned radio, television, and newspapers; and

- ✓ A political party cannot sponsor a candidate for election to a District Assembly or a lower local government unit;

- ✓ Only a citizen of Ghana can contribute to the funds of a political party;

- ✓ All presidential candidates should be given the same amount of time and space on the state-owned radio and television, and in the state-owned press; and

- ✓ The EC was entrusted with supervising the transition and electoral processes, compiling new voters register and establishing a new and substantive EC whose membership would include the appointed staff and representatives of the parties.

Party Structure and Organization

The lifting of the ban on political parties saw the resurgence of parties of all sizes and ideologies. Political parties are indispensable mechanisms for promoting democratic governance and the main agents of mobilizing people for participation. Political parties did play significant roles in Ghana's struggle for independence, and against the authoritarianism of the 1960s, 1970s and 1980s. In their discussion of the importance of party development in democracy, Russell Dalton and Martin Wattenburg noted that parties are inevitable aspect of democracy so democracy is "unthinkable" without parties. The importance of parties in democratic transition and consolidation is evidenced in the fact that some leading members of the parties greatly contributed to the democratic transition process in Ghana. While parties were banned under the authoritarian regimes, the leaders of the parties were very instrumental in resisting authoritarian rule and advocating a return to democratic rule. For example, Adu-Boahen's memorable speech at the Danquah Memorial Lectures in 1988 broke the "culture of silence" that was imposed on the Ghanaian polity by the PNDC regime.

The role of political parties in shaping public policies and programs cannot be overemphasized because they are the main agents of organizing, contesting and providing candidates for elections. Theorists such as Chandler, Siaroff and Cross confirm the important role parties play as the crucial intermediaries linking the state and society. For example, the formation of IPAC through joint action by the parties, the EC and the donors became an important mechanism for dialogue, consultation and consensus building, which greatly contributed to sustaining and putting Ghana's democracy back on track after the 1992 parliamentary election boycott by the opposition parties. The importance of political parties as the rallying point of the electorate in elections is seen in the limited number of independent candidates who are elected as Members of Parliament (MPs) to Ghana's parliament and the fact that no independent presidential candidate has ever been elected president in Ghana. For example, in the 1992 parliament, out of 200 MPs, there were only three independent parliamentarians. In the 1996 parliament there were no independent MPs and only four independent MPs in the 2000 parliament. As Hofferbert rightly argued, the structure, organization and performance of political parties are some of the most vital aspects of the road to democratic consolidation. Through political education, political parties help generate reliable information that raises the electorates' political awareness on public policy and government accountability, which generally contribute to the process of consolidating democracy.

Like other parties elsewhere, the fundamental aim of political parties in Ghana is to seek to control or influence the conduct of government, essentially by getting majority of its candidates elected to public office. As political organizations, parties are more effective means for people to articulate their views and have more influence in the political process than people who enter politics as independent candidates. The process of winning people's support for a party's platform involves a great deal of energy and expense involving communicating with the electorate, formulating and disseminating the party's platform as well as engaging in programs and activities for securing public support. Consequently, the survival and competitiveness of any party largely depends on its effective organization. Parties that have a large following often meet these needs

more easily than independent candidates, especially in countries like Ghana where the technology for communication is not well advanced. Hence a discussion of the structure and organization of the political parties in Ghana shows their similarities and differences in their background or formation, composition and organizational strategies.

Arguing that the structure, organization and performance of political parties are some of the most significant aspects of a party's development, David F. Roth and Frank

Wilson concluded, "parties in different political settings differ dramatically in the task they perform, their organization, their style of operation, and their relationships to the overall political unit". In spite of the differences and similarities among political parties in Ghana, in terms of policy orientation, in recent years, all the political parties have moved to the center with regard to their public policy framework. Political parties' relentless effort to broaden their ideological and policy appeal to the electorate conforms to Kirchheimer's "catch-all" party model of party organization. As Maor noted in his discussion of the "catch-all" party model, the need to appeal to wide cross sections of the community meant that parties had to move away from their strict ideological-based policies to the center of the political spectrum in order to attract more voters. Table 6. 1 below shows the structure and organization of the four main political parties in Ghana that have representation in parliament.

Table 6. 1: Structure and Organization of the Four Main Political Parties

NPP	NDC	PNC	CPP
National Executive Chairperson Vice-chairpersons General Secretary Treasurer National Organizer Women's Organizer Men's Organizer Youth Organizer	National Executive Chairperson Vice-chairpersons General Secretary Treasurer National Organizer Women, Men and Youth Organizer Propaganda Secretary	National Executive Chairperson Vice-chairpersons General Secretary Treasurer National Organizer Youth Organizer	National Executive Chairperson Vice-chairpersons General Secretary Treasurer National Organizer Women's Organizer Youth Organizer

Organizers Council of Elders Disciplinary Committee Finance Committee Paid staff Volunteers	National Council Council of Elders Disciplinary Committee Finance Committee Paid staff Volunteers	Women's Organizer Limited paid staff Volunteers	Limited paid staff Volunteers
Regional Level Chairperson Vice-chairpersons Regional Secretary Regional Organizer Financial Secretary Women Organizer Men Organizer Youth Organizer Council of Elders Disciplinary Committee Paid staff Volunteers	Regional Level Chairperson Vice-chairpersons Regional Secretary Regional Organizer Treasurer Women Organizer Youth Organizer Propaganda Secretary Council of Elders Disciplinary Committee Finance Committee Paid staff Volunteers	Regional Level Chairperson Vice-chairpersons Regional secretary Regional organizer Treasurer Youth organizer Women's organizer Paid staff Volunteers	Regional Level Chairperson Vice-chairpersons Regional Secretary Regional Organizer Treasurer Youth Women's Organizer Paid staff Volunteers

NPP	NDC	PNC	CPP
Constituencies Chairperson Vice-chairperson Secretary Organizing secretary Treasurer Women's Organizer Youth Organizer Disciplinary Committee Paid staff Volunteers	Constituencies Chairperson Vice-chairperson Secretary District Organizer Treasurer Women's Organizer Youth Organizer Disciplinary Committee Paid staff Volunteers	Constituencies Chairperson Vice-chairperson Secretary District Organizer Treasurer Youth and Women's Organizers Paid staff Volunteers * The PNC does not have structures in some constituencies.	Constituencies Chairperson Vice-chairperson Secretary District Organizer Treasurer Women's Organizer Youth Organizer Paid staff Volunteers The CPP does not have structures in some constituencies.
Unit/Wards Chairperson Vice-chairperson General Secretary Treasurer Ward Organizer	Wards/Branches Chairperson Vice-chairperson General Secretary Treasurer Ward Organizer	Unit/Wards The PNC does not have structures in some constituencies	Unit/Wards CPP does not have structures in some constituencies

Women's Organizer Youth Organizer Disciplinary Committee	Women's Organizer Youth Organizer Disciplinary Committee

The Danquah-Busia's United Party (UP) Tradition: New Patriotic Party

The NPP bases its Constitution on respect for civil liberties and rule of law hence its party-slogan is "Development in Freedom" with an elephant as the party's symbol (refer to Table 6.2 on party symbols). Executives are chosen through party primaries at all levels of the party - national, regional, constituency, ward or unit levels (see Table 6.1 on party structure and organization). Article 5 (2) of the NPP Constitution states, the party's organizational structure is based on the Unit, Constituency, Regional, National and Overseas organizations. The officers at the helm of the various levels of the party's structure are elected at the Annual Delegates Conference. At the national level, there is the Chairperson, three vice-Chairpersons, the National General Secretary, National Organizer, Men's Organizer, Women's Organizer and Youth Organizer, at the National Headquarters in Accra. The national executive oversees the activities of the party at the national level and designates authority to the regional executive in the administration and organization of the party's affairs in all the ten regions. They also work in collaboration with the president or presidential candidate on issues such as campaign strategies and party policies. The national executive members are elected in a party primary or national congress in a city chosen by the party leaders. Besides, there are other bodies such as the Council of Elders, who are prominent members of the party appointed to this position by virtue of their political and professional experience and position within the society or the party. For example, Article 15 also provides for National Council of Elders. There are also Disciplinary and Finance Committees at the various levels. Article 9 of the party Constitution outlines the structure of the party at the national level as follows:

- ✓ The National Annual Delegates Conference
- ✓ The National Congress
- ✓ The National Council
- ✓ The National Executive Committee

Article 14 of the party's constitution provides for additional structures of the party, which among others include the National Women's wing, the National Youth Wing and the Tertiary Educational Schools Congress (TESCON), and various regional and district branches of the youth wings known as the Young Elephants.

The organization of the party at the national level is as follows: The National Annual Delegates Conference is the supreme governing body of the party, which is held once every year, at least, four weeks after the last of the Regional Annual Delegates Conference. At the national congress, five members of the party from each constituency, comprising two executives and three ordinary members, vote to elect members of the national executive body. The National Annual Delegates Conference consists of members of the National Council, two delegates from each constituency, and one representative of the Founding Members from each region, one representative of the Patrons from each region as well as one representative from each overseas branch of the party. The National Congress is responsible for the election of the presidential candidate of the party in accordance with the provisions of Article 12 of the party's Constitution. The congress is held not later than 24 months prior to the national election date. Ten delegates from each constituency, one representative from the founding members from each region, and one representative of each of the overseas branches of the party are eligible to vote to elect the presidential candidate at the National Delegates Congress. The party has regional offices in all the ten regional capitals. Article 7 of the party's Constitution describes the structure of the regional level with constituency Chairpersons, a representative of the Regional Council of Elders, and sitting parliamentarians or parliamentary candidates from the region are members of the regional executive. The MPs or candidates do not have the right to vote at executive committee meetings. Regional officers are elected at the Annual Delegates Conference. The structure of the party's regional leadership is similar to that of the national level except that the national level has three Vice Chairpersons. Each regional branch has nine elected executive officers - Regional Chairperson, two Vice-Chairpersons, Regional Secretary, Regional Organizer, Men's Organizer, Women's Organizer and Youth Organizer, as well as a Financial Secretary. For example, as the one National Vice-Chairperson of the party noted, the executive's work is voluntary and there are other party members who work as volunteers in the regional offices, but they may receive some form of incentives and benefits from the party in situations where the party can afford to do so.

The number of volunteers who work in the party offices depends on the period. During election periods, many party members volunteer to work in the party offices, but the number reduces between elections, and there is limited paid staff such as the secretary and driver. An arrangement similar to the national congress is used to elect the regional executives. Ten members of the party consisting of four executives and six members from each constituency in the region vote to elect the regional executives. The main difference is that only representatives from the constituencies within the region participate in the congress/primaries. When the party is in power, the regional party executives work with the Regional Minister (RM) on issues that affect the interests of the party at the regional level. However, the position of the RM, who is the government's appointed representative in the region and head of the regional administration, is not an elected position. The RM may be appointed by the President from the national parliament or outside of parliament, usually a ruling party member to be vetted by the parliamentary vetting committee and voted on in parliament before being confirmed.

Article 6 (2) also states each constituency shall have a Constituency Executive Committee. Each constituency at the district level also has nine elected executives and a financial secretary. The leader of the Constituency or district level executives of the party is the constituency Chairperson, assisted by a Vice-chairperson, Secretary, Organizing Secretary, Men and Women's Organizers and Youth Organizer, paid staff and volunteers. The constituency executive committee appoints the Financial Secretary after its election. The constituency/district executives work in consultation with the MP on various issues at the constituency level. In a situation where the constituency executives could not cooperate with the MP, the party can be divided and may lose the parliamentary seat to another party. The election of the constituency executives takes the form of an Electoral College. The chairpersons from the wards or polling stations within the constituency vote to elect the constituency executives. In order to be able to represent the constituency as an MP in the national parliament, one has to meet the conditions set in the party manifesto regarding parliamentary candidacy, which include among others, being a member in good standing in the party, being a citizen or resident in the constituency or community, having no criminal record, and being of sound mind.

A prospective candidate files for his/her nomination at the constituency level by completing the party's application forms and attaching curriculum vitae with a GHC1,000 (About US$1,025) non-refundable fee during the 2004 election. The nominee is then vetted and approved by the party's Constituency, Regional and National Councils before he/she is qualified to participate in the primaries. Eleven executives from the various polling stations in the constituency vote to elect the parliamentary candidate. The candidate who secures a majority of the votes becomes the party's parliamentary candidate for the constituency. Below the constituency level is the grassroots or community level party organization, that is, the electoral areas or wards that are small unit cells or polling stations/zones, which are responsible for organizing grassroots support for the party. Each ward or party polling station also has five local executives consisting of the Chairperson, Secretary, Women's Organizer, Youth Organizer and Treasurer, and some members from the wards or units vote to elect the ward executives. The NPP prides itself as a party of the liberal democratic tradition. Like its predecessor parties of the Danquah-Busia tradition, it claims to be the epitome of liberalism among the political parties in Ghana and emphasizes free enterprise as the foundation of social development. It believes that creating the enabling environment for the private sector to flourish is the basis for the growth of a dynamic private sector for wealth creation and national progress. Hence the government's popular slogan "the golden age of business". The NPP claims to share political traditions with the Republican Party in the United States. Apart from their policy orientation, one significant commonality is that both parties have the elephant as their symbols. Since the Danquah- Busia has a long-standing tradition of implementing neo-liberal economic policies, the NPP believes that getting the economic fundamentals right is the ultimate feature of successful free market reforms.

Hence in pursuit of its democratic tradition and free market policies, since assuming power, the NPP has implemented the neo-liberal economic policy framework prescribed by the IFIs and the donor countries. In this regard, the party's overriding economic policy objective is to create macroeconomic stability through fiscal discipline, a low inflation rate, a low bank interest rate and a strong currency. The party also implements policies that are also geared toward attracting foreign investors to create jobs to help offset the high unemployment rate and the achievement of other economic indicators that could help bolster Ghana's economic stability. There is a general perception that NPP has been one of the governments that have implemented the most extensive social policies alongside its macro-economic policies since Nkrumah and

Busia's CPP and PP governments respectively. Nonetheless, the government's commitments in the Highly Indebted Poor Country (HIPC) initiative and the continued influence of the IFIs' conditionalities on national policies make social implications of public policy secondary to the achievement of the objectives of free market reforms.

The Rawlings Tradition: National Democratic Congress

The NDC party bases its Constitution and party manifesto on social democracy. As shown in Table 6.2 below, the party uses an umbrella as the party's symbol. The structure and organization of the major political parties is not markedly different. One of the main differences is that the NDC has Rawlings as the founder and permanent leader of the party. The structure of the NDC is as follows: National Executive Committee, Regional Executive Committees, District Coordinating Committees, Constituency Committees and Ward Committees. At the national level, there is the Chairperson, two Vice-Chairpersons, the General Secretary, National Organizer, National Treasurer, Women's Organizer, Youth Organizer and a Propaganda Secretary at the National Headquarters in Accra. Similar to the NPP, the NDC party also has a Council of Elders, which consists of some leading members of the party appointed to this position by virtue of their contribution toward the development of the party or their political and professional experience or status in the society.

There are also Disciplinary Committees at all levels of the party structure. Similar to the NPP, the NDC has additional wings such as the Tertiary Educational Institutions Network (TEIN), the DWM, the Verandah Boys and Girls Club, the Cadres in the June 4 Movement that are broadly spread across the country. (Refer to Table 6.1 on party structure and organization). The National Executive Committee of the NDC has a broad mandate with various functions, which include carrying out the policies and programmes of the party adopted by the National Congress. The National Executive

Committee presents an annual report to the National Congress on the party activities and accounts as stipulated in the Political Parties Law. The power of approving of candidates to contest national elections is also vested in the National Executive

Committee. The National Congress elects the members of the National Executive Committee and the presidential candidate of the party. The National Congress of the party is composed of the following:

- ✓ Two delegates from each constituency elected by the constituency conference
- ✓ All members of the National Executive Committee
- ✓ The president of the republic and his vice-president where they are members of the party
- ✓ The party presidential candidate and his vice in an election year
- ✓ Past presidents and vice-presidents of the republic who are members of the party
- ✓ Ministers of state and deputy ministers who are members of the party
- ✓ District chief executives who are members of the party
- ✓ All members of the parliamentary caucus
- ✓ All party parliamentary candidates in an election year
- ✓ All founding members of the party

Regional Executive Committee members; and a representative of each such other integral party organs formed by the National Congress.

Executives are chosen through party elections at all levels of the party - the national, regional, constituency, ward or unit levels. There are also paid-staff such as administrative secretaries, drivers and security guards, and some members of the party work as volunteers in the party office. The national executives are elected in primaries or a national congress in a city chosen by the party leaders and oversee the activities of the party at the national level and delegate authority to the Regional Executives in the administration and organization of the party's affairs in all the ten regions. At the congress, some members and executives from each constituency participate in the election of the national executives. The elected executives work in collaboration with the presidential candidate on issues such as campaign strategies and party programmes. The NDC also has regional offices in all the ten regional capitals. The structure of the party's regional leadership is similar to that of the national level. The regions have eight functional executives and each regional branch has a Regional Chairperson, two vice-Chairpersons, the Regional Secretary, the Regional Organizer, Women's Organizer, Youth Organizer and a Propaganda Secretary. There are also paid staff and party members who work as volunteers in the regional offices. When the party was in power, the regional party executives worked with the RM on issues that affected the interests of the party at the regional level. An arrangement similar to the national congress is used to elect the regional executives. Five members from each constituency within the region, consisting of executives and party members, vote in the primaries to elect the regional executives. The main difference between the national and regional primaries is that only representatives from the constituencies within the region participate in the congress/elections.

The leader of the constituency or district level executives of the party is the constituency Chairperson, assisted by a Vice-chairperson, Secretary, Organizing Secretary, Men's Organizer, Women's Organizer and Youth Organizer, paid staff and volunteers. The constituency/district executives work in consultation with the MP on various issues at the constituency level. Where the constituency executives could not cooperate with the MP, the party can be divided and face the danger of losing the elections. The election of the constituency executives takes a similar format to that at the regional level, except that only representatives from the wards within the constituency

participate in the election. Below the Constituency level is the grassroots or community level party organization, these are the wards or branches, which are responsible for organizing grassroots support for the party. The branches and zones have local executives or zonal officers such as the Chairperson, Secretary, Women's Organizer, Youth Organizer and Treasurer. The branches have about fifteen executive members. These grassroots level units also have the same system of electing officers.

Representatives from the various wards or branches elect the executives in the wards. To stand as an MP, one has to meet the conditions set in the party manifesto regarding parliamentary candidacy. The basic conditions for qualifying as a party candidate are among others, be a member in good standing in the party, a citizen or resident in the constituency, have no criminal record, and be of sound mind. An aspiring candidate files for his/her nomination at the constituency level by filling party application forms and a non-refundable fee determined by the constituency. As one constituency chairman noted, until the party lost power in 2000, the party's parliamentary candidates were not required to pay registration fees. A confidential report is submitted on the nominee who is then vetted and approved by the National Council before he/she is qualified to participate in the primaries. Party nominations are normally open for thirty days. Two members from every branch or polling stations form an

Electoral College for the primaries to elect the parliamentary candidate. The candidate who secures a majority of the votes becomes the party's candidate for the constituency. The NDC, which is the major opposition party and second largest party after the NPP, claims to be a social democratic party, the same ideology espoused by the two Nkrumahist parties represented in parliament – the CPP and the PNC. The NDC also associates itself with democratic left parties in some Western countries such as Britain's

Labour Party and the Democratic Party in the United States. Despite its socialist background and its claim as a social democratic party, the NDC strictly implemented the neo-liberal economic policies when it was in power. It was also inclined to balance the pursuit of tough macro-economic stabilization measures with social policies, what the government termed "human-centered market reforms". For example, the party's firm belief in the PNDC's populist inclination obliged the government to succumb to pressures for salary increases, social development and its refusal to remove government subsidies on fuel despite rising crude oil price on the international commodities market, which plunged the country into a renewed economic crisis and led to the government's resounding defeat in the 2000 election.

The Nkrumahist Tradition Parties: The Convention Peoples Party and the Peoples National Convention

Although the CPP and the PNC, which are parties in the Nkrumah political tradition, do not have nation-wide party offices and organization, they have some form of party organization at the national and regional levels and in some constituencies, but do not have structures in some constituencies. Both parties claim to represent a revival of Nkrumah's ideals and social policy. The CPP has as its symbol a cockerel and the PNC's symbol is a coconut tree. The executives of both parties are chosen through party primaries at all levels of the parties' structures- the national, regional, constituency, and branch levels. At the national level, there is the Chairperson, two Vice-Chairperson(s), the General Secretary, National Organizer, Women's Organizer and the Youth Organizer at the parties' National Headquarters in Accra. Unlike the NPP and NDC parties, due to financial constraints, there is a limited number of paid staff in the party's national and regional offices, mainly one secretary or office administrator. The staff in the party offices consists mainly of members of the party who work in the office on voluntary basis. The National Executive oversees the activities of the party at the national level and delegates authority to the Regional Executive in the administration and organization of the parties' affairs. The national executives work in collaboration with the presidential candidate on issues such as campaign strategies and party organization. The national executives are elected in primaries held in a city chosen by the party leaders, where members from the party's constituencies vote to elect the national executives. The two parties have regional offices in all the regional capitals and the structure of their national and regional leadership is similar to the NPP and NDC parties, but they do not have nationwide constituency offices like the NPP and NDC, reflecting their lack of nationwide support. While the EC requires all registered political parties to have offices or presence on the ground in constituencies in all the ten regions, the Nkrumahist parties have sporadic support in some specific constituencies across the country. Apart from its regional offices, the PNC mainly has its constituency offices in the Upper West, Upper East and Northern regions, and other constituencies sparsely scattered across the country. The CPP also has offices in the constituencies where it has representation in parliament and some constituencies in parts of the country. The two parties' low levels of institutionalization partly accounts for their poor showing in all the presidential and parliamentary elections that have been held since the democratic transition. As Panebianco noted, the importance of institutionalization in party organization is underscored by the degree of interdependence and participation among its internal actors. If we compare the two parties, the CPP is a more widespread and a more popular party with a larger support across the country than the PNC. Each regional branch of the PNC and CPP parties has a Regional Chairperson, two Vice-Chairpersons, the Regional Secretary, the Regional Organizer, Women's Organizer, and Youth

Organizer. There is also a limited number of paid staff and party members who work as volunteers in the regional offices. Like the NPP and NDC, the CPP and PNC have other bodies such as the National Women's wing, the National Youth Wing and the Tertiary Educational Schools Congress (TESCON). An arrangement similar to the national congress is used to elect the regional executives.

The leader of the Constituency or District level of the party is the constituency Chairperson, who is assisted by a Vice-chairperson, Secretary, Organizing Secretary, Women's Organizer and Youth Organizer, paid staff and volunteers. In constituencies where the party has an MP, the constituency/district executives work in consultation with the MP on various issues. The election of the constituency executives takes a similar format at the regional level except that only representatives from the parties' branches within the constituency participate in the election of the constituency executives. Below the constituency level is the grassroots or community level party organization, that is, the branches, which are responsible for organizing grassroots support for the party. While the political parties' internal organization often remains the same, their policies vary over time to keep pace with the changing international environment. One main difficulty facing the Nkrumahist parties is how to merge the various small parties together to form a formidable opposition to the two major parties - NDC and NPP. For example, when the NRP and CPP joined together to form the New CPP, the PNC refused to join the new alliance. This continues to divide the base of the Nkrumahist tradition. Table 6. 2 below shows the respective political parties in Ghana and their symbols.

Table 6. 2: Political Parties' Symbols

Political Parties   Party Symbols

New Patriotic Party   (NPP)

National Democratic Congress   (NDC)

Convention Peoples Party   (CPP)

Peoples National Convention   (PNC)

Every Ghanaian Living Everywhere (EGLE)

United Ghana Movement   (UGM)

National Reform Party   (NRP)

Great Consolidated Popular Party   (GCPP)

Democratic Peoples Party   (DPP)

Ghana Democratic Republican Party   (GDRP)   N/A

Democratic Freedom Party (DFP) N/A

Ghana National Party

Political Party Strategies for Recruiting Members

Political parties in Ghana recruit members through informal and formal means. Membership in parties offers certain opportunities for influence or rising through the parties' ranks at the national and local levels that would otherwise not be easily available to others who are not party members. In the review of the literature on party development, Randall and Theobald underlined the important role of parties in party development such as parties providing opportunities for political participation and as the medium for political recruitment, thus creating opportunities for upward social mobility. Hague et al also emphasized the importance of membership recruitment as an important aspect of party development. Apart from members who join parties on their own, political parties in Ghana use common strategies to recruit members. Parties recruit new members by organizing rallies to educate the public about the parties' programs, manifestos and policies. Another method of gathering support and increasing party membership, especially during elections is through town-to-town, village-to-village and door-to-door campaigns by the parties' grassroots organizations and supporters. In this regard, the organizers for men, women and youth set up programs and organize functions that are geared toward attracting support from new members.

Other methods used to solicit membership are, among others, outreach programs, and campaigns to talk to people about the party. Party members also do advocacy work by organizing meetings at the grassroots level to inform people about the party's policies. Members are also recruited through advertising on radio and television, establishing youth and women's wings and other programs to attract people into these groups. Parties use the symbols on uniforms, flags, caps, scarves, banners, songs and other emblems and paraphernalia to attract support of the electorate and recruit new members. While these strategies help the parties attract support and membership, the use of Internet sources for membership recruitment and fundraising purposes as is widely used by parties in most developed countries such as the United States has not been introduced in Ghana's party system. Such party symbols and other party paraphernalia have become an indispensable part of party campaigns in Ghana (see Table 6. 2 on party symbols), and are important

means of convincing many rural-based uneducated voters, some of whom base their voting decision on such symbols and candidates' personalities rather than issues.

Hence some parties use their symbols as a campaigning strategy to solicit voters' support through psychological appeals and propaganda against other parties. For example, in the 1979 elections when Ghana was facing economic hardships, some supporters of the PNP convinced some voters that their symbol, the "palm tree" which can serve as both a food and cash crop, is more useful than the opposing parties' symbols. Also, in the 1992 and 1996 elections, supporters of the NDC argued in some villages in the rural areas that their symbol the "umbrella" protects people from rainfall and the scorching sun, while the NPP's symbol the "elephant" is destructive to their crops. Regardless of the name or symbol of the party, its ideology is used to distinguish it from the other parties and to clearly explain its agenda to the public and make the party appealing to voters. These arguments that are based on the parties' symbols signify a metaphor of the opportunities or vision of the party.

This also signifies that parties use their symbols as tools for propaganda in election campaigns. In recent times, some parties have provided transportation to their supporters to convey them to and from campaign rallies to boost the parties' visible support and in some cases to polling centers to enable their supporters to vote, especially in constituencies where a party does not have a strong support base. The supporters of the political parties in Ghana can be classified into three categories: the leaders (both at the local and national levels), the party staff, and the grassroots members. At the top of the party membership is the national leadership, which is mainly drawn from the elite groups in the society. A majority of the party leaders interviewed either have a university education or are successful businesspersons who rose to the top of the party through their qualifications and socio-economic position within society or their financial support of the party.

The second category of the party members is the party workers and party activists, consisting of paid staff and volunteers who work in various capacities in the parties' offices. Many of these members are staunch supporters of the party's ideals and will support the party whether in power or in opposition. Their role is vital and indispensable to the leaders and the party's electoral fortunes. This group of party members and the leadership constitute the mainstay of the party in terms of its organizational setup. The third group of party supporters is the grassroots members who have strong allegiance to the party and will support the party regardless of whether they are in favour of the party's policies or not. The importance of grassroots members to party organization cannot be underestimated. Grass roots members provide vital voluntary work to canvass for votes, attend party meetings, rallies and campaigns. They are often responsible for canvassing for votes, distributing leaflets, party memorabilia and persuading supporters to go out to vote for the party during campaigns and during elections. Members also contribute to party organization by providing essential funds in the form of dues and fundraising for party organization. Grass roots members also contribute to the recruiting and training of future political leaders at the local level of the party organizational structure. Another important role of members in political parties is their role as "opinion carriers". They provide a voice in the community, often becoming key communication links between the party and the community.

Party members help to set the political agenda and legitimize certain opinions and contribute to policy-making. The importance of having majority in the various

representative institutions and branches at the local and national levels and the role of party members in leadership and candidate selection at party primaries show the necessity for a party to have a large active and committed membership. Membership in political parties does not imply paying dues and having a party identification card. Many of the party leaders interviewed admitted that while formal membership of a party implies a responsibility to contribute and support the party's activities, many of the supporters do not register or obtain identification cards, neither do they pay regular dues, but only vote for the party in elections. It is only a few of the party members that are fully committed and motivated to contribute financially and materially to the parties and help in the organization of the parties on a day-to-day basis. A CDD poll in 2002 shows that a substantial majority, 71% of Ghanaians identified with political parties, but only 26% are

registered or card bearing members of parties. The men, women and youth organizers of the political parties play key roles in recruiting members for a particular party. Other membership drive strategies include the promotion of personalities within the party,

especially the presidential candidate as the embodiment of unity and good leadership to the electorate.

All the political parties in Ghana are organized along the lines of the mass party, electoral party and "catch all" party models. Strategies used in membership drive and securing voters' support is in line with the strategies discussed in Duverger's mass party, Epstein's electoral party Kirchheimer's catch-all party models in the literature review. Each of the parties combines card bearing or fee-paying membership with informal or floating membership. Formal and informal membership in political parties is consistent with the Ghanaian political tradition since the inception of party politics in Ghana in the 1950s. The 1992 Constitution and the Political Parties Act 2000, Act 574 recognize the fact that parties have formal and informal membership. As the deputy chairman of the EC noted, this open and flexible membership of political parties is consistent with the liberal ideological orientation of Ghanaian political parties since the parties understand that membership of a political party is not compulsory. Hence citizens are free to join any party of their choice and leave when they wish to do so. A large majority of the informal supporters do not attend party meetings but spring to active political life during the campaign season and voting period during elections. In this regard, membership of a political party does not impose a rigid contractual obligation, but just verbal support and voting for the party during elections. Thus political parties in Ghana depend on the vote of a large pool of uncommitted members whose vote they desperately seek to capture through various campaigning strategies including financial and material inducements.

Political Parties Financing

One of the issues that hinder the development of the party system in Ghana is the problem of political party financing. Party financing remains a major bottleneck in promoting democracy and the party system in Ghana. The establishment and operation of a political party is a very expensive undertaking and is increasingly becoming more and more expensive in all democracies. The desire of parties to generate more income is evidently driven by the increasingly high cost of contesting electoral campaigns. Although democracy is perceived to be the best system of government in the world, the huge sums of money involved for its effective organization does not make it an easy form of government to practice anywhere around the globe. In Ghana, despite the huge

expenditures incurred by parties, such as expenditures on campaigns, transportation for people to party meetings, rallies and conventions, communication equipment and other logistical and administrative necessities needed for the effective functioning of a party, there is no financial support from the state for them. It also involves the maintenance of offices and staff at the national and ten regional levels, the 230 constituencies or district levels, and at the unit or grassroots level, some of whom are paid-staff. In view of the fact that the effectiveness of a party depends on how it is able to communicate its ideas to the voters through election campaigns, along with newspaper, radio and television advertisement, to persuade them to support the party's ideology and programs, make elections and practicing democracy a very expensive system. Since funding plays a significant role in the day-to-day functioning of parties, much of the energies of the party leaders, and volunteers are directed toward mobilizing financial and logistic resources from local and international sources to support the party.

Four main sources of funding are available to political parties in Ghana. These include: funding from the following private sources: members' contributions in the form of registration fees and annual membership dues; donations and grants or gifts from members and sympathizers; sale of party paraphernalia; and income from party fundraising activities. As noted elsewhere, parties like the NPP charged GHC1,000 fees (approximately US$1,025) from members who wish to stand for parliamentary elections. While the NDC did not charge prospective parliamentary candidates any fee for registration whilst in power during the 1992, 1996 and 2000 elections, due to financial constraints, the party charged fees from candidates in the 2004 elections. Interview with some leaders of the NPP and NDC confirmed that the parties receive support from the parties' branches abroad, which consists of Ghanaians abroad who are sympathetic to the parties. While the NDC used to receive kickbacks from some contractors, with the change of government, this source of funding has shifted to the NPP party. No funding is given directly to the parties by international organizations. External support to the parties is in the form of seminars and programs for all the political parties and such logistics as voting accessories and training for the EC staff. Due to the numerous financial challenges involved, operating a political party is not an easy enterprise. The money raised is spent on salaries to party staff and volunteers' allowances, payment of office rent and utilities, administrative and stationery expenses, election campaigns, rallies and other political activities, bicycles, billboards, transportation and other logistics. To be registered by the EC, a party needs to satisfy conditions like having offices in many constituencies across the country. Party offices need to be managed by both paid and voluntary staff. In some cases, parties engage the services of professionals to strategize and design policies for them at the local and national levels. Political parties also fund their election campaigns through media advertisements, organizing and hosting rallies, and paying for the services of polling agents. Interviews with the party leaders strongly confirmed a general consensus among the parties that the sources of funding available to the parties are woefully inadequate for running the day-to-day activities and effective organization of the parties. As one party leader noted, "inadequate funding of political parties and limited fundraising strategies undermines party competitiveness and the possibility of rotating only the well-resourced parties in government periodically through elections".

In spite of all the above expenditures, parties in Ghana are mainly supported by donations from a few wealthy party members to meet their operational expenses and for campaigning in elections. The 1992 Political Parties Law prohibits or limits contributions from certain types of sources such as non-citizens, companies, partnerships, firms or business enterprises. One of the reasons for imposing this limitation was to reduce the monetary influence on Ghana's elections. It was also to prevent large contributions from non-citizens and businesses to support parties, which often comes with demands for contracts, tax evasion and granting of licenses, leading to high-level corruption and impeding political development. The Political Parties Act states the following sources of funding and criteria for raising funds for parties' activities: Only a citizen of Ghana may contribute in cash or in kind to the funds of a political party. Citizens include a Ghanaian owned firm, partnership or company that is registered in Ghana and is at least 75% Ghanaian owned.

The Political Parties Act has disclosure laws concerning the raising and expenditure of funds by political parties. Part II of the Act focuses on the operation of political parties and specifies what needs to be disclosed. Section 13 of the same law, discusses matters relating to political parties' initial assets, and further contributions and donations made to the party. Subsection 1, states that within three months of being issued with a final certificate of registration, or longer periods as the EC may allow, a political party is required by law to submit to the Commission a written declaration giving details of all its assets and expenditure, including contributions or donations in cash or kind, made to the initial assets of the party by its founding members. Subsection 2 also states that the declaration submitted to the Commission under subsection 1 "shall state the sources of funding and other assets of the political party." Subsection 3 states that within 21 days before a general election, a political party shall submit to the EC a statement of its assets and liabilities and other particulars in such a form as the Commission may demand in writing. Subsections 3 and 4 also require the statement to be supported by a statutory declaration made by the General Secretary and the National Treasurer of the party. The Commission publishes this information in the Gazette to make it a public document within thirty days of receiving the declaration. Subsection 6 states, "where a political party (a) refuses or neglects to comply with this section; or (b) submits a false declaration, the Commission may cancel the registration of that political party. "Subsection 14 has disclosure requirements on election campaigns. A political party shall submit to the Commission, within six months after a general election or a by-election in which it has participated, a detailed statement of all expenditure incurred during the election, in such a form as the Commission may direct. Section 21 also has a fairly comprehensive provision on Returns and Accounts of Political Parties. Within six months from 31 December of each year, a political party shall file with the Commission a return in the form specified by the Commission indicating the state of its accounts, the sources of its funds, membership dues paid, contributions or donations in cash or kind, the properties of the party at the time of acquisition, and such other particulars as the Commission may reasonably require; and audited accounts of the party for the year. Apart from these annual returns, the Commission may, at any time, upon reasonable grounds, order the accounts of a political party to be audited by an auditor appointed, and paid for, by the Commission. Concern for the rising expenditure needed to successfully run a political party is growing in Ghana. In the CDD's 2002 Afro barometer poll, 51% of the general public cited lack of adequate funding as the leading problem facing political parties and 70% of respondents are of the view that political parties would perform their roles more

effectively if they were well resourced. While 53% support state funding, a significant minority, 43%, is opposed to the idea and 62% said parties should be allowed to receive contributions from foreign sources. A significant minority, 47%, of respondents mentioned that the total votes won by each party in the previous election should be the criteria for disbursing funds to the political parties. Since 2000, the idea of state funding for political parties has been a major public issue and has provoked a great deal of controversy. There are no limits to individual donations, or the circumstances under which funds can or cannot be given to parties. To help create a level playing field in party fundraising, the 2000 Political Parties Amendment Act amended one of the inconsistencies in the 1992 Political Parties Law by removing the limits on the financial contributions that members could pay to a party, and placed outright restriction on corporate and foreign contributions to parties.

There is a high demand for political parties' financial transparency, accountability, and full disclosure of funds received (78%) and expenditures (79%), while 80% of respondents strongly believe that there is corruption in political parties. Respondents also cited 'unfair business' (42%), and kickbacks (40%) as the greatest manifestations of political corruption. A majority, 54%, cited personal favours as the main reason why people donate to political parties, followed by 31% who said it was for winning government contracts and 17% cited gaining political appointment as the third reason. A strong majority, 62%, believes that public donations have some effect or influence on political decisions and public policy, while 53% do not believe that state funding will reduce corruption. Corruption in the political parties adversely affects governments' ability to promote anti-corruption measures and institutional performance as well as the country's democratic consolidation process. In the review of the literature, theorists such as Diamond argued that combating corruption is a major challenge to regime performance in the process of democratic consolidation, which requires political institutionalization and an effective civil society. Although parties are not supported with direct financial payments, through the EC, the state supports political parties indirectly with some basic necessities for campaigning during elections, such as making available to parties a limited number of vehicles during election years for campaign activities. The 1992 Constitution also guarantees all political parties equal access to the state owned media. In all the elections that have taken place in the Fourth Republic, the state media supported the political parties with free airtime and print pages, especially during election years, although not equally. Political parties are also supported indirectly through tax exemptions by the state. Some foreign donor agencies also support the political parties indirectly through seminars, capacity building and training programs organized for party leaders together with the EC. Although some leading members of the NPP interviewed expressed their support for public funding for political parties, they also noted that "the issue of public funding for parties does not command majority support among NPP members, especially the rank and file of the party, who believe that the NDC government intentionally left out public funding in the 1992 Constitution to the deny the opposition parties access to funding."

Funding of political parties' election campaigns continue to be one of the main issues facing Ghana's democracy. While some parties support state funding of political parties and advocate the banning of private funding for parties and the establishment of an independent commission or the EC to administer the funding of parties from state coffers under arrangements that are fully acceptable to all the political parties, others argue that private funding should be allowed to fund parties in order not to overburden the state. Even in a situation whereby workable and satisfactory regulations are enacted, enforcing limits on private funding of political parties and elections in Ghana would continue to face formidable challenges due to lack of strict monitoring systems to apply the rule. For this reason, in 2003, the EC undertook nationwide consultative meetings to solicit views on financing political parties and the electoral process in Ghana. The outcome of the consultative debates emphasized the need for public funding for parties as a way of enhancing multi-party politics and the development of democracy in Ghana.

In addition to the unresolved questions is the key question of the source of the funds. In a meeting held on April 2007 in Accra, representatives from the leading political parties in Ghana and Togo stressed the need for political parties to be funded by the state to create a level playing field for all parties and effective participation in the democratic process. The nationwide debates on party financing compelled President Kufour to add his voice when he stated in an address to representatives of Ghanaian parties that political parties must be partially, if not fully, funded through budgetary allocations, but cautiously added a caveat that the real challenge is 'when, how and how much'. The National Secretary of the NPP, "cited public opinion on the issue as one of the main impediments that delayed the party from passing the Political Parties Amendment Bill into law, since it could lead to a huge public relations backlash for the party". For example, while there is high recognition that parties would perform more effectively if they were well resourced in the CDD poll, many Ghanaians rejected state funding and cited personal funding by the parties' leadership as their preferred source of funding the political parties.

Factors that Shape Party Development and Democracy in Ghana Candidate Selection Methods in the Political Parties

Candidate selection is a very significant aspect of the political parties' internal organization in Ghana. What makes the process more interesting and vital is that candidate selection methods are institutional mechanisms that reflect power dynamics within the party, or in other words, the level of internal democracy within a party and the nature of a party's dispensation toward promoting democratic principles such as respect for civil liberties and the rule of law when it wins power. Hence the contrasting modes of selecting leaders and presidential candidates in the party seem to underlie the level of internal democracy in the parties. Article 55 (5) of the Constitution prescribes certain basic standards and requirements to which all political parties must adhere, by stating that "the internal organization of a political party shall conform to democratic principles and its actions and purposes shall not contravene or be inconsistent with this Constitution or any other law." The article further states that to be eligible to stand for parliamentary elections in a constituency, the person has to come from or reside in the community, not be declared bankrupt, of sound mind, and have no criminal convictions. The underlying view of this constitutional provision is that since parties are the basic

foundation of democracy and the avenues through which political leaders are recruited, it is important that they develop and strictly abide by democratic standards by educating their members to be tolerant, and accommodate other peoples' opinions and dissent.

Some leading members of the NDC admitted that the party lost the 2000 elections massively because it failed to abide by democratic principles in the selection of its parliamentary candidates, since candidates were imposed on many of the constituencies by the party's leadership. For example, the former chairman of the party, Obed Asamoah, who was then the head of the Reorganization Committee, noted, "if the NDC ever hopes to come to power, then it must do things like what the NPP did while in opposition. The NPP who are now in power did not use election by acclamation, why should we do that in our party?" For example, in the 2000 elections, many disappointed candidates also contested the parliamentary elections as independents to challenge the party's nominees. In Anlo in the Volta region, the former Foreign Minister in the NDC era, Victor Gbeho, stood as an independent candidate against Kwasi Sowu and won with a huge margin. Nationwide, there were more than twenty constituencies where newspaper reports indicated that conflicts within the NDC regarding the selection of candidates led to demonstrations, conflicting public statements, mass defections, candidates standing as independents and even some violent confrontations. The party lost in twelve of the twenty constituencies in total. Overall 31% of the NDC's seats went to the NPP, 10% of the lost seats were directly as a result of some of its members standing as independents. It was reported in the *Daily Graphic* newspaper that when some party members in the Jomoro constituency defied Rawlings and gave their support to another candidate, the party congress in the constituency was postponed. In sharp contrast to the procedures used by the NDC in its candidate selection, the NPP uses competitive democratic methods to select its presidential and parliamentary candidates in its primaries. This may be due to the fact that since the party was formed in 1991, there has been relatively equitable distribution of power within the party and power did not evolve around one personality, as is the case in the NDC. The method used in the party's candidate selection shows the NPP's commitment to open competition, and to the rights and freedoms of the individual, which form the basis of the party's manifesto. Although in the 1996 and in 2000, about 90% of popular sitting MPs were selected unopposed, but this was a strategic policy agreed upon by the party leadership and the constituencies to maintain more seats. As explained by the National Chairman of the party, the system used to select candidates for the parliamentary elections is, the candidates are elected at a party congress at the constituency level in which representatives of the various grassroots units, mainly the party chairpersons in the constituency, are allowed to vote for their preferred candidate. As the party's National Chairman noted, when candidates contest for positions, it prepares them for the general elections and strengthens the party to be more competitive. This strategy is one of the main factors that enabled the NPP to wrestle power from the NDC, despite the latter's unlimited access to state resources.

Despite its democratic procedures in selecting candidates, the NPP system is not perfect and there were allegations of lack of democratic procedures in the party's primaries. For example, in the 1996 NPP primaries, Adu Boahen accused some of the presidential aspirants of bribing some of the delegates. In the period leading to the 2004 elections, during the candidate selection process, several dozen aggrieved NPP supporters carrying placards with inscriptions like "stop imposing candidates on us" and "grassroots is the power," rushed to the NPP National Headquarters to protest against certain actions of the national executives, which they considered as imposing unpopular decisions on some constituencies. Hence one of the major problems facing many parties in Ghana is lack of democratic procedures in their candidate selection methods and their internal organization. Candidate selection methods used by some political parties may lead to internal divisions among members of the same party or constituency, the emergence of independent candidates and even secession from some political parties.

Experiences of both the NDC and NPP have shown that choosing a candidate through undemocratic means can harm the party's fortunes in the general elections, since it makes the party candidates look illegitimate and those dissatisfied with the candidate selection process may stand as independents and split the party's votes. The process of selecting candidates has a major impact on a party's development and is more likely to determine its fortunes during elections. For example, in the 2004 election, some NDC and NPP candidates lost their seats due to a split in the votes that was a direct result of other party members running as independents. Also, some party activists may be reluctant to campaign for any candidate they do not support and in whose selection they did not participate. There is a general consensus among past and present MPs interviewed that even when the party leadership supports a candidate, he should be acceptable to the party members at the grassroots levels, that is, members in the constituency and unit levels who will cast the election ballots because a participatory system of candidate selection not only helps the party win elections, but also strengthens the party internally. For example, questions posed to some NPP, NDC, CPP and PNC MPs on the selection of candidates by the political parties showed a general consensus that despite the improvement in the selection of candidates, there are still some concerns in the selection processes.

Apart from making gains in elections, an effective system of candidate selection strengthens the democratic base of a party, promotes popular participation and helps the party to grow in membership, strength and in its policy-making capabilities. I therefore disagree with Magnus Ohman's emphasis on election outcomes – winning or losing elections - as the only purpose of candidate selection. For example, in large measure, due to the Danquah-Busia tradition's democratic practices, the NPP became a stronger force to be reckoned with and avoided disintegration, even when it was in opposition. On the contrary, the NDC, even with its unlimited access to state funds has weakened considerably over the years, even prior to the 2000 elections, and is plagued by numerous internal feuds and power struggles. Despite the view of many of the party leadership that the party is changing and becoming more democratic, assault on some party leaders and members by Rawlings' supporters at the 2006 NDC party leadership convention in Koforidua shows that the NDC has not yet developed into a full-blown democratic party and due to this, it is often disrupted by internal power struggles.

Very often, parties are faced with a dilemma when it comes to candidate selection because they are interested in giving representation to their supporters and selecting candidates who are popular and appealing to the electorate and capable of winning the general elections, or risking defeat in the presidential and parliamentary

elections. At the same time, the parties also monitor who is selected to represent them since their interest is to select candidates who will not only represent the party in elections, but also are willing to promote the party's interests and its ideology. Some issues that emerged at the NDC and NPP primaries were vote buying and improper inducement;

interference from constituency, regional and national party executives; and hosting of delegates by candidates as an inducement for their vote.

Internal Party Democracy: Democratic Procedures in the Parties' Organization

Another important issue in the political parties' organization that shape party development, but has not been given prominence by parties in Ghana is lack of internal party democracy, which is central to the promotion of democracy. In analyzing differing perspectives on the importance of internal democracy in the 1970s, William Wright highlighted different schools of thought on the issue. He described theorists who regard internal party democracy as beneficial and see parties as central to the political system as advocates of the "party democracy model," and those who describe parties as one of many actors in a democratic arena he labeled the "rational-efficient model". Internal party democracy helps to instill in party members, especially those who may aspire to assume public office at the national level, a sense of democratic values as part of the parties' political training of their members. It is also vital for establishing sustainable parties, and for promoting participatory practices in Ghana's democracy. As Essuman- Johnson noted, "one yardstick of a party's internal democratic structure is how party leaders are chosen to contest national office and run the party's affairs". Although some democratic theorists, like Robert Dahl and Samuel Huntington were silent on the issue of internal party democracy in their writings, the need for internal democracy for the development of the party system and promotion of democracy is underlined by the need for people to freely join or leave political parties, contest elections, participate in decision-making or present their views on issues within the parties and in national affairs. The question one may ask is, if a party is not internally democratic, how could it promote democratic principles with regard to encouraging participation in decision-making, respecting the rule of law and civil liberties as well as promoting checks and balances in government.

Lack of internal party democracy could negatively or positively impact a party's unity and its support base, and yet has not received widespread attention in Ghana's democratic consolidation. Some African theorists such as Kwame Boafo-Arthur and Joseph Aryee argued that institutionalization of political parties must involve the building of internal democracy within the parties and restraining the power of leaders who may use their power to control the grassroots members. As Boafo-Arthur noted, it involves the direct participation of the grassroots members of the party in decision-making, its organization and in its leadership selection processes. Experiences from Ghana's political history show that democratic governments in Ghana that promoted internal democracy were more democratic when they assumed power than those that adopted control and authoritarian strategies. For example, Nkrumah's CPP and Rawlings' NDC governments were not internally democratic and failed to promote democratic principles in many respects during the period of their rule. In contrast, during Limann's PNP term of office in the Second Republic, despite its Nkrumahist traditions, the party respected democratic values, both internally and as the ruling government. Busia's PP and the present NPP governments have promoted democratic principles within the parties and in governance. This problem of internal democracy of political parties is a reflection of how power is organized and distributed in the parties. Democratic consolidation theorists such as Aryee argued that the concentration of the power of policy making in the hands of party members might prevent abuse of power by over-zealous party officials who might exploit their power advantages in the party over the grassroots members. While some scholars see internal party democracy as unnecessary for the promotion of democratic development, others like Magnus Ohman give credence to its role in democratic development.

NDC and Internal Party Democracy

When it comes to internal party democracy, the NDC is severely handicapped, since some key members of the national leadership have often displayed intolerance of opposition within both the top and the lower levels of the party, especially since one person claimed ownership of the party. Another reason for the party's lack of internal democracy is the body of fundamental ideals that underline the party's principles. For example, whereas the NDC has social development as its core principle, it lacks the ideals of individual freedom, respect for rule of law and freedom of expression. Interviews with constituency party leaders in the NDC brought to light a number of

pressing issues concerning internal democracy that have been left unsettled by the party leadership because the issues affect their interests or concerns some of their key supporters. All the NDC constituency party leaders interviewed complained about decisions being centered on a small group of people in the top hierarchy at the national level without consultation with local executives, which they see as the main reason for the declining fortunes of the NDC party in elections. The top-down approach to party organization led to the NDC leadership's imposition of parliamentary candidates on the various constituencies in the 1992, 1996, and 2000 elections. Although the NDC's parliamentary candidate selection process has often been based on primaries, Rawlings and a few leaders at the national level played major roles in influencing candidate selection processes in all the party's constituencies across the country, especially in the 1992, 1996 and 2000 elections. However, they also noted that due to the internal reforms that have been taking place since the party lost power in 2000, they saw a reduction in the influence of the party's founder in the 2004 elections. The chairman of the Ajumako- Enyan-Denkyira constituency also noted, "the leadership of the party makes decisions without consultation with grassroots members and in 1996, the party's top hierarchy overturned the results of about seventy parliamentary primaries. All decisions pertaining to the party organization are made at the national level and the leadership does not listen to the views of the people at the grassroots. This is not good for our party's development and our chance of wrestling power from the NPP".

Article 41 of the NDC party constitution states that "except as otherwise stated in this constitution, at any party meeting, decisions should be taken by consensus, and in case of failure to reach a consensus, by a majority of the votes cast," and the National Executive Committee also clearly stated "it should be noted that deep, frank and open consultations and consensus building are equally important in democratic process as elections. "Nonetheless, the lack of popular participation in the party's candidate selection process characterizes the NDC's lack of internal democracy since its inception, and led to the formation of the NRP and DFP to further weaken the party's support base. In spite of these developments, the National Organizing Secretary of the NDC argued that while the critics of the party have labeled it as undemocratic, the party's internal discipline remains one of its greatest strengths and that should not be confused with lack of internal democracy. While one group led by the former chairman of the party, agitated for democratic reforms to loosen Rawlings' grip on the party's decision making, another group led by Rawlings have fiercely resisted any changes to the party's status quo. This has led to further divisions and resignations by some leading members from the party, while others have vehemently, but quietly criticized the leadership of the NDC's intolerance of participation, freedom of speech and choice. For example, many of the NDC party's constituency chairpersons admitted that the party needs to improve its democratic culture to help it regain nation-wide support and enable it win the 2008 presidential and parliamentary elections. The lack of internal democracy was also the cause for the confrontation between some key members of the executive branch during the NDC's second term in power. For example, due to some disagreements between the President and the Vice President, K. N Arkaah, the latter was not allowed to chair cabinet meetings in the absence of the President. Instead, the Presidential Advisor on Government Affairs, P. V. Obeng, who was a non-cabinet member, was appointed by the then President to chair the meetings on his behalf. This led to some major allegations by the Vice President against the President, and eventually resulted in the former being assaulted by Rawlings at a 1995 cabinet meeting. The lack of internal democracy in the party has continued since the party's inception and was prevalent in the NDCs 2004 congress in which Kwasi Botchwey, who was supported by the party's former chairman, Obed Asamoah, challenged Atta-Mills, the party founder's (Rawlings) favourite. At this congress, some placard inscriptions displayed by pro-Mills and Rawlings supporters stated "NO Rawlings, NO NDC" and other threatening messages. It was alleged that several of Botchwey's supporters were assaulted and/or injured.

While this may be seen as an internal party issue, it indicates Rawlings' grip over the party even in his retirement as president. This raises some complex questions as to whether the NDC and its key leaders are ready for internal party reforms and whether the party has the capacity to build enduring democratic structures like the NPP's more liberal attitude towards internal democracy. While the congress was criticized for its lack of democracy, the rift that occurred between the party chairman and the Botchwey camp on the one hand, and Rawlings and the Mills camp, on the other, became the basis for aggrieved members within the party voicing their opposition to the party's style of operation and agitating for tolerance and internal reforms. The NDC Regional Organizer for the Kumasi constituency also reiterated the need for internal reforms and grassroots participation in decision-making since lack of internal democracy in the party created a long-standing rift between the former National Chairman, Obed Asamoah, and the Founder, Rawlings, and that has weakened the party both at the top and at the grassroots.

The lack of internal democracy and the numerous internal squabbles that plagued the party was evident in an assertion by the former Women's Organizer, Frances Asiam that she was bribed by Mrs. Rawlings to insult and embarrass the national chairman of the party, Obed Asamoah, and accused Rawlings of being a murderer whose hands are soiled with blood. In a Regional Congress of the NDC party in Tamale, Rawlings accused some of the party's regional executives of distributing machetes to party activists to intimidate their opponents, and described the election of Alhaji Sumani Zakari over his preferred candidate, Alhaji Ibrahim Adam, as fraudulent and the congress as nothing but a charade. He further suggested that his archrival, Obed Asamoah and his supporters must be flushed out of the party. For example, there were reports of intimidation, harassment and bully tactics against supporters of candidates who opposed Rawlings' favoured candidates in the 2000 presidential candidate primaries in Accra, and during the 2006 leadership convention in Koforidua, some perceived Rawlings' supporters allegedly assaulted supporters of the former National Chairman and the former Women's Organizer of the party. Allegations of intimidation and assault at the NDC's Sixth National Delegates' Congress, led to the resignation of key personalities from the party such as, the former National Chairman, Obed Asamoah, the former National Women's Organizer, Frances Essiam, and the former Second Vice-Chairman, Kwaku Baah, from the party after the congress. The former MP for Tamale, Wayo Seini, the NDC Chairman in the Jaman District in Brong Ahafo and four executive members of the NDC at Offuman Zongo in the Techiman Municipality defected to the NPP in 2006, stating the lack of democratic principles in the NDC and the NPP government's impressive development projects in the northern part of the country as their reason. The resignation of key members of the NDC national leadership shows deep cracks within the party's unity. The NDC was reported to have experienced similar internal strife in some constituencies such as the Wenchi East and Agona East constituencies among others. For example, there were allegations of bribery in the NDC party's primary at Tafo. Also, there were defections of several members of the NDC party to the NPP in the 2000 and 2004 elections. Some candidates and party executives accused some of the NDC leaders of being biased in favour of some primary contestants and of manipulation during the primaries. To complicate matters, some NDC MPs and members have expressed their misgivings about the party's presidential candidate and more importantly, the party's founder's actions and stated emphatically "just as Rawlings overthrew the 1981 Constitution through senseless military adventurism, so has he overthrown the party's constitution and hijacked it to suit his personal schemes". Due to the power struggle with the party, the conflict between Asamoah and

Rawlings could not be resolved, which eventually led to the resignation of the former from the party. This compelled a segment of the party's supporters, led by Asamoah, to sever ties with the NDC to form the Democratic Freedom Party (DFP). Apart from the breakaway parties, several NDC members have defected to the NPP and other opposition parties. Although the NDC now appears to be embracing democratic principles and has shown the desire to shed the tradition of militant authoritarianism inherited from its parent PNDC regime, the power struggles, infighting and undemocratic practices, especially by Rawlings and his supporters, does not augur well for the party's future and long-term sustainability. Addressing the first youth congress of the party after its defeat in the 2000 elections, Kwamena Ahwoi, the former minister for regional integration admitted that the bickering and factionalism politics in the party are the major "internal conflicts that are sending confusing signals to our members and supporters, that have lowered morale, made it difficult to mobilize the impossible to organize for street action. "In a popular television programme dubbed *kweku-one-on-one*, the former NDC

Minister for Presidential Affairs, Iddrisu Mahama, stated that the party has learnt its lesson from its mistakes and would never impose parliamentary candidates on constituencies; it would rather adhere strictly to the norms of internal party democracy "because that is the only way the party can win back disenchanted supporters and thereby survive. "Due to the party leaders' realization that there is a need to shed its undemocratic character after the 2000 election defeat, its fifth congress and national leadership race held on 27 April 2002, was contested based on democratic principles, and despite Rawlings' opposition to his candidacy, Obed Asamoah's candidacy, emerged the winner and chairman of the party, defeating Iddrisu Mahama by 334 to 332 votes. Since the 2000 election, the party has elected its presidential candidate and many of its parliamentary candidates based on the primary system and attempted to reduce the rate at which candidates opposing Rawlings' preferred candidates, and their supporters, are harassed and intimidated. Despite the improvements in internal democracy in the party, some undemocratic practices still remain.

NPP and Internal Party Democracy

While the NPP is noted for practicing democratic procedures in its internal organization, there have been cases of disagreements between the leadership and some party members on a number of issues. For example, during my research, some executive members in some constituencies such as the Koforidua and the Assin North constituencies of the NPP expressed their disappointment with the former National General Secretary and Information Minister, Dan Botwe, the President and the national leadership of the party for their failure to resolve conflicts between the executives in the above constituencies and the MP for Koforidua and the former Central Regional Minister respectively, in a fair and transparent manner. Dissatisfaction with the party organization, policies and some undemocratic practices led to defections and resignations by some NPP party members. For example, the

2000 election was marked by some high- profile defections to the ruling NDC party. The NPP presidential candidate's former campaign manager, Alhaji Inusah, joined the NDC, and was immediately made a leading member of that party. Also, an NPP youth activist, Kakra Essamuah, after his unsuccessful bid for the position of NPP general secretary dramatically, endorsed the NDC presidential candidate, John Atta Mills. Dr. Gilbert Bluwey, who was an NPP member and the then acting Head of the Legon Center for International Affairs, also defected to the NDC. On October 25, 2004, 500 NPP youth from the Sokpayiri section of the Wa municipality defected to the PNC and about 250 supporters of the ruling NPP at Bimbila defected to the NDC.

In the 2004 NPP party primaries, there were reports of intra-party conflicts due to unfair practices by some executives in the Okaikwei North, Ledzokuku, Offinsu South, Navrongo Central, Bole Bamboi and Yendi constituencies. In the Wenchi East, Agona west, Bawku Central, Ho East, Navrongo Central, Offinsu South and Obuasi constituencies, discontent with the outcome of the primaries led some defeated candidates to run as independent parliamentary candidates. Some primaries like the Ayawaso West Wuogon, Sunyani East and Anlo were rescheduled on several occasions to enable the executives to resolve the impasse by convincing some candidates to step down for preferred candidates. In Garu/Tempane and Wa Central constituency, some NPP supporters accused the national executives of the alleged imposition of parliamentary candidates. Also, in the NPP primaries in the Akwatia constituency, there were allegations of vote buying in the form of "camping of delegates in hotels. "These intra- party conflicts were a result of lack of internal democracy within the parties due to unfair manipulation of party primaries. It is apparent from our discussion of party democracy and candidate selection in Ghana that the characteristics of party organization or factors that shape a party's internal dynamics contribute to issues of internal democracy.

Patronage and Patron/Client Relations in Membership Drive and Elections

Patronage is a central issue in Ghana's party structures, organization and membership drive strategies, and electoral competitions. Both the political parties and the electorate see patronage as an opportunity to gain some advantages. Some forms of patronage are acceptable and even occur in the developed countries. Political parties' campaign platforms in elections, and communities and voters' electoral decisions are guided by patronage. Patronage relations between the ruling parties and a society guide voters' support for parties. This is to express a community's collective interest and its confidence in a party to meet its socio-economic needs. It is also a way of forging a new social contract with an elected government, which means benefiting from the distribution of development projects and patronage to groups and individuals. As Ninsin noted, through this kind of relationship, voters create opportunities for their communities' improvement by soliciting development programs and simultaneously trying to achieve the maximum material gains to improve their living conditions. Parties solicit support and membership by campaigning across the country to convince eligible voters to vote for them based on a party's platform on a promise to deliver development projects for communities and other financial and material incentives and other material goods to potential voters and supporters, and in the case of a ruling party, on its political and socio-economic achievements. One acceptable common strategy that is used by parties in Ghana to solicit membership is through interpersonal contacts within communities such as festivals, funerals, traditional gatherings, churches and church conventions, and child naming ceremonies. Candidates and party leaders who attend such community ceremonies may give monetary or logistical inducements to individuals and/or communities during such occasions to support development in the community, and to use the occasion to solicit support by promoting their party's ideology and development policies to attract the support of the people.

Such gatherings are seen to be ideal settings for spreading a party's message and donations made to communities are indirectly intended to offer the party leadership the opportunity to promote their party's interest and to influence would-be members or voters' decision to support one party over another. For example, leading members of

Ghana's political parties also use funerals of prominent members or their relatives to explain their party's platform and criticize the other parties' agendas. The funeral for the late influential Paramount Chief of Dormaa, Osagyefo Agyeman Badu, was taken over by the NDC political leadership and used the occasion to canvass for votes. Similarly, the NPP used the funeral of some of its prominent members like the late Obeng Manu to promote the party as a better alternative to the NDC. All the party leaders interviewed mentioned similar strategies for soliciting membership and indicated that they are satisfied with the other parties' campaign strategies, and how they solicit membership and funding. As a result of this patronage system, voters' choice of candidates or parties is very often guided by the view that the candidates or parties should serve as a link between them and the state in the distribution or allocation of financial and material resources in the form of goods and services. For example, in a strategic move to win support in NDC strongholds, the ruling NPP government has been providing development projects to both communities that voted for the party and those that supported the NDC. Even in the Volta region where NDC had a clean sweep in the 1992, 1996, and 2000 elections, the NPP embarked on major projects like the Keta Sea Defence construction and other road networks in the hope of making electoral in-roads in the region. In this regard, there is a linkage between an individual and a community's willingness to support a party and its candidates, and the expectation of reward in the form of financial and material incentives, or in development projects for the community, after winning the election.

Whereas some forms of patronage are acceptable for party organization in modern democracies, other patronage practices in Ghana are unacceptable and illegal.

Some parties and party leaders coerce individuals and communities to support their party and deny unyielding communities their basic human rights to have equal access to development and opportunities. For example, the NDC used the "divide and conquer" strategy to win votes by denying communities that failed to vote for the party development projects in order to coerce them to support the party. Pronouncements by the President and his wife, Nana Konadu Agyeman-Rawlings, justified this discriminatory distribution of development projects in their speeches. While MPs should be able to demand projects from the executive as part of pursuing their constituents' rights, after the 1996 elections, Rawlings threatened opposition MPs that they should not expect their development demands to be met.

It is alleged that under the NPP government, in the Northern region, a Self Help Electrification Project was denied one village in favour of another, because as the administrator admitted, the other village did not support the NPP. The Volta Regional Minister allegedly made a similar statement. This confirms how some politicians use development projects to force people and communities to vote for their party or punish the community for not supporting the incumbent party. Also, in some cases, positions and contracts are given to undeserving individuals and groups based on their political affiliation during both the NDC and NPP rule. The CDD noted that during the NDC era, contracts were awarded to individuals "not for reason of professional competence, but political partisanship," and it is alleged that some undeserving NPP members received huge contracts without going through competitive bidding during the "Ghana at 50" celebration. These acts are a clear example of undue abuse of incumbency and are unfair to the opposition parties.

Another form of patronage in the political parties that is unacceptable is the patron-client relationship between the party elites and the grassroots members. Personalities and clientelist networks predominate in Ghana's party system, and many public officials regard politics and public office as a means to personal enrichment by dubious means. Especially, at the local level, there is a strong presence of patron-client relationship between the party leaders and the grass roots members. As C. Clapham noted in his discussion of African politics, the patron-client relationship is fundamentally a relationship of exchange in which a superior (patron), provides financial and material support to the inferior, (the client) and the client, in turn, provides support for the patron. This relationship is based on an unequal relationship between patrons and clients, and the benefits accruing to each of them from the exchange may be uneven. Membership in Ghana's political parties is categorized into two main classes, namely the "Big Men and Small Boys."

The so-called "big men" who constitute the leadership and wealthy members of the party enter politics to acquire wealth and/or increase their wealth to enable them to control decision-making within the parties and dictate to the grassroots members. This group distributes part of its financial and material acquisitions in the form of patronage to the lower classes, who have been termed "small boys" - uneducated, poor and grassroots supporters in the urban areas and mostly, in the rural areas. In this way, power is concentrated in the hands of the "big men" and the members in the lower ranks of the party not only serve the interest of the leaders, but also have little chance of upward

mobility in the party hierarchy. As Jonathan Fox rightly noted, clientelism is a form of social and political control. Political parties and some voters see patron-client relations as an exchange of favours between the parties and the electorate - some individuals or organized groups are co-opted by the political parties through various forms of patronage. In Ghana, this practice has so permeated the party system that the party leaders and supporters do not see anything wrong with promoting patron/client relations.

Weaknesses in the Party Financing and Declaration Law

In assessing the rules governing elections in Ghana, it is necessary to examine how were the rules and procedures for financing elections and party candidates streamlined in the parties to create a level playing field for all of them? Although for obviously good intentions, such as preventing too much monetary influence in Ghanaian politics, Article 55 Section 16 of the Constitution restricts funding of political parties to citizens of Ghana, the Constitution failed to specify emphatically how political parties should be funded. The Political Parties Act, 2000 (Act 574) also does not regulate funding of political parties, aside from prohibiting funding by non-citizens. One ambiguity about this law is that, despite its ban on donations by foreigners, it also states that a corporate citizen, defined by the Act as a company registered in Ghana and whose capital is at least 75% Ghanaian-owned, can contribute in cash or kind without any limits or any other regulations. This gives some foreigners and businesses some leeway to exploit the law for favours from public officials and a ruling party. The law has also failed to regulate the private funding of election campaigns by citizens since individuals and interest groups often pay huge sums of money to parties and their candidates to finance election campaigns. This has made the parties find their own ways and means of funding their activities, and made it extremely difficult for some parties to raise funds.

Many of the party supporters such as contractors who donate to parties often expect to receive rewards in the form of contracts, jobs and favours. The practice whereby the ruling parties give contracts to their favorites and receive kickbacks from the contractors leads to decrease in budget for the contractors, results in shoddy work on government projects, and a cycle of corruption. Since one of the key tenets of democracy is equality of access to political resources, permitting unregulated private funding of political parties and candidates renders the playing field for competitive elections unequal between the ruling party and the opposition parties that are already cash-strapped. As Gyimah-Boadi noted, in the 1996 elections, there was a highly disproportionate funding ratio between the ruling NDC and the opposition parties of some fifteen to one. There is also the threat to internal party democracy, since those who contribute heavily to support parties directly or indirectly influence party-decisions by dictating to the rest of the party members without debate or consensus. Such party donors may insist that they or their nominees occupy key party positions, whether they are qualified or not. For example, the NDC's heavy dependence on Rawlings' financial support led to his attempts to dictate to the party leadership and members and forcibly influences the parties' electoral processes to ensure that his supporters occupy its key leadership positions. Similarly, leading some members of the NPP, PNC and CPP such as the President and chairpersons influence certain key decisions in their parties.

There are pros and cons to the argument on the issue of setting limits on how much one can donate to a party. Whereas advocates in favour of restricting party funding argue that it turns the democratic process into a money-raising machine, deprives poor but well-deserving and qualified citizens from standing for a public office, and over- represents the interests of the rich, others argue that since mass membership dues are inadequate to fund parties or non-existent in the case of some minority parties, enacting such a law to put a cap on donations to the parties would not only phase out some opposition parties, but also limit citizens' right to free speech in the shaping of public opinion. One other problem with the law on disclosure of sources of funds is the requirement that opposition parties must reveal the names of their individual and organizational contributors could lead to backlash and reprisals from the ruling party, especially in the award of government contracts and restricted access to business opportunities and public sector jobs. This is an indication that there is a need to regulate corporate funding of parties to reduce the risk of big corporations and wealthy interests influencing elections in Ghana, as in the United States.

Another major problem with party financing is the weaknesses in the law guiding political party fundraising activities and the inability of the EC to monitor how parties in Ghana are able to evade disclosure laws through secretive operations. Attempts to gather information on parties' income and expenditures from the EC confirmed that the documents were either unavailable or the financial information disclosed by the parties were very scanty and inaccurate. According to the Deputy Electoral Commissioner, despite the existing law requiring political parties to declare their incomes and expenditures, due to parties' suspicion on monetary issues, lack of record keeping and their unwillingness to openly divulge their total incomes and expenditures to the EC the documents filed since the 1992 election show inconsistencies. Since parties do not strictly abide by the constitutional provisions, and some contributors preference to remain anonymous, due to victimization from the ruling party, as happened to some businessmen during the NDC era, some parties failed to declare all their income and expenditures during some of the election years, while in most cases, the declared income is very unreliable. Due to the weaknesses in the implementation of laws in the country, the EC is unable to enforce disclosure. Some forms of fundraising by parties in Ghana leave much to be desired because some parties use their incumbency advantage as the ruling government to exploit public sector appointees and businesses, which promotes patronage in the political parties. One breach of this political parties law was that while the political parties were barred from forcibly soliciting funds from businesses, the NDC received kickbacks from the Ghana Association of Contractors to finance the party. Utterances by the former chairman of the NPP, Haruna Esseku, also confirm the perception that the NPP has used similar strategies to raise funds into the party's coffers. This practice does not augur well for the development of democracy in Ghana. While the Political Parties Act 2000 (Act 574) was enacted into Ghana's Constitution to remove restrictions on individual contributions to a party and to promote public trust in the electoral process, the issues discussed above prove that there are still some major problems with political party financing in Ghana. For example, PNDC Law Act 281 of the 1992 Political Parties Law was found to be too rigid and deemed to have been calculated by the PNDC to stifle the development and sustainability of the opposition parties in order not to pose a threat to the NDC. Despite the constitutional provisions that stipulate the sources from which parties can solicit funds and the EC's monitoring of parties to ensure that they are playing by the rules and regulations guiding all political parties on their sources of funding and expenditures, the parties flout these rules. For example, section 9 (a) of the Political Parties Act (Act

574) 2000, empowers the EC to refuse the registration of any political party unless "the internal organization of the party conforms to democratic principles and its actions and purposes are not contrary to or inconsistent with the Constitution". Party funding continue to be one of the major pressing issues in Ghana's democratic development. Many party leaders argued that the importance of the parties in Ghana's democracy must be regarded like other democratic institutions such as the EC that are funded by the state. While proponents of state funding for parties argue that having such a policy in Ghana will help curb corruption in the political parties and help them

organize more effectively, those against the idea have vehemently expressed their opposition to it for a number of reasons. One argument against providing state funding for parties is that since political parties will still be free to raise funds from private sources, there will still be party contributors who will demand contracts and offer kickbacks to the party to continue the cycle of corruption within the parties, and decrease the internal democratic processes in the parties. Another argument against funding of political parties is, if parties rely on state funding, it will reduce the influence of party members and civic groups, since there will be little incentive to encourage the participation of grassroots members in party decisions.

There is also the possibility that when parties are funded by the state, it could promote "party-entrepreneurs" and lead to the mushrooming of parties with the intention of gaining access to funding. Some leaders of CSOs also argue that the media and other civic groups that play significant roles in safeguarding Ghana's democracy should also be funded if parties should have access to state funding. Others also question whether independent candidates will also receive state funding. Based on the arguments on both sides of the issue, regarding public funding of political parties, this study argues that state funding of political parties is a necessity to help merging parties to compete effectively against the major parties in elections. Nonetheless, there should be a caveat or among others a threshold such as the percentage of votes or parliamentary seats won by a party to qualify for state funding. Otherwise, it will not be beneficial to the development of Ghana's democracy because people could abuse the system for the purpose of receiving state funding for personal gains.

Lack of Participation in the Parties' Structure and Organization

Another weakness of the political parties in Ghana is found in the realm of participation and representation. Despite the immense role of the political parties in Ghana's democratic development over the years, as channels through which citizens express their social and economic demands on the state, the political parties have shown that their capacity to act as true intermediaries between society and the state is limited because they are elitist in terms of their recruitment and organization. The lack of popular participation in the political parties is an indication that one of the major problems facing the party system in Ghana in contemporary times is that majority of Ghanaians lack in- depth political knowledge, which highlights the deficit in civic and political education by the political parties, the NCCE and civic groups. While the distribution of the educational background of the respective political parties' MPs in Ghana's 2005 Parliament indicates that a greater number of MPs have post-secondary diplomas, bachelors and masters degrees, it indicates that political parties in Ghana are gradually becoming elite-led because there is increasing elite collaboration and circulation of elites in the emerging two-party system in Ghana. A majority of MPs, (73. 4%) have at least a first degree, 49 MPs or 22. 6% have a second degree and 11 MPs or 5. 6% have a third degree. Only two MPs did not go beyond the Middle School Leaving Certificate (MSLC) level, whilst 13 MPs or 4. 7% possess GCE 'O' or 'A' Levels and 12 or 5. 2% of MPs have a teachers Certificate 'A' qualification. In extreme cases, this results in depriving the majority of people of their political participation in the decision-making at the top hierarchy of the party organization. Table 6. 3 below shows the educational background of the MPs in the 2005 parliament.

Table 6. 3: Educational Background of the MPs in the 2005 Parliament

Political Parties	High School Certificate	Diploma/ Certificate	Bachelors Degree	Masters Degree	Ph. D.
NPP	2	25	53	35	6
NDC	10	26	38	14	4
PNC	1	2	1		
CPP			2		1

From my observation of political party activities and campaigning in Ghana, it became evident that the level of participation of grassroots members in the parties is restricted to insignificant roles, such as attending political rallies and voting in elections. Political parties integrate the minority groups and rural-based grassroots supporters in a subordinate way to make them play minor roles in the parties. Incorporating the grassroots members and rural-based supporters into the lower strata of the party structures without allowing them to occupy important positions reduces their influence in decision-making. For example, the NDC, which prides itself as a party of the grassroots,

does not promote participation at the grassroots level. Interview with many NDC chairpersons at the district level brought to light the rigid centralization of power in the party. While the NPP is more liberal than the NDC when it comes to participation in decision making at the grassroots, the party also has participation and representation issues to deal with in some of its constituencies. This situation is prevalent in the other minority parties in parliament - PNC and CPP. The problem with participation and representation in the parties stems from the fact that most political parties in Ghana are controlled in an exclusive way by a small group of elites more concerned with remaining in power than identifying and dealing with the people's demands and problems. Many party leaders do not promote popular participation in decision-making and often do not represent the interests of majority of their members. It is necessary to point out that to build and sustain strong state/society relations requires promoting participation and effective representation.

An additional flaw in the structure of political parties regarding representation is the gender inequality in the positions within the parties. Gender representation constitutes one of the major issues that need attention in Ghana's political system. Women played significant roles in the independence struggles and continue to play key roles in Ghana's democratic development. Due to the influence of women's groups such as the Federation of Women Lawyers, the National Commission on Women and Development, and the DWM, women's participation in politics in Ghana has seen some improvements in recent years, especially in the 2000 and 2004 elections. Nonetheless, the participation of women candidates in the 1992, 1996, 2000 and 2004 elections and the number of women candidates in the respective political parties was limited. The NPP government has made a visible progress in gender equity in its ministerial and DCE appointments significantly increasing the number of women appointed to various ministerial and deputy ministerial positions, in comparison with previous governments. The government has also appointed women to head some key public institutions, which were dominated previously by men, such as the Internal Revenue Service, the Immigration Service, Registrar-General's Department. Georgina Wood was recently appointed as Ghana's first female Chief Justice. The government also made progress establishing, for the first time in the history of Ghana, the Ministry of Women and Children's Affairs to address women and children's issues. Since its assumption of power, the NPP government has increased the appointed membership of district assemblies reserved for women from 30% as originally prescribed by the NDC government to 50%. Nonetheless, out of the about 91 Ministers in the NPP administration, only nineteen are women, which represents about 21%. Of the 43 full ministers, only four are women, that is, 10%, and 16 deputy ministers out of 51, making up about 30% of the total number of deputy ministers. In the first term of the NPP government, 2000-2004, there were only 7 women among the 110 DCEs. Some advocates of women's empowerment have questioned the NPP government's commitment to improving women's political participation. They regard the small increase in female appointments to ministerial portfolios as a piecemeal effort to pacify women, but not to give them equal opportunities as their male counterparts in the parties. Although the NPP has made significant strides in women's appointments, the NDC also appointed some women to high-level ministerial and managerial positions during its term in office.

The issue of representation and participation also encompasses the gender gap in the leadership roles in the parties and government appointments. There is still a major gap in the appointment of women as compared to men in the government and other sectors of the public service. Only about 10% of MPs in the second parliament under the Fourth Republic were women, despite the fact that women constitute about

52% of the population. Out of the female candidates who filed nominations for the 2000 elections, the NDC had 20 parliamentary candidates, and the NPP fielded 20 women. The NRP had 17, 16 for the CPP and 4 for the UGM. Currently, the ruling NPP has 20 female MPs and NDC has 5 female MPs, so that the 2005 parliament consists of 205 males and only 25 females. The lack of women's involvement in public life is not only reflected in the president's appointments, but also in other political spaces. The 24 member Council of State that serves as an advisory body to the president has only three women. The recent ministerial appointments and the representation of women in parliament show that Ghana has a long road to achieving gender equality in its public and political life at a time when many countries in sub-Saharan African are making greater strides in women's political and socio-economic empowerment. For example, Liberia, which just emerged from a civil war, now has a woman president. Namibia, which gained independence just 17 years ago, has a woman deputy speaker of parliament who was sworn into office in March 2005. Rwanda, which experienced one of the worst civil wars in Africa, has 40% of women in its parliament.

This democratic deficit in gender representation shows that the proliferation of political parties in Ghana has not strengthened the role of poor and minority groups such as women because there is unfair representation in the party system. While recent developments in Ghana have encouraged women's participation in politics, most women are kept in the rank and file of the political parties without playing significant roles. The lack of women participation in politics prompted some local NGOs like Community Action, FIDA and the Center for Sustainable Development Initiatives (CENSUDI) to organize a number of workshops for women's capacity building initiatives. This encouraged more women to participate in the elections and run as parliamentary candidates in the 2004 election, but the percentage of women to men who actually participated and won is marginal. Experiences from different countries in Africa have shown that it is difficult to increase the proportion of women in political institutions unless special measures and methods such as affirmative action and quotas are employed. For example, in Tanzania, 25% and 20% of seats at the local and national levels respectively are reserved for women. In Uganda, one parliamentary seat for each of the forty-five districts is reserved for women, that is, 45 out of 280 seats, representing 14%. In South Africa, one-third of candidates on the ANC party list are women.

Conclusion

The above analysis of party organization shows that the activities of parties constitute an integral part of the process of developing democracy in Ghana. Some important issues that have been identified in this chapter to hinder Ghana's democratic development include the lack of internal party democracy and democratic procedures in candidate selection, the prevalence of patron/client relations and lack of participation in the parties' leadership structures. It is also apparent that some opposition parties' activities and organization are restricted by lack of financial and logistical resources, which has resulted in major institutional weaknesses in the parties. The context in which some of the parties operate does not augur well for promoting civil liberties and

participation in the political parties. For example, analysis of the parties' organization showed the level of internal democracy within the two parties. Despite the general consensus on the NPP's respect for democratic principles, there have been cases of non- inclusive tendencies by the leadership in recent times, as shown in the dissatisfaction by some constituency executives with certain decisions by the national executives.

It is apparent that the internal party democratic culture within the NPP was far from perfect, its candidate selection procedures and organization encouraged competition and fairness in comparison with that of the NDC. This deficit in participation signifies the lack of democratic culture, which continues to hinder unity in the NDC party. One possible explanation for the party's authoritarian character is that the NDC emerged from an authoritarian regime, and the leadership adopted a "culture of control and silence. " For this reason, some of the party leaders at the national level find it difficult to give up their coercive powers and the party's dictatorial characteristics. As one constituency chairman noted, "many voters are shunning the NDC not because we do not have any good organizational machinery, but power struggle among some of the high-ranking members is hurting the image of the party among the electorate and led to the party's poor performance in the polls. "While the NPP has a high level of institutionalization, the NDC has a medium level of institutionalization since it has more internal problems in the selection of its candidates and organization, but the party is still strong and united, despite the secession of the NRP and the DFP.

Chapter Seven

Parties Representation in Ghana's New Socio-Political Matrix

Introduction

The first part of the chapter focuses on the role of parties as representatives of the pubic. Since the 1992 democratic transition, parties have been one of the main focal points for aggregating citizens' interests and an important link between state and society. The second section of this chapter examines the relationship between the political parties and society in terms of respect for basic human rights and their promotion of the rule of law. The re-introduction of multi-party system of government in 1992 and the period preceding the 2000 elections witnessed gross abuse of people's human rights despite the transition to democracy, and a confrontational relationship between the ruling NDC party and the opposition parties. The lack of respect for the rule of law and civil liberties also led to the victimization of some members of the opposition parties and civic groups who openly criticized the ruling government. In spite of the power alternation in 2001 and the NPP's promotion of civil liberties, there have been cases of abuse of power by some party officials, which aroused public sentiments and criticism. Strengthening of state/society relations plays an important role in democratic consolidation.

Do parties in Ghana create the enabling environment for representation and participation of members at all levels of party organization? How robust is the relationship between the state, political parties and society.

NDC and Society Linkage: 1992-2000

The significant role of the political parties in nurturing democracy is evident in the fact that it is commonly assumed that after elections, the ruling party will establish and maintain a harmonious relationship with civic groups and society in general, as well as promote democratic values in governance. Nonetheless, the political environment in Ghana after the 1992 and 1996 elections under the NDC government proved that multi- party elections alone do not guarantee the promotion of democratic principles and accountability. For this reason, the success of a democratic system should not only be considered in terms of the success of elections alone, but also the existence of a law- abiding government, an autonomous legislature and judiciary. A dynamic party system and strengthened democracy also limit the ability of the ruling party to unfairly control the electoral process, and promote effective guarantees against police brutality, arbitrary arrest, detention without trial and press censorship. Grugel argues that to consolidate democracy, democratic values must be widely accepted by all political and civil actors and the state must have institutions that translate citizen preferences into policy, protect democratic rights and principles, and promote a strong participatory and critical civil society. With regard to the NDC party, its record on representation was very poor. One area in which the NDC government flagrantly failed in promoting fair representation was its failure to promote government accountability. The *de facto* one party parliament became the government's rubber stamp after the 1992 election. One of the major problems that the *de facto* one party parliament under the NDC rule posed to sustaining Ghana's democracy after the 1992 election was the difficulty faced by the parliament and the judiciary in holding the government, which was a reincarnation of the authoritarian PNDC regime, accountable. Interviews with four former MPs of the National Convention Party (NCP) who were in the 1992 parliament described the difficulties they faced with the executive and parliament in the performance of their oversight and representative functions as a minority party that was far outnumbered by the NDC MPs. Interviews with ten NPP MPs who were in the 1996 parliament also revealed a similar experience. The NDC party, through various strategies managed to thwart the parliament from effectively performing its oversight function. As one MP noted, although the opposition parties were fully represented in the 1996 parliament, with about two-thirds of MPs belonging to the NDC, the ruling party exploited its numerical strength over the opposition to its advantage. This enabled the government to pass several unpopular bills presented by the government. The party exploited the advantage of having a one party dominated 1992 parliament to pass some controversial bills under what they termed as a "certificate of urgency." In this way, the party would deliberately delay some important legislation until close to recess, and then parliament would rush certain bills through to meet the executive's desires. In the NDC era, there was little or no attempt to incorporate some opposition members in the government for effective representation, inclusiveness, and to build a harmonious relationship with the opposition parties. According to a former NPP MP, suggestions from the opposition parties on policies were always received with suspicion and often rejected without examining them thoroughly to determine the viability of such views. Unlike the Public Forum instituted by the NPP government, there was little or no attempt by the

NDC to open up spaces for the public to directly communicate their problems and concerns to the President, his Ministers, and other appointed officials.

The rule of law is an important feature of democracy because it ensures that the relationships between the citizens within a country, and the citizens and their

government, are well and fairly regulated to prevent abuse of power and oppression. Nonetheless, the NDC government lacked credibility with regard to respect for the rule of law because under the democratic system promoted by the NDC in the post-transition era, the right to personal security and freedom was only weakly established. As Linz and Stepan argued:

Unless the behaviour of public officials are constrained by a network of laws, courts, independent review and control agencies as well as civil- society norms of transparency and accountability, democracy will be diminished by political abuse and cynicism, and political actors will fail to commit themselves to the rules of the game.

Between 1992 and 2000, flagrant abuses of human rights occurred. For example, political prisoners convicted by a partisan Public Tribunal during the PNDC era in the early 1980s remained in prison long after the transition, without the right to appeal to an independent court, and some individuals, mainly opposition supporters, were detained for varying lengths of time without due process of law. For example, despite the change of government from authoritarian rule to democracy in 1992, the NDC government continued its unlawful arrest and detention of its opponents without going through laid down institutional and legal procedures. The weakness of the official commitment to the rule of law was underscored by the failure of the NDC government to disband partisan security and paramilitary organs, such as the ACDRs, that were used to harass, torture, arrest and detain opposition members and dissenters without trial. A major problem posed by the NDC government was its restrictions on civil liberties, especially freedom of speech and association as well as its intolerance of dissent and criticism. In a multi-party system of government, every person within the society should have the right to express his/her opinion no matter how unpopular they might be and whether or not the government and/or the parties disagree with the views and the expression of such differences in ideas should be tolerated by those in power. On many occasions, the government's actions infringed on the civil liberties of some individual citizens and civic groups such as NUGS and the media.

Between 1992 and 2000, students and workers' peaceful protests were met with violent reactions from the police, the ACDR and other government paramilitary bodies on a number of occasions. The lack of participation made criticisms against government policies a criminal offence that was punishable by detention and sometimes imprisonment. The behavioural dimension of democratic consolidation advocated by Plasser, Ulram and Waldrauch argues for strong and intensified state-society relations. It also highlights the importance of social organization by social and political groups, and their participation in decision-making processes is encouraged and not hindered by political actors since it ensures the concrete implementation of basic civil liberties and political rights. While it is largely the police who patrol the boundary between the lawful and unlawful exercise of these rights, it is the ruling party that controls the state security apparatus that often instructs or allow the police and other state security institutions to infringe on people's rights. For example, the NDC government used the police and the Bureau of National Investigations (BNI) to arbitrarily arrest, detain, and imprison its opponents and critics, as well as members of the press, for lengthy periods without trial by the courts. As a leading member of the NPP puts it, "in the PNDC/NDC era, if you were a vocal critic of the government, you feared for your life and you always looked over your shoulders to see if someone was after you. If you were a public service employee, you got worried about the prospects of being arbitrarily sacked from your job, and if you were a businessman, you always feared that the government would destroy your business. Due to these fears, many people who did not support the NDC were either forced to obtain the NDC's party card or did that to disguise themselves as NDC members to protect their businesses. "The level of abuse under the NDC government even extended to some high-level public officials in the government. For example, media reports alleged that former President Rawlings assaulted his finance minister, Kwesi Botwey, and a minister of trade and industries, Emma Mitchell, as well as the late Vice President, K. N. Arkaah, during a cabinet meeting. When the Alliance for Change (AFC) held demonstrations on May 11 and 25 1995, in Accra and Kumasi respectively, and later in Takoradi and the other regional capitals, in reaction to the government's disregard for the deplorable economic plight of majority of the people, and to protest the Value Added Tax (VAT).

The ACDR, which was the NDC government's paramilitary body, and thugs hired by the government violently suppressed a peaceful demonstration against the government's introduction of the VAT tax system, which led to the killing of four demonstrators in what was referred to as the *"kume preko"* incident. This act of brutality became a stigma on the government's record, and led to the public and the international community's distrust of the NDC's commitment to democratic ideals. As a former NPP MP noted, the killing of peaceful demonstrators by government agents was a major turning point for the promotion of democracy and human rights under the multi-party system. The U. S. government report on Ghana's 1995 Human Rights situation alleged that the then Minister for Youth and Sports, E. T. Mensah was responsible for the deaths, which occurred during the *kume preko* demonstration on May 11 1995. Since various democratic theorists agree that "civil society greases the wheels of democracy" theorists such as Diamond, Whitehead, Putnam and Dahl discussed the central role of CSOs as a driving force behind democratic consolidation and the need for the state to cooperate with civic groups to establish a firm democratic political culture.

In a democratic system, the state must promote democratic principles and establish institutions that encourage and not curtail democratic freedoms and participation in decision-making. While the introduction of democracy helped to reduce the secret killings and flagrant abuse of human rights under the PNDC, the NDC government was also plagued with accusations of various forms of human rights abuses. For example, one case that attracted international attention was the one involving the conflict between the Djentuh family and the Rawlings family. This led to the imprisonment of the Djentuh family members involved in the case without any proper trial and for no apparent offence other than a trivial family feud. In the Djentuh case, during the NDC administration, the family was found guilty, but after the defeat of the NDC government, an independent judge found the first trial to be severely flawed, and overturned the previous judgment. This incident shows that there could be gross arbitrariness and infringement of the individual's rights by those in authority even under an ostensibly democratic government.

These infringements of people's rights and allegations of brutality by security forces, as well as the police, through the use of torture, especially against the government's political opponents, were frequent.

One of the most critical problems was the NDC's disdain for press freedom and scrutiny. It is noteworthy that unlike the PNDC era, after the 1992 transition, a certain level of press freedom was promoted by the NDC, since the media published stories that they previously could not publish under the PNDC regime. New FM stations thrived and they played an important role in educating people on a number of political and socio-economic issues. While Ghana's independent press was vocal in its criticism of the activities and policies of the government, journalists were often harassed and threatened. In the post-1992 election era, the media was subjected to increasing intimidation, harassment and the threat to their political and civil rights, even under a democratic government. Press censorship and threats to journalists and newspaper publishers threatened the sustainability of Ghana's democracy. The government's favourite tool for intimidating journalists, editors, and publishers was Section 185 of the penal code, which makes any publication by the media that the government considers "seditious" information to be libel and a criminal offence.

Many of the government officials and party members' abused the criminal libel law against journalists who were critical of the government and also weakened the independence of the media. This led to the unlawful arrests, detention and imprisonment of numerous journalists and newspaper publishers. The use and abuse of the seditious libel law by the NDC government and some public officials was inconsistent with the constitutional provision that stipulates the freedom and independence of the media. In May 1994, the then NDC Publicity Secretary filled a libel suit against Kwaku Sakyi-Addo, acting editor of the *Ghanaian Chronicle* newspaper and its publishers at the Tema

High Court. In 1996, the government charged three prominent editors and publishers with publishing a report that carried a maximum of ten years in prison, a case that dragged on into 1998. Also, in 1997, four other journalists were arrested on charges of criminal libel. The publisher and editor-in-chief of the "Ghanaian Chronicle," Nana Kofi Koomson and the publisher of the "Free Press", Tommy Thompson and his editor, Eben Quaicoo were arrested and remanded in custody for ten days for publishing allegations of drug dealing by some government officials reported in a foreign newspaper. Theorists such as Putnam argued that the emergence of a rich civic culture is indispensable for democratic consolidation since it leads to the development of trust relations. Hence while it was necessary that the NDC government developed trust relations with the media, it rather antagonized journalists for doing their work.

In 1996, a columnist of the "Free Press" newspaper was also jailed for thirty days for libeling the Chief Justice and another columnist of the "Free Press" was picked up by military personnel and detained in the guardroom for criminal libel, and the then president of the African Journalists Association, Kabral Amihere was picked up at night for writing stories that were not favourable to the military. This was an orchestrated strategy by the NDC to put fear in journalists who were out to expose the political and financial misdeeds of government officials. During this and other trials, some members of the bench sided with the government to incarcerate innocent journalists. Also, the state media that had a national reach were under government control and were often used for official propaganda. Court rulings in favour of granting equal access to opposition parties and CSOs were not effectively enforced and the government disregarded the National Media Commission (NMC), which was established under the Constitution to serve as an independent mediator of media-government relations. Other issues that emerged under the NDC rule were the unlawful seizure and/or destruction of opponents' personal property to serve as a deterrent to critics of the government. An example was the government's unlawful demolition of an opposition supporter's five million dollar hotel complex in Accra on April 12, 1999. The NDC appointed several women to various government and public portfolios such as Emma Mitchel as the minister of trade and promoted women's rights through the activities of the DWM and signed a number of international conventions, as well as its active participation in the Beijing Conference on women. Nonetheless, the activities of the DWM were purely politically motivated and directed towards promoting the interest of the NDC party and its supporters. As a leader of a women's credit union group noted, the DWM deprived the majority of women who were not members of the NDC party and the DWM of financial and material assistance that were received by the organization. Some members of the opposition parties and private business-owners alleged that some government contracts were awarded on the basis of ruling party membership and that government officials pressured businesses to steer contracts toward favoured companies and individuals.

On many occasions, the NDC government impeded the work of constitutional bodies, such as the National Commission on Civic Education (NCCE) and the CHRAJ was its frequent interference with decisions of these bodies against public officials. For example, Rawlings issued a "white paper" on CHRAJ's decisions against P. V. Obeng, Colonel Osei-Owusu and some leading members of the NDC who were found guilty of corruption, and in 1997, Rawlings' disdain for human rights and the rule of law made him criticize the NCCE for organizing a symposium on human rights. Democracy under the NDC was more of a hybrid regime than a full blown democratic system because low levels of accountability characterized the regime. It was what O'Donnell described as "delegative democracy," and Steven Levitsky and Lucan Way, termed a "competitive authoritarian regime," due to its electoral, legislative, judicial and media restrictions and manipulations. The government's disregard for participation, human rights and the rule of law tainted the party's image and reduced its support among the people. Since the defeat of the NDC in the 2000 presidential and parliamentary elections, in the last seven years, the parties opposition status in parliament have shown its increasing commitment toward promoting human rights, civil liberties and the rule of law through its scrutiny of the NPP government's policies and actions of government officials that contravene the 1992 Constitution. Nonetheless, the pace at which internal democracy is promoted within the party is painfully slow.

NPP and Society Nexus: 2001-2008

The period after the 2000 election witnessed an attempt by the NPP to encourage participation in decision-making by creating an enabling environment for people to express their views on issues and to actively involve civil society in public policies. The

NPP government's attitude to public opinion is characterized by accommodation of criticism from opponents and the public. As the vice-chairperson noted, "after assuming office the government realized that it is harmful to Ghana's fledgling democracy if it suppresses the differences of opinion expressed by the electorate and the opposition parties. "On the issue of representation, the approach adopted by the government in handling differences in opinion by critics and the general public was far different and more accommodating of dissent and criticism than the NDC government's strategy.

One novel institutional process that has been introduced by the NPP government to enhance representation and bring government to the doorsteps of the people is the Public Forum concept. Meetings are held in all the district and regional capitals across the country, as well as in the national capital and attended by the president, ministers, MPs and DCEs. Through the Annual People's Assembly and the Meet-The-Press program for Ministers of State, freedom of information has been encouraged. The People's Assembly or Public Forums has afforded the president, ministers, regional ministers, DCEs and, especially, MPs the opportunity to interact frequently with the public and the press to explain government policies to their constituents, and to answer questions from the public and the press on issues that affect the interests of the general public. The public forum is also intended to answer questions relating to allegations against government officials, and to inform people about the government's policies and the progress made in addressing some of the major problems facing the people and communities in Ghana. As one minister noted, "aware of the importance of the directive principles of governance, the MPs and other public officials attend such Town Hall meetings give people the opportunity to air their views on government policies, make the communities' needs known to the government, and for action to be taken to address them in an effective manner. "This concept of participation has created the atmosphere for expanding political spaces for the CSOs and the public in the design and implementation of policies, since the general public is at liberty to criticize government policies and participate in decision-making at the Town Hall meetings. As the Minister of Information acknowledged, the NPP believes that the public forums are necessary because a government that is open to listening to sincere complaints and grievances of the people and taking steps to act and redress such grievances is a positive step towards government responsiveness. The NPP government's policy of "all-inclusive government" has opened an important avenue for cooperation and compromise among some leading members of the political parties and representation of some opposition members in the government. Through this initiative, the President has appointed a number of people from the opposition parties to various high level local and international positions. Some examples are the appointment of the former Minister of the Youth and Sport from the PNC party; the appointment of a former member of the PNDC/NDC, Joyce Aryee, as the Chief Executive Officer of the Ghana Chamber of Mines, and Paa Kwesi Nduom, a leading member of the CPP as the Minister of State for Public Sector Reforms. Also, the government endorsed the appointment of the former deputy Minister of Foreign Affairs, Ibn Chambas, and Ekow Spio Garbrah, the former Minister of Education in the NDC era as the Secretary-General of the ECOWAS and the Commonwealth Telecommunications Organization in U. K. respectively.

The incorporation of former high level PNDC/NDC members by government such as P. V. Obeng into the public service by the NPP government show a commitment toward structural and institutional reform in the political process and strengthening of Ghana's democratic stability and consolidation. The NPP government has also given due attention to gender representation and minority rights in the Ghanaian society. To continue the initiatives of the NDC on the rights of women and children, the NPP has taken further steps in this direction by establishing a Ministry of Women and Children Affairs. The NPP government has also appointed some women to high-level positions in the Ministries and public corporations as Ministers and Managing Directors or Directors, respectively and for the first time in the country's independence history, a woman (Justice Georgina Wood) has been appointed as the Chief Justice. In addition, some local think tanks such as the IEA, CDD and the CEPA are freely involved in policy-making processes and led to increased public trust in public officials.

Another area that has been improved upon by the NPP government to promote active representation and participation is the process of vetting Ministers of state. The NPP government also strengthened the process of vetting ministers started under the NDC after the 2000 and 2004 elections, which took a more open form with increasing public participation in the process. The Ghanaian public's show of keen interest in the 2001 and 2005 ministerial vetting processes, and the citizens' initiative in submitting petitions and information about nominees to the Appointments Committee was a marked departure from the previous ministerial vetting processes, which were more or less ceremonial since the people only observed the process without any active participation. The fact that some of these petitions were given serious attention signifies the concern of the public about standards of probity, ethics and accountability that goes with the position of a Minister and the extent of freedom of expression that people enjoy. The enthusiasm

shown by the media is also notable since the vetting process was broadcast live on GBC television and other local radio and television networks.

The role of the media was significant, because a widely publicized vetting process provided, among other things, an opportunity for the public to dispute and challenge claims made by nominees before the Committee and also to discipline the conduct of nominees by drawing the public's attention to them. For example, the openness of the NPP Ministers' vetting process and public participation brought to the limelight, some issues of ethical and increasing public confidence in the democratic process and the NPP government. Due the government's efforts in resolving the political and socio-economic problems facing the country, people are now more patient with the pace at which the government is addressing problems facing the people. For example, in a CDD poll, about four out of five of those polled by the CDD believe that the current system of democratic government should be given more time to address the problems in the system. a majority of the people polled, about fifty-two percent, said they would still vote for the NPP. Eighty-one percent of respondents expressed trust in the ruling NPP and seventy-one percent in the opposition parties.

The emergence of the NPP to power has also witnessed the increased promotion of civil liberties, the rule of law, and human rights, as well as freedom of speech and association. Since 2001, the strengthening of the legal and institutional frameworks and a clear separation of powers has contributed to the strengthening of the democratic process. Many of the government's education and health policies has led to the abolition of user fees and the "cash and carry" health system. The government continues to implement the Ghana Education Trust Fund (GETFund), which was approved under the NDC government in August 2000, the free primary education, free bus transportation for school children and the school feeding programme as well as the National Health

Insurance Scheme (NHIS) and stabilization of the economy through various macro and micro economic measures to help address the problems facing the people.

Other policies embarked upon by the government are infrastructure development programmes such as the construction of schools and road networks to facilitate transportation and economic development. The NPP government's introduction of these social policies shows that although the donors agencies and countries continue to pressure the government to cut spending, the NPP is gradually moving away from the strict neo- liberal adjustment policies implemented by the PNDC/NDC government, which led to cuts in social spending on education and health services, which resulted in extreme hardships on the people. In this regard, Ayee argued that the NPP government's programs and policies such as promotion of national reconciliation, joining of the HIPC initiative, repeal of the Seditious Libel Law, formation of a government of "inclusiveness", and the participation of civic groups in local and national policies and its "zero tolerance" for corruption policy are all meant to promote democratic governance and are in the right direction towards democratic consolidation. It is important to note that the party's zero tolerance policy on corruption has not been effective in the fight against corruption.

With the power alternation in Ghana, the NPP government has shown respect for the rule of law and attempted to practice responsive and accountable government in a manner that was lacking in the NDC government. The recognition by the public of the new government's tremendous boost of civil liberties may be attributed to a wide variety of policy actions instituted since the inception of NPP rule, such as the abolition of the Criminal Libel Law, the discontinuation of all pending cases that were brought against journalists in the previous regime and the introduction of the freedom of information bill, which the government and parliament have been reluctant to pass, because it is not in their favour pass a law that could be used by the public against them. With the change of government on January 72001, reports of arbitrary arrests and detention without trial of individuals who criticized the PNDC/NDC government in the notorious "Castle Guardroom" ceased.

In the CDD 2002 poll, many respondents argued that with the re-introduction of democratic rule and the emergence of the NPP to power respect for their civil liberties has generally increased. 69% of the respondents said they feel less fearful of being arrested unlawfully than in the past and that their freedom of expression has increased. 68% believe that there is greater freedom of association; 67% feel that their right to vote as they choose is more secure; and 54% feel that equal treatment of citizens before the law has improved. The NPP government's promotion of civil liberties and rule of law has strengthened the democratic system in Ghana. People are able to express their views more freely without fear of retribution. For example, in a speech to the Ghana Journalist Association and all media personnel on the occasion of World Press Freedom Day in 2002, President Kufuor noted:

"Let me take this opportunity to re-affirm the government's commitment to the enhancement of the fundamental human right of freedom of expression, without which the human spirit is deprived of its vital breath," he said. The President further noted, the repeal by the NPP government of the criminal libel law that sought to criminalize speech attested to the government's commitment to freedom and rule of law. "

To a greater extent, the NPP government has addressed past and present issues of human rights abuses since its ascension to power in January 2001. The 1992 Constitution places emphasis on fundamental human rights and freedoms and further buttresses these rights with the establishment of the CHRAJ. Supported by international human rights organizations such as the United Nations High Commission on Refugees (UNHCR), Amnesty International and Human Rights Watch (HRW), the NPP government has been addressing past and present human rights abuses by some public officials and state institutions. As proof of the NPP government's commitment to reconcile the country, especially those who have suffered arbitrary physical abuses as well as financial and material losses since Ghana's independence, the President on May 7, 2002, inaugurated Ghana's National Reconciliation Commission (NRC) to enable a national dialogue to re- examine the pain of the preceding years. The NRC was to investigate violations of human rights and had extensive powers to gather documentary evidence and compel the attendance of witnesses. The NRC received and heard about 4,211 petitions across the country between 2002 and 2004 and appealed to victims of past atrocities to desist from seeking vengeance. Positive steps are being taken to safeguarded human rights in Ghana because the NRC's work is a major step in the right direction toward democratic consolidation.

Under the NPP, government appointees are held accountable for their actions and subjected to high standards. An IEA Research Poll on popular perception of the NPP government indicated, fifty-nine per cent of respondents noted that arbitrary arrest had gone down, with about fifty per cent noting it had gone down considerably. Some events that support the view that democracy and the rule of law are working in Ghana were the resignation of the Minister of Interior, the Northern Regional Minister and the National Security Advisor in 2002 over their alleged involvement in the Yendi conflict, to enable a fair and independent investigation to take place. This is possibly the first time that Ministers in a ruling government have either resigned voluntarily or been forced to resign for their suspected involvement in an issue to enable an independent investigation to take place. In July 2001, the former Minister for Sports in the NPP government was jailed for four years on two counts of misappropriation of funds and

causing financial loss to the state. Also, the former Deputy Minister of Finance in the NDC government faced charges of corruption and was sentenced to eight years in jail. Other acts of corruption, arbitrariness and abuse of power that occurred during the NDC administration were also investigated by the Fast Track Court (FTC). However, there have been criticisms against the NPP government of practicing selective justice, because no NPP government appointee has been charged of corruption, that is not to say that none of the government appointees is corrupt.

Unlike the NDC regime, the NPP government has respected the independence of the judiciary and the rule of law, since decisions by the judiciary are either accepted or challenged under the normal legal procedures. A case in point is the Supreme Court ruling against the FTC that was established by the NDC government. The FTC, through which the case involving the former Chief Executive of the Ghana National Petroleum Company (GNPC) and Advisor to former President Rawlings, Tsatsu Tsikata, was being tried, was declared illegal and unconstitutional. Although the ruling was a major blow to the NPP government, it accepted the decision and appealed the case through the normal legal process. The Supreme Court, by a six to five majority verdict reversed its earlier decision on the constitutionality of the FTC. One problem with this ruling is the constitutional provision that empowers the president to appoint any number of judges to the Supreme Court because the president increased the number of Supreme Court judges to tilt the balance after the first ruling on the case. Both the NDC and NPP governments have exploited this leeway to their advantage, which indirectly compromise the independence of the judiciary. This shows some of the weaknesses in Ghana's 1992 Constitution that allow the president to appoint any number of judges to the bench. The NPP government has also exploited this constitutional leeway except that the president has not used his position to victimize judges such as forcibly retiring them through unlawful means, as was the case of Justice Amoah Sekyi during the NDC era. In spite of some lapses in the government's promotion of democracy, on the whole, the promotion of representation and participation, and respect for human rights, the rule of law and the constitutional provisions show that the NPP is contributing toward Ghana's democratic consolidation. The US Annual Human Rights Report on Ghana for 2007 released in 2008 indicated that although there were problems in some areas, the Ghana government generally respected human rights and made significant improvements during 2007.

Some Weaknesses in NPP's Representation Functions

Regardless of the numerous positive measures to improve governance by the NPP government such as its respect for the rule of law, civil liberties and freedoms, a review of the developments after the 2000 election and the power alternation that followed shows that some major democratic deficits still remain to be redressed by the ruling party. While the NPP deserves to be credited for the democratic development described above, there are other areas in which the government falls short. With the state's entire investigative apparatus at the President's disposal, it was expected that the

President would seek clarification of certain basic claims on a nominee's background by requesting authentic documentation from candidates, and that issues of abuse of power and corruption would be investigated thoroughly before announcement of the position and the vetting process. Even when some NPP members supported these allegations, the president failed to withdraw the ministerial nominees who were entangled in various ethical improprieties. For example, some NPP members and the press brought corruption and abuse of power charges against the former Central Regional Minister, Isaac Edumadze, and the Minister of Roads and Transportation, Richard Anane. The number of petitions filed against some nominees and evidence that emerged in the vetting process show that little or no pre-screening and background checks were done by the executive before the names of the nominees were announced and presented to parliament. Another weakness in the process was that the composition of the Appointments Committee undermined the integrity and neutrality of the process, since some MPs who had been nominated for Ministerial positions were also members of the Committee and participated in the vetting of ministerial appointees. Another challenge that faces Ghana's democratic consolidation and the NPP government is how to meet the needs of justice, truth and reconciliation through the role of the NRC in a viable and progressive democratic project, so that the public could have justice for past and present wrongs. Despite the fact that the NRC was of momentous historical importance, since it was established to provide some public acknowledgement of the gross abuses committed by Ghana's post-independence authoritarian regimes, calls from the media and other groups to the NPP government to act on the recommendations of the NRC Report have fallen on deaf ears. After eighteen months of public hearings on about 4,211 petitions received across the country, the NRC Report was submitted to the government on October 12, 2004, but the government unduly delayed in implementing the recommendations in the report, which caused needless pain to the victims and public cynicism about politicians' concern for their problems. The government's effort to compensate the victims and the families of people who lost their lives or property and/or suffered in one way or another under the PNDC/NDC and other past authoritarian regimes has been painfully slow.

The delay in the payment of compensation to all the victims also undermined the government's long-term commitment to addressing human rights violations and cast some doubts in the minds of the local and international "transitional justice observers. " There is also the issue of formulating a policy to restoring and rehabilitating the lives of victims and survivors of human rights violations. Also lacking is an amnesty policy to

grant amnesty to people who have made a full disclosure of the facts and shown remorse for their actions to insulate them from future prosecution. The NPP government's failure to redress these issues with the utmost urgency as was done in South Africa after the fall of the apartheid regime, have raised doubts about its commitment to reconcile the victims of the human rights atrocities. Some NDC members alleged that the NPP government used the NRC to conduct an anti-NDC witch-hunt and political vendetta to tarnish the image of the NDC for electoral gains in the 2004 elections. Despite the NPPs overall promotion of civil liberties, some NPP government officials and some overzealous police personnel have been involved in cases of abuse of power, which could taint the government's image if appropriate measures are not implemented to check these practices. One case in point was the matter in which some police officers in Kumasi reportedly arrested a mechanic for making derogatory remarks about President Kufour, when he was on a tour of the Ashanti region August 2003, and for resisting arrest. The mechanic, Yaw Kusi was arraigned before a magistrate court and was reportedly convicted and jailed for the supposed offence. Although the victim was later released on the president's orders, his conviction points to the fact that despite the abolition of the obnoxious Criminal Libel Law, some statutes that infringe on individual liberties still remain that must be addressed by the NPP.

In 2004, some incidents involving the government's role in the state media institutions provoked accusations of media politicization, such as government interference in the media in April 2004, in which the National Communications Authority

(NCA) closed down Light FM radio station in the Volta Region, for non-payment of accrued licensing fees, although the action was alleged to be politically motivated. Another case involved an incident in which the former Central Regional Minister, Isaac Edumadze, seized a transport owner's taxi for several days because the driver drove carelessly and literally crossed his vehicle. Although the taxi was released to its owner, public outcry over these cases embarrassed the government and almost tainted the record of the NPP regarding respect for civil liberties. In another development, the same Minister is alleged to have used brutal force on an employee of the Cape Coast Municipal Assembly for attempting to tow his vehicle, including other cases of victimization, threat and assault on innocent people. While such incidents of flagrant Ministerial abuse of power is rare in recent times, police brutality and extortion is still prevalent, hence there is an urgent need that the NPP make increased and sustained effort to resolve the problem of abuse of power by the state security personnel.

MPs as Representatives of the Political Parties and the People

One of the limitations on the power of any ruling party is the development of an effective legislative body; hence, the role of elected MPs is critical to the success of every democracy. In Ghana, MPs' functions include; representation of their constituents and promotion of development projects in their communities, as well as parliamentary law- making and oversight functions, including determining the sources of state revenue and taxation, determining and monitoring how state funds are spent, ratifying treaties, approving loans negotiated by the government, approving state appointments, and endorsing the declaration of a state of emergency. Based on the functions outlined above,

this section of the study will examine how accessible the parties and elected representatives are to their constituents and other members of the public, and how effectively MPs perform their representative, law-making and oversight duties.

MPs play important functions as representatives of the people and the political parties in parliament and while many of the losing parties are often inactive after elections, parliament enables MPs from both the ruling and opposition parties to represent their constituencies and participate in governance in the years between elections. As one MP put it, parties and parliament are important avenues of representation for the people. A vital individual and collective responsibility of MPs centers on bringing the problems facing their constituents to the government's attention and protecting them against unlawful violation of their rights and freedoms by the government and its security agencies, as well as by other people within the community. The participation of opposition parties in the second parliament under Ghana's Fourth Republic saw a considerable improvement in the level of debate, as compared to the first parliament where there was no opposition. As the representatives of the people, MPs protect the people's rights and liberties that are enshrined in the Constitution by protecting them from abuse of power by the institutions under the executive, such as the police. The importance of parliament's oversight function in promoting government accountability is evidenced in the fact that while public accountability through elections occur every four years, MPs in the performance of their oversight functions frequently check the ruling party to promote accountable government. The Constitution confers on parliament the power to undertake a variety of responsibilities and functions within the context of legislative, deliberative, investigative and regulatory functions.

The importance of the MP's role in parliament is therefore seen in the exertion of public control through the right to scrutinize government policies. In spite of the NDC's huge majority in the 1997 parliamentary session over the NPP (133 to 61 MPs), the minority opposition leader, "shadow" ministers and parliamentary spokesmen for various government ministries and departments critically analyzed government policies and put forward alternatives. For example, in 1996, the opposition parties held press conferences to outline their alternative budget after the national budget was presented. The input of the minority parties in the 1997 parliament especially in financial, constitutional, and legal issues, helped to refine most of the bills that were presented to Parliament to be debated and voted on. A number of NPP MPs who were in the 1996 parliament noted that despite the NDC's huge majority in parliament in the 1996 parliamentary session, opposition MPs critically analyzed government policies and put forward alternative policies to improve the quality of public policy. There is no doubt that the input of the minority MPs in the 1997, 2001 and the 2005 parliaments, especially in financial, constitutional and legal issues helped to refine most of the bills laid before parliament. Opposition parties' MPs contribute to discussing issues in parliament and their alternative views on policies form part of the process towards achieving government accountability.

In both the 1997 and 2001 parliaments, the opposition MPs boycotted some parliamentary proceedings for some days to register their objections to certain government policies and draw the attention of the public to the matter. For example, in the debate on the VAT Bill in 1995, the opposition staged a walkout, because it argued that the tax would bring hardship to most Ghanaians. Also, in the 2005 parliament, the opposition MPs staged a walkout for two weeks against the Representative of the

People's Amendment Bill (ROPAB). This bill, which was later passed into law, is intended to enable Ghanaians living abroad to vote in presidential elections. While the ruling party argued that it is meant to restore the deprived rights of Ghanaians abroad, the opposition counter-argued that it was intended to boost the ruling party's votes in future elections. Article 242 (b) of the Constitution provides that MPs are ex-officio members of the District Assemblies (DA) in their respective constituencies.

MPs are required to work in collaboration with the members of the DAs and the District Chief executives (DCEs) to promote development in their constituencies. To avoid mismanagement, waste and corruption, MPs serve as representatives of their constituency in both the national and local level parliaments and ensure that the local officials use state resources judiciously. Another primary function of MPs is the passing of laws proposed by the government. MPs' power to legislate laws is noted in Article 106 of the Constitution. Parliament is also granted legislative power under Article 93 of the Constitution, which specifies that except where a matter is specifically excluded from the legislative reach of parliament, such as in Articles 3, 56 and 107, parliament has the power to legislate on any issue, especially in the administration of justice. The power of parliamentarians was thus strengthened in the Constitution to provide greater powers to the constituencies in the legislative process and improve levels of government accountability at all levels of government - national, regional and district levels. MPs also serve as watchdogs of the constitutional provisions to protect the interest of their constituents and the general public. For example, in January 1997, the minority leader asked the Supreme Court to give a proper interpretation of some constitutional provisions on ministerial appointments and retained ministerial portfolios in the second parliament of the Fourth Republic. This was done to bloc the NDC government from maintaining some ministers and deputy ministers from the 1992 administration without parliamentary approval. The basis of the opposition parties' complaint was that ministers and deputy ministers had exhausted the mandate given to them in the 1992 parliamentary approval, but continued to exercise their functions with the President's approval. By a majority vote of four to one, the Supreme Court ruled in favour of the opposition parties in parliament. As an NPP MP noted, the opposition MPs in parliament have also used the courts to seek interpretation of government acts they believe are in contravention of the constitutional provisions to promote public interest. For example, in the cases involving challenging the requirement of a police permit for political parties and civic groups to hold demonstrations; requiring the Ghana Broadcasting

Corporation to accord the parties equal coverage; challenging the commemoration of 31December as a public holiday; and the ability of the NDC government to use District Assemblies in the manner in which they were constituted before the introduction of constitutional rule to approve the appointment of DCEs. The impact of these and other important rulings by the Supreme Court in favour of the opposition parties against the NDC government showed that despite the frequent disbanding of Ghana's parliament by authoritarian regimes over the past decades, MPs in parliament now have the capacity to oppose, influence and/or check the conduct of the government. Opposition MPs in the 2001 and 2005 parliaments have also played comparable oversight functions to scrutinize the NPP government's policies. In the CDD 2002 poll, 57% of respondents said they approve of the performance of their MPs and fifty-four percent approve the job of the Regional Ministers and DCEs. 63% believe they could command the attention of their elected representatives, which is a significant increase over the 49% that responded in the 1999 poll on the same issue.

Challenges to Ghana's Democratic Consolidation

Problems Associated with MPs Representation Functions, the Office Holders' Assets Declaration Law and the 1992 Constitution

One of the major challenges that sapped the vitality and efficiency of Ghana's parliament in the pre-1992 era was the political instability in Ghana. At the time of the transition to democratic rule, Ghana's parliament was very weak, compared to the ruling NDC party that wielded considerable power to suppress the powers and functions of parliament in playing its oversight functions. The dissolution of parliament after the 1966, 1972, 1979 and 1981 coups disrupted the systematic and sustained development of Ghana's parliamentary institutions. While there have been a number of programs by both local think tanks such as the CDD and international organizations such as the USAID and the Canadian Parliamentary Centre to help Ghana's parliament to rebuild its institutional capacity, it continues to show some weaknesses in its oversight functions and other related roles. As one MP admitted, the 1992 Parliament showed a weak capacity to initiate and scrutinize bills proposed by the NDC government and the opposition boycott of the elections at the time also deprived parliament of the opportunity to perform its oversight functions effectively since there were no opposition members in the one-party dominated parliament that was more or less used by the NDC to its advantage. In 1992 alone, nine proposals for constitutional amendments were submitted by the then Attorney General to parliament for approval. In the 1996 parliament, the opposition MPs were far outnumbered by the NDC MPs, so their views made little impact on the government's position on a number of public policy issues. For example, when President Rawlings refused to propose a Freedom of Information Law and an Official Secrets Act and ignored the press and public request for the abolition of the Criminal Libel Law of 1960. Opposition parties in parliament were incapable of checking the government's abuse of a law that infringed on people's rights and was widely used by state officials to harass some opposition members and the press. While there are wide-ranging constitutional provisions regarding parliament's legislative functions, the conventions and procedures for holding a ruling government accountable were not sufficiently developed.

One of the primary challenges facing MPs in carrying out their representation functions is the incessant financial and material demand coming from their constituents. The role of MPs in Ghana goes beyond just representing the community and the interest of constituents in parliament because constituents expect more than just representation from MPs. Apart from getting funding from the government for development projects, and due to the inadequacy of such government funding, constituencies rely on MPs to get funding from the NGOs, some diplomatic missions accredited to Ghana, and bilateral and multi-lateral organizations for development. As one MP noted, the high expectation of many constituents makes MPs' work more complex and challenging. Most often, MPs are flooded with personal and community appeals and demands for money and other material goods. Some constituents approach their MPs with various demands including payment of their children's school fees and hospital bills, as well as money for clothing, food and other personal needs. Voters often threaten MPs who are not able to meet these demands that they will not vote for them in the future elections. Some MPs interviewed claimed that these incessant personal demands from their constituents deter them from visiting their constituencies regularly. Hence within their communities, the MP's role includes ceremonial representation, such as attending and chairing social functions like weddings, child naming ceremonies, engagements, funerals and birthdays, to support the community's activities. The constituents, on their part, use such occasions as an informal meeting to convey their grievances to their representatives and other government officials. While these added roles have been a major financial strain on MPs, they have also used such occasions to enlighten their constituents about government policies, impending projects to be undertaken in the area, and even to solicit votes. MPs also keep in touch with their constituents regularly identifying problems facing their communities. This practice has led to significant improvements in MPs' service delivery functions to their communities under the Fourth Republic. MPs who fail to stay in touch with the people regularly to keep abreast with their problems or are unable to obtain funding from any of the above- mentioned sources for development are regarded by their constituents as ineffective and may not be re-elected either at the party primaries or in the general parliamentary elections. For example, among some of the fundamental reasons why thirty-nine NPP MPs and nineteen NDC MPs lost their seats in the 2004 party primaries was the lack of contact with the constituents to address their problems. One of the issues associated with Ghana's MPs is their lack of concern to amend the constitutional provision that gives undue financial incentives to MPs at the expense of the public interest. Notwithstanding the high rate of poverty in the country, parliamentarians' self interest often takes precedence over the general suffering of majority of the poor. Despite Ghana's indebtedness that led to the NPP government's

decision to opt for the Highly Indebted Poor Country (HIPC) initiative, MPs were granted US$20,000 as government guaranteed loans to purchase cars to facilitate their work after every parliamentary election since the re-introduction of democracy in the 1993, 1997 and 2001 parliaments. In 2005, this figure was increased to US$25,000. A number of MPs interviewed on this issue explained, "the US$25,000 is a compensation for their low salaries. " If this is justified, then every worker in Ghana deserves to have a government guaranteed loan to compensate for their low salaries. The irony and controversy over this issue is that MPs who have been in parliament for three or four consecutive terms benefited from this loan scheme every four years, and as a result, have been silent about its unfairness to other public service workers. Another problem with MPs' representation role is the failure of parliament to amend the constitutional provision that allows for the appointment of majority of ministers from parliament and place limitations on the President regarding the number of ministries and ministerial appointments. Although the Constitution does not put a cap on the number of ministers the president can appoint, parliament also has a responsibility to check the president from abusing this power by restraining him from appointing an excessive number of ministers by voting against the president's request for the creation of more ministries and rejecting unethical or unqualified ministerial appointees. However, since MPs are likely to benefit personally through ministerial appointments, MPs in the 1993, 1997, 2001 and 2005 parliaments under the NDC and NPP governments have been silent over the large number of ministers, which are unnecessary drain on the country's

budget. An additional weakness in Ghana's parliamentary procedures and the 1992 Constitution regarding parliament's power to approve or reject the President's ministerial nominations is that nominations by the executive are voted on through open rather than secret balloting. Although ministerial nominees were investigated in the 1993, 1997, 2001 and 2005 vetting processes, despite public opinion and adverse media findings against some of the ministerial nominees, due to the open ballot system and the prospect of benefiting from ministerial appointments, MPs are not able to exercise their voting power based on their personal and professional discretion, which confirms that there are still some major flaws in parliamentary appointment processes, which significantly impact the effectiveness of parliamentary representation in Ghana.

Yet another critical problem facing Ghana's MPs is lack of financial and logistical support and other administrative facilities from the government to facilitate their work. As one MP puts it, "despite the fact that parliament's role is considered crucial for the development of an open, accountable and responsive democratic system, support services for MPs such as assistance of research personnel, library facilities, books, data, office spaces, and paid constituency staff are provided by the state on a minimal basis or are virtually non-existent. "MPs in Ghana rely on information and statistics provided by the government to debate policies in parliament. As an MP noted, "the lack of financial and logistical support has weakened parliamentarians' capacity to make an independent analysis and objective judgment on various critical issues and policies, and impedes their effort to address the problems facing their constituents. "The Office Holders Assets Declaration Law that prevents MPs and other public officials from acquiring wealth illegally is also flawed, because immediate family members, such as spouses of public officials, are not included in the law and are often used as front persons. Excluding the spouses of public officials and civil servants from the asset declaration law means that state officials could have an opening for hiding corrupt gains.

One constitutional provision that has attracted a lot of criticism in various circles is the President's power to appoint an unlimited number of ministers from parliament, thus weakening the oversight function of parliament. While the appointment of a majority of ministers from parliament provides an opportunity for a cordial relationship between the executive and legislature, it poses some significant problems for the performance of parliament's oversight functions. The adoption of the Westminster model, which permits the appointment of MPs as ministers, has led to the inability of parliament to perform its oversight function to ensure greater accountability of the executive. This constitutional provision, coupled with MPs desire to get ministerial positions, has weakened the oversight functions of parliament, because ministerial positions and the patronage that comes with it confers the status of a "big man," which emphasizes the culture of superiority in the Ghanaian society. For example, a report released by African leaders on Ghana's performance in the country's democratic development as part of the African Peer Review Mechanism (APRM), applauded the country's success in consolidating democracy, but criticized the lack of separation of powers between the legislature and the executive.

The 2005 ministerial vetting process also highlighted some fundamental procedural and institutional weaknesses in Ghana's democratic system. Although the vetting process signified great strides in Ghana's democracy, the president's reluctance to withdraw certain nominees who were found wanting by the Appointments Committee, and parliament's subsequent approval of the entire first batch of ministerial nominees, despite some of the nominees' failure to answer adequately a number of disturbing questions raised about their suitability of holding such high public offices, contributed to the disillusionment of many Ghanaians in the process. This also shows some of the weaknesses in parliament's oversight functions and flaws in the 1992 Constitution. A number of NPP, NDC, CPP and PNC party leaders interviewed expressed their dissatisfaction with the president's handling of allegations leveled against some of the nominees in the vetting process, especially Isaac Edumadze, the former Central Regional

Minister. A lack of checks and balances in the appointment of ministers and DCEs is a matter of concern in Ghana's democracy because the appointment power of the president as stipulated in the Constitution could easily be abused. In the appointment of public officials, parliament completes its work once the approval is completed and communicated to the president. When parliament approved a nomination, it was up to the president to proceed with the appointment of that Minister. Therefore, the approval by parliament does not constitute an order to the president to appoint the nominee.

Under-representation due to Uneven Distribution of Parliamentary Seats

One of the structural problems facing Ghana's electoral system that impedes the effectiveness of MPs representation of their constituents is the uneven distribution of parliamentary seats. This has created uneven population and vote distribution in some districts. In the process of re-demarcating the constituencies, the EC failed to ensure that the population in some of the constituencies with large populations is relatively equivalent to the size of the other electoral districts. The unequal size of parliamentary constituencies due to the unequal distribution of voters leads to the problem of significant under-representation, especially in the regions dominated by large urban populations, such as in Ashanti and Greater Accra. This discrepancy in the voter distribution could also be a potential source of electoral disputes in some of the affected constituencies, and above all, some MPs inability to meet most of their constituents' needs. For example, in the 2001 parliament, the NPP's 100 MPs represented on average about 61,000 registered voters per constituency, whereas the 92 NDC MPs served less than 46,000 voters per constituency. While an average constituency has 53,495 registered voters, there are 20 constituencies with over 90,000 voters, and the smallest twenty constituencies have less than 27,500 registered voters. Apart from one constituency, all the twenty largest constituencies are in the Greater Accra and Ashanti Regions, mainly in the Accra and Kumasi metropolis respectively and their suburbs. The average number of registered voters in the twenty-two constituencies in the Greater Accra region is roughly 83,904 voters, which is considerably higher than the national average. Despite the creation of thirty new constituencies prior to the 2004 elections, and over thirty additional seats to be contested in the 2008 election, the distribution of parliamentary seats still favour the NDC party that designed the initial constituency redistricting. This unequal distribution of population in relation to the number of parliamentary seats is against Article 47 (3) of the Constitution stipulates that constituencies should be fairly distributed. About ten percent of the constituencies in Ghana have over 90, 000 registered voters, which is much higher than the population in many of the 230 constituencies. Some constituencies in the Greater Accra and Ashanti Regions, such as the Bantama constituency, which has been termed the NPP's "Florida," are too densely populated to remain under a single constituency, yet during the 2004 electoral redistricting by the EC, it failed to re-district some of these very densely populated constituencies. This has led to discrepancies in the distribution of legislative seats across the country. Additionally, the highly populated Greater Accra Region has only five District Assemblies, which has an equal number of seats as the sparsely populated Upper West Region. According to the 2000 census, an average of 103, 025 people live in each of the 45 most highly populated constituencies, which is higher than the national population average of 92,061 people for the then 200 constituencies.

The 2000 census has also shown that there are five constituencies with over 140,000 residents, and five with less than 75,000 people. For example, whereas the Krachi constituency in the Volta Region has over 159,591 residents, the Kajebi constituency has only 52, 849 people. Size and population distribution have affected the registered voter rates, since the populations are highly imbalanced even across the 45 constituencies. The size of some constituencies made it difficult for some MP's and candidates with limited resources to effectively campaign or to actively visit all parts of the constituency regularly to address their constituents' needs and immensely contributed to their defeat in the 2004 party primaries and elections. A former MP, Nana Asante-Frimpong, highlighted this problem when he argued that his Kwabre constituency in the Ashanti Region should be re-demarcated, because it is difficult to visit all the villages and towns to interact with his constituents. The NDC candidate for Ablekumah South Constituency in Accra, Dr. Nii Armah Josiah Aryeh, who lost to the NPP's MP, Theresa Tagoe, won more votes than a candidate who won in a sparsely populated constituency with about 20,000 voters. Considering the present number of parliamentary seats, each constituency should have about 47,000 voters.

Corruption and Abuse of Power by Party Leaders and Public Officials

Under Ghana's new political dispensation, besides promoting democracy and socio-economic development, combating corruption presents a major pressing issue for Ghana's democratic consolidation. Due to the political instability that besieged the country after independence and the successive military coups, Ghana's party system did not have the opportunity to deal effectively with corruption by developing effective mechanisms of checks and balances, or to institutionalize anti-corruption measures to promote ethical behaviour, civic responsibility, and accountability in the parties and government institutions. Theorists such as Diamond argued that combating corruption is a major challenge to the process of democratic consolidation, which requires political institutionalization and an effective civil society. Many public officials and politicians in Ghana fail to use their political power effectively, competently and responsibly to achieve social change. The questions that need to be addressed in this section with regard to the effort being made by the political parties toward reducing corruption in Ghana are how effective are the policies and institutional mechanisms for preventing public officials and the public from involvement in bribery and other forms of corruption? And how have the policies of the NDC and NPP governments affected the fight against corruption?

It was in the light of the widespread corruption that the 1992 Constitution made provisions for the establishment of anti-corruption bodies such as the Commission on Human Right and Administrative Justice (CHRAJ), established under Section 18 of Act 456, while the Serious Fraud Office (SFO) was also established under Act 466 of the Constitution. The problem of deterioration of the morality of public officials and the widespread belief in the endemic abuse of public office also motivated the Consultative Assembly that designed the 1992 Constitution to include a code of conduct for public officials in the Constitution to help check corrupt practices in the society. The code covers conflict of interest, declaration of assets and liabilities and the institution to handle complaints about contravention. Article 284 of the Constitution is explicit on "conflict of interest," which states "a public officer shall not put himself in a position where his interest conflicts or is likely to conflict with the performance of the functions of his office. "The CHRAJ is responsible for handling contravention and non-compliance with the Code, checking and redressing incidents of mismanagement and malfeasance, and for promoting human rights. The code's financial disclosure provisions require that public officers submit to the Auditor-General a written declaration of property, assets and liabilities to the office of the Public Accounts Committee in the Accountant General's Department.

NDC's Record on Corruption Eradication

Ghana's 1992 democratic transition was expected to usher in a new system of government and method of ruling under the NDC government. While there were some minor changes and improvements after the transition, in the form of reduction in the abuse of executive power, the NDC government continued the same policies and methods through which the PNDC had ruled the country. The lack of transparency and the executive's dominance of the legislature in the 1992 and 1996 parliaments made it difficult for the public and media to have access to government information, which enabled some party leaders and government officials to engage in corrupt activities without regard for public and media criticisms. For example, during the NDC era, the Auditor General's Report on government accountability consistently pointed to escalating embezzlement, corruption, malpractice, and other improprieties in many government institutions.

In January 1996, the persistence of corruption and the unethical behaviour of some leading NDC officials led the CHRAJ to investigate ten top government officials, including five Ministers of state and some Chief Executives of public corporations, on allegations of corruption and illegal acquisition of wealth. At that time, the then Minister of the Interior,

Colonel Osei Owusu, and another member of the presidential staff, allegedly owned houses worth over 500 million cedis (about US$200,000). Another Minister was charged that his annual salary was 3.6 million cedis (approx. US$2,000) at the time, but his expenditure was one billion cedis (about US$400,000), over four years.

P. V. Obeng, who was the then Minister for Presidential Affairs and a leading member of the PNDC/NDC, and Flt. Lt. Joseph Bampo Atiemo, the then Chief Executive of the Ghana Cocoa Board were all probed by CHRAJ for embezzlement of state funds and illegally acquiring assets. While many of the defendants were found guilty of the charges they were accused of, in all the cases cited, the NDC government failed to act upon CHRAJ's findings against these officials, and that showed the government's lack of commitment to combating corruption. The then President, Rawlings, issued a "white paper" which sought to undermine the work of the CHRAJ and openly condemned the Commissioner, Emile Short, for "witch-hunting" against members of his government.

It is ironic that a government that claimed to have its foundations in accountability, anti-corruption, public morality, integrity and patriotism, should attack a constitutionally mandated independent body for investigating its members and shield them from public accountability and corruption investigations. In several instances, the government overturned the Commission's rulings and intimidated and arrested journalists for reporting corrupt practices of state officials. As Ayee noted, while the Commission's recommendations led to the resignation of some Ministers, the code of conduct in the 1992 Constitution did not promote ethical behaviour because the government lacked the political will to enforce it. The lack of measures to check corruption in the state-owned enterprises

(SOEs) divestiture program enabled some public officials to use their families and friends as front-persons to purchase some of the public corporations at undervalued prices. For example, it was alleged that the former First Lady, Nana Konadu-Agyemang Rawlings, used front persons to purchase the Nsawam Cannery factory section of the Ghana Industrial Holding Corporation (GIHOC) with government funds amounting to US$500,000.00 dollars and failed to pay any taxes to the state. Not surprisingly, the CDD's 1999 Afrobarometer survey indicated a very high public awareness about official corruption in Ghana. In the survey, 76.2% of respondents noted that most government officials and politicians are mainly concerned with enriching themselves, and 84.9% of respondents believed that bribery was a common practice among public officials. The widespread public perception of political and bureaucratic corruption of public officials made people lose trust and confidence in the government's willingness and ability to fight corruption.

NPP's "Zero Tolerance" Policy on Corruption

The period following the power alternation in 2001 brought a great deal of public optimism about not only the promotion of democratic principles and social policies, but also the fight against political and bureaucratic corruption in Ghana. It was in response to public sentiments against corruption and abuse of power that President Kufour's NPP government declared a "zero tolerance" policy on corruption. This was the most promising and popular aspect of the President's inaugural speech, which signified a reflection of the depth of popular concern with the problem of corruption in the Ghanaian society, and the desire of majority of the people to see corruption in the public service eradicated or drastically curtailed. A number of policy initiatives in the initial years of the NPP government showed positive signs of government commitment to implementing policies that were geared towards achieving its declared "zero tolerance" for corruption.

To achieve its objective, the government initiated some transparency-enhancing measures, such as the repeal of the criminal libel law, expanded media access to public officials and executive employees and frequent explanation of government actions and policies through announcements placed in the print and electronic press. In 2003, the government implemented some institutional reforms to curb corruption by passing three laws governing public finance. These are, the Internal Audit Agency Act, the Procurement Act and the Financial Administration Act to create central boards designed to oversee some of the fundamental financial functions of government. The government also introduced the Public Procurement bill and a Whistleblower Protection bill both of which were passed into law, but parliament has not yet passed the freedom of information bill. The government also solicited public views on public policies issues through the introduction of the public forum concept or town hall meeting, in which the President, Ministers and parliamentarians meet with the people periodically at the national, regional and district levels to explain government policies and answer questions from the public and the media. Another strategy, through which the NPP made efforts to check corruption, was the prosecution of some of the party's own Ministers of state for their involvement in some corrupt and fraudulent deals that caused financial losses to the state. For example, in July 2001, the former Minister for Sports in the NPP government was jailed for four years on two counts of misappropriation of funds and causing financial loss to the state. The Fast Track Court (FTC) also convicted the late former deputy Finance Minister in the NDC administration, Victor Selormey, who was sentenced to eight years imprisonment for embezzling US$1,297,500. Some critics considered his prison sentence for an offence that caused the nation a substantial loss to be too lenient and a slap on the wrist because petty criminals suffer a worse fate than what the ex-Minister was given, but it was a significant step in the fight against official corruption. The FTC also sentenced the former Minister for Agriculture, Ibrahim Adam, the former Finance

Minster, Kwame Peprah, and other high-ranking members of the NDC government to various prison terms for their role in the Quality Grain Scandal. In another case, the present Minority Leader of Parliament, Alban Bagbin, was charged with abuse of power and was asked to refund to the state certain unauthorized expenditures involving the use of vehicles belonging to the Ghana Ports and Harbours Authority for purposes unrelated to his official business as a Board Member in the NDC era that allegedly benefited his 1996 and 2000 parliamentary election campaigns. In his defense, the Minority leader

insisted that using state resources for personal benefit is a perk that comes with his position, and a standard operating procedure in the public service.

Is the NPP's "Zero Tolerance" Policy Working?

The NPP's initial effort to combat corruption through the prosecution and imprisonment of some Ministers by the FTC created an atmosphere of public relief and the feeling that a new era of swift and robust action against corruption and abuse of public office had emerged, and was a sign of the administration's determination to fight corruption in accordance with the rule of law and due process. Regardless of the modest achievements that have been recorded by the NPP government, CHRAJ, SFO and the Ghana Anti-Corruption Coalition (GAAC), reducing corruption is still one of the daunting challenges facing the government. For example, out of 21 countries in Africa surveyed by the World Economic Forum and published by the Accra Daily Mail, Ghana placed 10as the least corrupt country in Africa. Although this trend is an improvement over Ghana's ratings in the past years, it is clear that the country has quite a distance to go to improve its record on corruption. Despite the government's efforts, allegations and some evidence of corruption have plagued some NPP Ministers and other government officials since the party assumed power in 2001. This shows that the success of the government's zero tolerance for corruption policy has been limited, if not completely ineffective.

The opposition NDC party also made a number of allegations of abuse of power and financial impropriety against some NPP officials in various situations. Some of the alleged cases of potential conflict of interest and corruption were the Sahara oil lifting contract in the 2002 Sahara Energy Resources Company, a Nigerian oil business, which was the sole sourcing agency and the lack of transparency in its crude oil deal with the Tema Oil Refinery earned the Nigerian Company an undeserved US$1. 5 million. Apart from these cases, there have also been a number of high-level corruption cases under the NPP government. For example, in 2004, the deputy Minister of State at the Presidency and Member of Parliament for Wenchi East, Alhaji Moctor Bamba, resigned his position after numerous investigative reports by the Chronicle newspaper revealed that he had used his office to facilitate visa fraud and forged signatures of various Ministers of state to obtain loan guarantees for a private company, of which he was the director, shareholder and secretary. In addition, allegations of impropriety and conflict of interest have been raised against some NPP officials during the 2005 ministerial vetting process and in the press. For example, some party members and the press allegedly accused the former Central Regional Minister, Isaac Edumadze of amassing wealth through bribery and extortion during his tenure of office.

In these cases, the President ignored calls from party members and the media to investigate and/or terminate the appointment of the ex-Central Regional Minister, Isaac Edumadze, who was accused by some NPP members of corruption and abuse of power, which was later confirmed by the Audit Service. Regardless of these allegations and public misgivings about the candidate, his appointment was confirmed by parliament. This was a bad precedent for Ghana's democratic development, and reinforced allegations of corruption within the NPP government. Whereas during the 2006 government reshuffle, the ex-Central Regional Minister was dropped, While the Minister's firing was a demonstration of Ghana's growing democracy, this issue, together with the nomination and confirmation of some Ministers with questionable backgrounds, dented the NPP government's commitment to the "zero tolerance" for corruption, and shows that the Office of Accountability at the "Castle" has not lived up to its duties and public expectations. Other cases of corruption, and drug-dealing cases have been linked to some public officials both under the NDC and NPP governments and some members of the police service. One case that reflects breach of office and abuse of power occurred in November 2005, when an MP, Eric Amoateng, was arrested with his accomplices in the United States for illegally importing $US6 million worth of heroine into that country and has been found guilty and jailed for 10 years. This has caused severe damage to the integrity and credibility of government officials and Ghana in general. The irony is that when the case broke, some leading members of the party admitted receiving complaints about the candidate's suspicion of drug dealing during the nomination process made them skeptical about his honesty, but some chiefs from his area coerced them into accepting his candidacy. There have also been some cases of missing seized cocaine in police custody in recent times.

Despite the president's pledge to stamp out corruption during his inauguration speech, the recent Transparency International Corruption Perception Index (TI-CPI) shows that Ghana's corruption index has stagnated or retrogressed in recent years. In the TI-CPI report, Ghana dropped from its high rating in the 1999 and 2002 TI-CPI ratings, in which it scored a 3.9 rating and placed fiftieth, out of 102 countries assessed by the corruption monitoring body. In the 2003 Report, Ghana placed seventy-two out of 133 countries on the World Corruption Perception Index and obtained a score of 3.3 out of 10, with 10.0 denoting least corrupt and 1.0 representing the most corrupt. In 2004 Ghana was rated 3.6 out of 10, and 63, which dropped to 3.5 in 2005 and to 65 out of 159 countries ranked. Since Ghana's inclusion in the survey in 2000, its rating has fluctuated between 3.3 and 3.9, which is just slightly above the 2.9 average score of sub-Saharan Africa. A number of recent public opinion polls by the CDD and Ghana Integrity Initiative (GII) that were conducted since the president's declaration of his "zero tolerance" policy, indicated that the fight against corruption has stagnated and it is again on the rise. In the CDD's Afrobarometer poll in March 2005, in which 1200 people were selected randomly from all ten regions of the country without regard to ethnic, religion or party affiliation, 81% of the participants responded that the Ghana Police is the most corrupt institution, 72% of respondents believe judges and magistrates are corrupt and regarded the judiciary as a mistrusted institution, and 71% cited corruption among tax officials. 56% of the respondents believe there is corruption in the presidential office, compared to 38% of respondents in 2002. There is an increase in the number of people from 62% in 2002 to 67% in the 2005 poll, who admitted that public officials are corrupt. 59% agreed in the 2005 poll that MPs are corrupt, which shows an increase of 7% from the 2002 poll.

Institutional Corruption and Inequitable Administration of Justice

One of the prevalent critical issues of corruption in Ghana is institutional abuse of power and corruption by the police and judiciary. In December 2005, the Ghana Integrity Initiative noted that a Transparency International survey on corruption in Ghana as measured by the Global Corruption Barometer sequentially ranked the police, customs, political parties, the judiciary, utilities and tax collecting institutions, education, business and private sectors, registry and permit services as well as the media as the most corrupt institutions in the country. A survey consisting of 2000 respondents conducted by the Commission on Human Rights Initiative's (CHRI) Africa Office in 2002 showed a very high percentage of respondents (71%) had not seen Ghana's 1992 Constitution. The question is how can people who have low level of awareness defend their rights when violated or access the court system for redress?

Police Abuse of Power

Despite the fact that the government has achieved significant successes in promoting civil liberties, abuse of power by personnel from the police and judicial institutions charged with enforcing the law and/or administering justice continue to adversely affect the promotion of civil liberties and the rule of law in Ghana. Interview with some journalists across the country described the pervasive corrupt practices that have permeated the police service, as "a social disease the government has not yet found a cure". One of the main issues that were emphasized by the journalists was that the police continue to accept bribes from both complainants and suspects, and sometimes keep suspects for more than the stipulated 48 hours without any charges, bail or trail. The journalists also narrated stories about people who have been in remand for periods ranging from several days, months and years. This action contravenes Article 17 of Ghana's 1992 Constitution, which guarantees equality before the law and non- discrimination. While the rule of law gives people detained by the authorities the right to apply to the courts for immediate release from custody, torture and detention without trial for longer than 48 hours, failure to obtain warrants for arrest by the police are some of the dents in the respect for civil liberties and rule of law being promoted by the NPP government. It is also alleged to be common police practice that before taking a complainant's statement, some police personnel demand money for pen and paper, and for transportation before arresting suspects. Drivers have also been some of the major victims of police personnel dubious strategies to extort money, which include unnecessary delays, and sometimes using various intimidation tactics. Evidence of police abuse of power is also seen in the U. S. Government's Country Report on Human Rights Practices in Ghana report for 2003 released by the U. S. Bureau of Democracy, Human Rights and Labour on February 25, 2004 cited police brutality with excessive force against criminal suspects. Incidents of police brutality, negligence and corruption report issued by the Commission on Human Right and Administrative Justice on a study sponsored by the Commission on Human Rights Initiative and the U. S. State Department Country Report on human rights practices for Ghana between 2000 and 2004, stated that human rights violations continue to occur in Ghana by the police and in the prisons. The report indicated that some prisoners have been on remand for lengthy periods at the James Fort Prison and 399 prisoners were on remand in the Kumasi Central Prisons, while the US-SDCR on Ghana for the same year also stated there were 1,270 remand prisoners in Ghana whose warrants had expired. The US-SDCR also stated 20% or about 2,000 of the 9,783 prisoners nationwide, were on remand. On December 10, 2005, the CHRAJ Commissioner also stated that "annual inspections of police cells revealed greater compliance with the 48-hour rule and that fewer suspects were detained for more than 48 hours, but added that the police personnel demanded money from suspects as a precondition of their release on bail."For example, a Commission on Human Rights Initiative (CHRI) report indicated that a prosecutor at the Odorkor police station in Accra refused to bail a woman with four children who had been granted bail by a court of law. There is evidence of pervasive bribery and corruption in the police and judicial service, but successive governments in Ghana have not been able to introduce any clear policy to remedy these unwarranted practices, which are more widespread in the rural areas, where many people are ignorant of the constitutional provisions and their rights. Whereas government officials publicly stated that the government's "zero tolerance for corruption" policy applied to the police and other security officials, the Police- Community Relations Survey found that 68% of respondents believed extortion or bribery occurred frequently within the police service. Of the number of respondents who admitted having offered a bribe, 92% reported that police officers accepted the bribe. Similarly, a public opinion survey conducted by the CDD in September 2002 and released in February 2003, indicated that citizens were most suspicious of the police, with 79% responding that at least some police personnel were corrupt, followed by customs officials by 74%, and judges and magistrates, by 70% of respondents. The report also indicated that many Ghanaians who have been arrested by the police believe they were not treated according to the law. A number of people arrested were not told about the charges against them, while 67% were not given an opportunity to contact a lawyer. The 2006 Report on Human Rights practices released by the United States Bureau of Democracy, Human Rights and Labour on March 6, 2007 also indicated that "although the NPP government generally respects human rights, and has made significant improvements since assuming office in 2001, human rights problems are still prevalent in Ghana, including "deaths resulting from excessive use of force by police, vigilante justice, harsh and life-threatening prison conditions, police corruption and arbitrary arrest

and detention of criminal suspects, prolonged pre-trial detention, police infringement on peoples' privacy rights, forcible dispersal of demonstrations, forced evictions and corruption in all branches of government". Another survey conducted by the CDD on Police-Community Relations, found that many of those arrested believed that they were not treated according to the law and there was a strong belief that police often violated the human rights of those arrested. Of those who stated that they were arrested, 46% were not informed of the charges against them, 51% were not read their rights, 67% reported they were not allowed to contact a lawyer, and 44% believed they were presumed guilty from the onset. The statistics on police abuse of power show that the problem is relentlessly acute and on-going.

Judicial Abuse of the Rule of Law

Another public institution that has been marked for being notorious for corruption is the judicial system. Due to the pervasive corruption in the judicial system, judges and magistrates' decisions on some cases brought to the courts are often based on monetary interest rather than the rule of law. Ignorance of the law and weak institutions have facilitated corruption in the judiciary's service delivery processes and created deep social injustice against many people in the society. The Constitution guarantees equal access to justice, for example, Article 19 states "the courts shall give every person charged with a criminal offence a fair hearing within a reasonable time. An adjudicating authority for the determination of a civil right or obligation shall be established by law and shall be independent and impartial, and proceedings shall be in public. "Nonetheless, a number of surveys conducted on the knowledge of people about rights show that many Ghanaians are not familiar with the human rights laws enshrined in the 1992 Constitution.

A major setback in Ghana's justice system is the undue adjournment of cases. The Judicial Service/CUSO report on cases in Ghanaian courts shows that there were adjournments in 70% of cases in Accra alone in 2003. While adjournment is sometimes necessary to enable the courts obtain some important facts in cases, cases are often delayed unnecessarily through adjournment and remanding suspects without any reasonable cause. Judges and prosecutors often abuse this system indirectly to punish suspects who are unable to pay their way by unduly prolonging the duration of cases. Coupled with the pervasive corruption in the court systems is the high fees charged in the mainstream courts, which is too high for most ordinary people, especially women and disabled persons. This discourages victims from pursing their cases in courts or gain access to the justice system. In a survey on corruption conducted by the Ghana Integrity Initiative in three regional capitals, Accra, Takoradi, and Kumasi in March/April 2005, an overwhelming majority of respondents, 90%, strongly agreed that corruption is rife in Ghana, 60% also responded that it is much worse, only 36% said the problem is much better or better. This trend in abuse of power by state institutions shows weaknesses in the parties' policy toward eradicating corruption.

Weaknesses in the Anti-Corruption Bodies' Mandate

While the role of the anti corruption bodies is to check corruption and abuse of power by public officials and state institutions, there are a number of institutional weaknesses in the mandate of the anti-corruption bodies. The government has failed to address a number of bureaucratic bottlenecks and institutional weaknesses that hinder the constitutionally mandated bodies like the SFO and CHRAJ's effort to combat corruption. While the CHRAJ and SFO are authorized to check political and administrative corruption, their dependence on the government for their budgetary allocations in many ways makes them less autonomous. Although Article 227 of the Constitution provides for financial autonomy of CHRAJ and the SFO, the executive has regularly cut budgetary allocations to these bodies. These agencies have been susceptible to manipulation through reduced funding and limiting the power of the organization and its personnel. For example, in 2003, out of the SFO's GHC720,000 budget, only GHC640,000 was actually given to the body for its expenditure. To make an already bad situation worse, the three public finance bills passed in 2003 failed to address some fundamental shortfalls of the agencies entrusted with checking corruption, such as their dependence on the government for operational resources, which makes them ineffective avenues of scrutinizing and sanctioning corrupt government officials. While the NPP government claimed to have increased the budgetary allocations of the constitutionally mandated bodies, the amount is often inadequate to meet the latter's full expenditures.

The willingness of the executive, parliament and the judiciary to cooperate with the constitutionally mandated bodies determines the extent to which they can effectively discharge their constitutional mandate. For example, one major weakness of the CHRAJ's power is that the coercive powers of the courts may not be invoked to enforce the recommendations of the Commission until three months have elapsed after the date those recommendations were communicated to the parties involved. If no action is taken to implement CHRAJ's recommendations, or the action taken is considered by the Commission to be inadequate, the Commission may take action in the courts to enforce the recommendations. For example, when CHRAJ found the former Transportation Minister, Richard Anane guilty on charges of conflict of interest and abuse of power, the Supreme Court later reversed the guilty verdict on technical grounds that CHRAJ investigated the Minister without a complainant.

This is a classic example of some of the loopholes of Act 456 in the Constitution and the weaknesses and lack of clarity regarding the power of the anti-corruption bodies. For example, whereas CHRAJ needs adequate power and capability to enforce its decisions, no concrete understanding has been reached between CHRAJ and the judicial system in cases where CHRAJ would have to go to court to enforce its decisions. As a result, cases prosecuted by CHRAJ that proceed to the regular courts may have to be dealt with as new cases. The SFO is not in reality autonomous of the ministry under which it was created and the government has refused to grant its director the security and independence that goes with a permanent appointment. The government's reluctance to give full legal autonomy and adequate disbursement of funding to the SFO and CHRAJ is a cause for concern in the fight against corruption. Organizations like the Ghana Integrity Initiative and the Ghana Anti-Corruption Coalition have joined together and launched the Ghana National Action Plan Against Corruption to pressure the government to change some constitutional provisions that impede the CHRAJ and SFO's duties.

Conclusion

Although the re-introduction of constitutional rule and the establishment of Ghana's parliament have led to some level of participation and generally improved the political parties' and MPs' accountability, the first part of the Fourth Republic under Rawlings' NDC government saw a continuation of the authoritarian practices by a democratically elected government. It is also apparent from the above discussion that between 1992 and 2000, excessive power amassed by the NDC government impeded the democratic process and the NDC's relationship with society. Based on the information gathered from the interviews and other methods employed in the research, it could be argued that although the NPP has promoted participation, human rights and rule of law to a greater extent, and is gradually re-building state/society relations, there are still some outstanding issues that needed to be addressed by the government to promote public trust in the political parties, government institutions and officials. Some of the main issues that continue to hinder Ghana's democratic consolidation are corruption and abuse of power by government officials and institutions, and the civil service, weaknesses in the anti- corruption bodies' mandate, weaknesses in MPs representation, law-making, and oversight functions, the office holders assets declaration law as well as under- representation due to uneven distribution of parliamentary seats.

The fact that the CDD poll cited political parties as the third most corrupt institution in Ghana after the police and customs shows the extent of corruption in Ghana's party system and state institutions. As Diamond noted, democratic consolidation must address the challenge of strengthening state administrative apparatus or bureaucracy, the institutions of democratic representation and governance, the judicial system and oversight agencies to audit the activities of governmental institutions. The inability of the government to design a viable strategy to stamp out corruption in the police and judicial services has undermined the reliability of state institutions and reduced the government's capacity to respond to the needs of the people in a more effective manner. Lack of political will to promote civic education for people's

empowerment against state institutions' encroachment on their rights and the inability of the state to reform Ghana's police and judiciary systems have led to the prevalent indiscipline and abuse of power in these institutions. The executive and legislative bodies have greater roles to play in streamlining these institutions to make them efficient and disciplined. When effective measures are instituted, such as a greater level of transparency in the political parties' activities and governmental processes and procedures for strengthening the legal and institutional frameworks, they help strengthen democracy in general. In so doing, it will help develop the social trust necessary for consolidating Ghana's democracy.

Chapter Eight

Summary

The main objective of this study was to examine two key questions. Firstly, political parties' role in Ghana's democratic consolidation, and secondly, the parties' structure and internal organization in terms of the achievements and the main challenges of party development in Ghana since the 1992 transition. The study examined the major political parties that have representation in parliament, particularly the NDC and NPP that have ruled Ghana since the democratic transition. This section also discusses the role of democratization in the development of political parties in Ghana. While the study shows that political parties in Ghana have improved their organization and functions over the years since the re-introduction of a multi-party democratic system, interviews conducted with the Regional and constituency chairpersons of the main political parties and other party leaders highlighted a number of problems. Among these are leadership failures, institutional problems and lack of logistical and financial support.

Some Major Findings of the Study in Comparative Perspective

Similarities in the Political Parties' Organization

Party Structure and Organization, Membership, Convergence Policy

In the process of examining political parties' structure and organization, and their role in Ghana's democratic transition and consolidation, the study identified some major issues that needed to be addressed by the political parties, civic groups, the EC and the government in order to accelerate Ghana's democratic consolidation process. The study also brought to light some similarities and differences in political parties' organization. One similarity that became evident in the study was that the leading political parties have similar hierarchies of power and processes for running their parties' affairs. Apart from the national congresses, each party has a national executive body headed by a chairman, general secretary, organizing secretary and other executive members who constitute the administrative nucleus of the party and council of elders. These national level bodies and functionaries in charge of the headquarters constitute the structures of power where actual decisions are made. Besides the secretaries, drivers, security guards and typists who are paid-staff, all the parties' executives work in the party offices as volunteers, although some are given financial and material incentives, such as business contacts, which promote patronage in Ghana's party system.

Another similarity in the political parties' organization that emerged in the study was that, apart from the national, regional and district level party organizations, the major political parties strive to organize branches in every town and village throughout the country. In recent times, parties in Ghana organize more at the constituency and unit levels as a strategic choice compelled by the need for effective mobilization of grassroots voters during elections. This has made the constituencies and local units/wards the most important organizational arenas for the political parties. It is also important to note that the party congresses held by all the major political parties is the highest party event and one of the most important avenues that enable the mass of the grassroots members across the country to participate in decision-making. The mandate of the party congress covers approval of the party constitution, the election of the national executive committee and other national officers, as well as the choice of presidential candidates. The national executive collaborates with the regional and constituency executives to set the modalities for choosing parliamentary candidates at the constituency level.

Another important common feature of parties in Ghana is that they are becoming more like "catch all" parties, as in many Western democracies, especially in the United States. Their efforts to embrace a broad spectrum of the society into their fold regardless of their political ideologies show that parties in Ghana have moved to the centre of the ideological issues and boundaries. Although the two major parties claim to have distinct ideological orientation, it is questionable whether there is any distinct variation in the pragmatic direction in the two major parties' policies. Despite the ideological differences between the NPP and NDC, the variation in their policy agenda is marginal. Since the two parties have alternated in the exercise of state power under Ghana's Fourth Republic they have implemented the same neo-liberal free market policies cushioned with social policies. Unlike the First, Second and Third Republics, in the present Fourth Republic, despite the differences in the three political traditions' ideological orientation, there are significant similarities in their platforms since almost all the political parties have adopted the same policies - centrist policies, emphasizing economic growth with redistribution.

Like parties in many developing countries, in contemporary times, rapid changes in the world economic systems and international political economy from the 1980s and 1990s have affected policies of parties and governments irrespective of their ideology. While the two parties' project their social policies to be human-centered, they are secondary to the achievement of the economic policy targets set by the IFI's. The difference is the degree to which one or the other party has successfully implemented the neo-liberal policies with little or no public opposition. In this regard, the NPP has been more successful than the NDC. With its popular slogan, "Development in Freedom," the party has successfully combined the implementation of free market and social policies such that the people have so far accepted all the policies implemented by the government without any major resistance. The CPP and the PNC, two of the major parties of the

Nkrumahist tradition, continue to pursue Nkrumah's Pan African ideology as their intended strategy for development in Ghana. While it is feasible to assess the performance and policies pursued by the NDC and NPP, it is difficult to assess the actual policies that the CPP and PNC would pursue when in power, since these parties of the Nkrumahist tradition are unlikely yet to assume power, after decades of defections and fragmentation. An assessment of the Nkrumahist parties, CPP and PNC shows low levels of institutionalization, due to their small size and the fact that they have not yet assumed power under the Fourth Republic. There is less tension and limited power struggles in the CPP and PNC. The main factor that has sustained the survival of the Nkrumahist tradition parties is their strong belief in Nkrumah's ideals and social policies.

Influence of Money, Patron-Client Relations and Corruption in the Party System

One main observation on Ghanaian politics during my field research relating to party financing in contemporary times is the excessive influence of money in elections. Party primaries and elections have become very competitive over the years, in terms of the number of aspiring candidates that compete for positions on the parties' ticket and the passion with which people participate in national and local elections. Nonetheless, the costs of election campaigns and standing for public office both at the local and national level have also skyrocketed to extreme levels, and the demands of the electorate on candidates and public officials have increased sharply. This ranges from invitations to funerals, babies' naming ceremonies, parties and other functions. At these functions officials are expected to donate financially and materially to families and communities. While candidates who compete in the presidential and parliamentary seats do campaign vigorously, access to funds has become an important factor in election campaigns. For example, in the NPP's 2008 presidential candidates' contest, each candidate paid

GHC25,000 (approx. USD$25,650) as registration fees. In addition, it was alleged that some of the candidates bought vehicles and other items for the party executive in the 230 constituencies.

This is an indication that in contemporary Ghanaian politics, money plays a significant role in the final choice of candidates because each candidate must have adequate funds to build a campaign machine, produce advertising materials and paraphernalia to sell him/herself to the electorate as well as meet all transportation expenses and pay his/her campaign staff. Each presidential candidate must tour the 230 constituencies, and campaign throughout the country. Much in the same way, a parliamentary candidate has to campaign across the district/constituency to promote his/her agenda and vision for development in the district and the people. Both presidential and parliamentary candidates offer financial inducements to would-be primary voters to influence them before and during party congresses. The power of money is increasingly becoming a decisive factor in Ghana's elections, as is the case in some Western countries such as the United States. This prevents qualified candidates with limited access to funding from competing in elections and/or win. In this case, a good and credible candidate who does not have sufficient access to funding to contribute to these functions, advertise his/her policies through radio, newspaper and television, buy campaign vehicles and pay people to work on his/her campaign can only dream of getting elected into public office. Hence the call for state funding of political parties is an attempt by advocates of election reforms to mitigate the escalation in the cost of election campaigns.

As a result, some factors that may be considered in the selection of candidates by parties include the influence, wealth and status of a person within the society, and their past or potential contribution to the party. This has made election competition a more challenging and an expensive endeavour. The excessive influence of money in elections has limited the grassroots members' upward mobility within the parties in leadership and candidacy positions. It follows that while organizational skills and strategic planning are important in election campaigns, very often, the candidate who is able to sell himself well to the electorate stands a better chance of winning because money is the critical wheel on which any successful organization moves forward effectively. In my interviews with MPs from all the parliamentary parties, they complained that it is becoming increasingly financially burdensome to stand in elections, due to the growing patronage costs. By the time a candidate qualifies in the primaries, the candidate has already spent a considerable amount of money on gifts and patronage such as paying children's school fees, hospital bills, contributing to funerals, and other campaign activities. They believe that the money could be used more usefully to challenge the other parties' candidates in the general elections. Apart from the influence of money in Ghanaian politics, another major problem identified in the study is patron-client relations, which has permeated all levels of the Ghanaian society. The predominance of patron-client relations corrupts elections in Ghana often prevents a well-qualified candidate from winning an election. The over reliance of individuals on MPs to solve their personal problems and the pressure to find ways and means to meet the community and individual needs promotes patronage networks and corruption among parliamentarians and public office holders who aspire to contest parliamentary elections. For example, the deputy chairman of the EC highlighted some of the main problems facing party organization and elections and admitted that bribing voters to vote for a candidate or party is illegal in Ghana. Nonetheless, due to the laxity in the implementation of laws and systemic failures, some of the laws guiding parties' conduct in elections are dormant and therefore not strictly followed. The predominance of patron-client relations in elections and political party organization adversely affects the practice of democratic procedures in the political parties. A survey by the CDD in collaboration with some international NGOs like the NDI, as part of the African Political Party Finance Initiative conducted between May 20 and 28, 2004 to build a national consensus as to the best approaches to financing political parties in Ghana, has revealed that 12% of voters admitted being offered money, or something in kind, to vote for a political party. This expectation is disturbing because it encourages political corruption and control of parties by the rich. The electorate's demand for material and financial incentives at every level of the party organization inflates the expenditures for candidates competing in an election. Some politicians also take advantage of the incessant demands from voters and distribute monetary and/or material favours to solicit the electorates' support and influence their voting decision.

Alongside the problem of patron/client relations is the issue of corruption in the parties and government institutions. While the idea of a multiparty system is good for the development of a sustainable democratic system in Ghana, corruption is obviously one of the major setbacks to achieving this goal. The predominance of corruption in the political parties, police and the judiciary is due the lack of enforcement of the constitutional provisions and legislation on corruption, and the inability of the government to implement existing laws to discourage state institutions and officials from indulging in it. Many party leaders, government officials and the general public openly admit that corruption is deeply ingrained in the society and expressed concern for its reduction or complete eradication, but how to achieve this goal is a problem for both the state and

society to figure out. For example, while the police and judiciary should be important institutions in the promotion and consolidation of democracy in Ghana, they are regarded as among the most corrupt institutions. Undue delays and undesirable influences in the administration of justice have facilitated the prevalence of corruption in state institutions that are charged with protecting the interests of the people, but instead prey on the ignorance of the majority of Ghanaians about their legal rights enshrined in the 1992 Constitution.

Leadership and Ethnicity in Ghana's Party System

Leadership plays a very important role in party organization and a party's success in electoral competitions. For example, despite the NDC's slack in promoting democratic principles, Rawlings' charisma and convincing power were contributing factors that enabled the party to sail through in the 1992 and 1996 elections. Thanks to the excellent leadership skills of President Kufour and his well-defined policies, the NPP has enjoyed wide popularity and won the 2000 and 2004 elections. Leadership skills also ensure unity among party members, party leaders and parliamentarians, as well as help to discourage secession by groups within the party. For example, apart from the formation of UGM by Wrekoh-Brobbey, which did not gain any major support from both the leadership and grassroots members of the party, the NPP, to a greater extent has stayed together throughout the sixteen years of Ghana's democratic transition. In contrast, Rawlings desire to control power in the NDC, and his lack of tact and diplomacy in managing the party has led to the breakaway of two groups at different times to form the NRP and the DFP, which has affected the party's electoral fortunes in recent years.

The importance of leadership in party organization and unity at the national, regional, constituency and unit levels also shows the level of unity in the parties. Whether the NPP can continue to retain that level of voter confidence and widespread support in the 2008 election and beyond, or whether the NDC or any of the opposition parties would be able to wrestle power from the NPP, depends on how the parties' leaders continue to promote democratic values within the parties and among the Ghanaian polity. Also, whether the NDC that has suffered many setbacks in recent years would continue to stay united should it lose the 2008 elections depends on the role of the leadership to deal with existing divisions within the party. Equally important is whether parties' policies are designed to effectively address the socio-economic needs of the people and the selection of astute parliamentary and presidential candidates who are able to explain the policies of the particular party to the electorate and articulate the party's vision for the country's future political and socio-economic development. More importantly, whether the leadership of the parties pays serious attention to the grievances and concerns of the supporters at the grassroots in the constituencies will be key factors in future elections. It also became evident in the study that while ethnicity plays a significant role in many African countries' party organization because some people may support or vote for a party and its candidates based on ethnic lines. Nonetheless, ethnicity does not pose a threat to Ghana's political system, although certain decisions in the parties may be taken due to ethnic reasons as a strategic political consideration. There is general perception that African nations naturally tend to bond strongly along ethnic lines and these are often carried into party politics, which enable some powerful individuals to exploit the tribal differences for their personal ambitions. Party driven ethnic conflict has undermined African countries' democratic processes in Kenya,

Sierra Leone, Rwanda, Liberia and Cote d'Ivoire. But Ghana's 1992 Constitution has been designed to prevent such problems from occurring. Several measures have been taken to safeguard the country's party and democratic systems from falling prey to ethnic rivalries. The 1992 Constitution states that it is against the law to establish and/or organize a party based on ethnicity.

Leaders of the political parties also ensure that the structure of the party executive reflects the national character by giving representation and equal opportunity to every tribe in Ghana. For example, a closer look at party organization shows that most of the major parties have ethnic balance in their structure. Very often, when a party's presidential candidate is from southern Ghana, the vice-president is chosen from one of the northern regions and vice versa. In this case, Ghana's Constitution and party organization strategies help prevent ethnicity from disrupting the democratic process or allowing some unscrupulous politicians to inflame ethic sentiments for political gains. Although people in various regions may vote for a party because of a candidate's ethnicity, this often leads to backlash against the candidates by voters in other regions who detest the practice of using the ethnic card to win votes. Hence it is difficult for a party that bases its campaign strategies on ethnic divisions to win support in all the regions. Due to the constitutional ban on parties with religious and ethnic identities, there is no religious fundamentalism to threaten Ghana's democracy, as in Nigeria, no serious threat of ethnic or class conflict, as in South Africa, and no clear and sharp division between the social classes, as in many Latin American countries such as Mexico and Brazil. While leadership and ethnicity are important to party development in many third-wave democracies, due to the measures instituted in Ghana, ethnicity does not pose a serious challenge to either local or national politics and the stability of the country's democracy.

The study further argues that the success of Ghana's democracy and many third- wave democracies in Africa challenges Jack Synder's view that there is a need to delay

democratization until well-developed parties and state institutions are established. Evidently, at the time of Ghana's democratic transition, its democratic institutions were not well developed. But the period after the transition has been marked by increasing improvement in the development and strengthening of the country's legal and institutional frameworks. My study argues that a country's democratic institutions can be developed in the process of consolidating its democracy, as Ghana illustrates. Experiencing democratic transition before fully developing a country's democratic structures has also contributed to Ghana's party development. Ghana's party system has undergone a lengthy process of struggle, resistance, reform and deliberation that has taken place since independence, and especially since 1992. These developments have also contributed to a number of reforms to institutionalize the party structures and their mode of organization. Additionally, the democratic transition and consolidation processes have increased majority of Ghanaians' acceptance of the democratic political culture as "the only game in town". Ghanaians continue to be committed to democratic governance, and have supported and sustained the effort to consolidate the country's democratic gains over the last fifteen years. My study further argues that in order to strengthen Ghana's democratic consolidation process, there is a need to continue to democratize state institutions such as the police and judiciary systems and also institutionalize the political parties by improving party structures and organizational strategies.

Variations in Party Organization

Candidate Selection Methods and Democratic Procedures

While there are striking similarities in the parties' structure, strategies for recruiting members, fundraising practices and some of the problems facing parties in

Ghana, there are also significant differences among the major parties on issues of internal party democracy and candidate selection processes. Two parallel issues dominate internal organization of Ghana's political parties: internal democracy and fairness in candidate selection processes. One of the major differences between the two main parties -NPP and NDC is the level of democratic procedures in their organization and in the selection of candidates - presidential and parliamentary candidates, chairpersons, secretaries and organizers. As an offspring of the Danquah-Busia tradition, the NPP embraces a large group of intellectuals and professionals, which seems to create a balance of power within the party, and gives little room for central control over whether MPs should be retained or not. Although the NPP is more democratic than the NDC, there have been instances of undemocratic tendencies in the party as well. For example, it is alleged that some members of the NPP also have used intimidation and harassment during the party's primaries or to settle scores with other party members, such as the clash between supporters of Moctar Bamba and other party members at a party congress and the recent conflict between supporters of Thesresa Tagoe, the NPP MP for Ablekuma and some constituency executives.

The NDC on the other hand, as a "socialist post-revolutionary party," carries the legacy and baggage of the revolutionary attitude into a democratic era, with a high degree of centralization of authority within the party. The complex leadership structure at the national level impedes democratic reforms within the party. For example, while John Atta-Mills was the presidential candidate of the NDC, Rawlings remained the Founder of the party, who is even more powerful than the chairman and presidential candidate, and his word is often final. While the NPP is under the control of the elected National Executive, Rawlings controls the NDC. Any party member who challenges his authority is seen as a dissident, and is in one way or another forced out of the party. Examples of these are the cases of Obed Asamoah, the former chairman of the NDC, Kwesi Botchwey and the former women's organizer of the party. While the NPP candidates compete, based on clearly laid down principles, the NDC often ignores the principles of democracy, and supporters of candidates often resort to intimidation, harassment and violence. For example, during one of the previous elections of the NDC's chairperson, supporters from the Rawlings' faction that supported Iddrisu Mahama intimidated, threatened and attacked supporters of Obed Asamoah. One of the main differences between the two parties is that whereas the NDC's candidates were not required to pay registration fees in the 1992, 1996 and 2000 elections, due to the party's access to state funds, the NPP charged fees. This is one of the main fundraising strategies adopted by the party in all the elections held under the Fourth Republic. The NDC, now in opposition, has started charging fees from parliamentary candidates to offset some of the party's election campaigning and administrative costs. The tendency of the party headquarters to impose candidates on some constituencies in complete disregard of local preferences is a major issue in promoting democracy within the parties. This tendency manifests itself at the party primaries when a candidate is imposed on the constituency rather than being elected by party members in it. While party leaders justify this by arguing that they want to ensure that their candidate wins the election at the constituency level, this trend has often led to many conflicts and rift in some party constituencies. Very often, when the people's favourite candidate is by- passed for a candidate favoured by the party headquarters, the rejected candidate contests the parliamentary elections as an independent candidate. The emergence of independent candidates demonstrates the dissatisfaction with the selection of candidates. For example, in the 1992 parliamentary election, 12 candidates stood as independents. The number of independent candidates in the parliamentary election increased by 375% to 57 in 1996 and further increased by 3.5% to 59 in the 2000 election. In the 2004 parliamentary election, the number of independent candidates increased by 113.5% to 126. The growing proliferation of independent candidates resulting from disputed candidate selection at the party constituency primaries points to the decreasing levels of internal democracy in some of the parties in Ghana. The NDC party's mechanisms for selecting a party leader have brought into question the parties' adherence to Section 9 (1)

(a) and Section 9 of PNDCL 218 and Act 574 respectively which deal with internal democracy. Despite the perception that the NPP uses open and competitive procedures to select its candidates, some unacceptable practices continue to hinder candidate selection in all the political parties. It is also apparent that the struggle for power has shaped party organization, the nature of political participation and internal democracy in the parties. Hence the contest for power dictates the need for party unity within the major parties, which are more united than the small and fragmented opposition parties. For this reason, different candidate selection methods and strategies adopted by the political parties often determine the level of internal democracy in the political party, and the extent of internal divisions and intra-party conflicts. This inevitably affects the performance of the party in presidential and parliamentary elections. Whilst all the parties face problems relating to internal party democracy, the NPP is more democratic than the NDC, due to its high level of institutionalization in its internal organization and candidate selection processes. The cohesion within the NPP can also be explained by the allegiance of the members of the UP tradition and its democratic ideals. Despite its numerous internal problems, the NDC continues to have strong showing in both parliamentary and presidential elections. This is due to the party's support from the remnants of its revolutionary structures during the PNDC era. The cohesion in the NDC is due to the grassroots support it enjoys from former members of the revolutionary cadres such as the CDRs, P/WDCs, ACDR, and the DWM established during the PNDC era.

While political parties' candidate selection methods are generally supposed to be based on democratic principles, various strategies adopted by some of the political parties call into question the issue of fairness and internal democracy. Problems associated with candidate selection and internal party democracy in the political parties is not unique to one party, although the extent of the problem differs significantly from one party to another. The lack of specific standards to guide parties' internal democracy and candidate selection processes has contributed to the party leaders' lack of attention to internal party democracy. This is due to the fact that the EC, which is charged with ensuring that parties conform to democratic principles, has not been very effective in playing this important role. So far, what happens within the parties is the parties' internal affair, and they are expected to resolve their issues through the leaderships' own conflict resolution strategies and efforts. Looking at the problems associated with political parties and the promotion of democratic consolidation in Ghana, it could be argued that Ghana's party system has made great strides in recent years. Nonetheless, the issue of internal party democracy in candidate selection and the lack of participation in decision-making by poor and minority groups are some of the key issues plaguing the development of Ghana's political system.

Ghana's Party System and Democratic Consolidation, and the Impact of Democratization on the Political Parties

The role of parties in Ghana's democratic consolidation examined in the preceding chapters shows that political parties are essential agents of democratic consolidation in Ghana. Their role in pressuring the NDC government to make pragmatic reforms in the legal and institutional frameworks and to create a level playing field for all the parties in elections was vital. For example, the opposition parties' protest against the 1992 presidential election outcomes and their participation in the IPAC negotiation processes led to major electoral reforms prior to the 1996 election and sustained Ghana's unstable democracy after the 1992 election debacle. The opposition parties' representatives in parliament also challenged the government on a number of issues, which they regarded as over-extension of the executive's influence such as on the issue of police permits to parties for holding rallies and demonstrations. Another way in which the parties contributed to the consolidation of democracy in Ghana is by using the legal system to challenge the NDC government on a number of issues, especially in electoral reforms, such as the introduction of transparent boxes and photo identification for voting.

Political parties in Ghana recruit election candidates at both the local and national level in the country and together with the EC and the NCCE have been educating voters on electoral rules and regulations. Parties have also served as a major source of influence in aggregating the peoples' interests and MPs have been the main agents for bringing problems facing communities to the government's attention. One other way in which parties have contributed to Ghana's democratic consolidation is by promoting tolerance, trust and cooperation between the political parties through the Chairperson's caucus. This important step has paved a way for dialogue among the party leaders and reduced tension and possible confrontation on election disputes among the parties. These organizational strategies and internal reforms have greatly contributed to facilitate the spread of the democratic political culture among party members and the public in general, and in turn, eased the progress of Ghana's democratic consolidation process.

The study also argues that democratization has contributed immensely to the development of political parties in Ghana. From the period following the 1992 democratic transition, legal, institutional and constitutional changes have gone a long way to help in the development of political parties and the consolidation of the country's

democracy. Among the major changes was the reform in the country's electoral institutions such as the establishment of a substantive EC to replace the Interim Electoral Commission, and the passing of the Political Parties' Law in parliament that compelled the ruling government to provide logistical support such as cars to all the political parties during elections. The process of democratizing the state has led to changes that have enhanced the practice of checks and balances and separation of powers among the executive, legislative and judiciary branches of government to drastically curtail the extensive executive interference in the duties of the other branches of government during the initial stages of the transition. This step created the enabling environment for the opposition parties to push forward their grievances and make inroads in their quest for increasing reforms, which led to the NPP's success in the 2000 elections. The NDC, as the main opposition party in parliament has also contributed to strengthening civil liberties, the rule of law and government accountability. It is apparent from the above discussion that political parties play a critical role in democratic consolidation and democratization. At the same time, democratization has spurred the development of political parties.

Concluding Remarks

While Ghana's parties have the potential to develop their internal organizations effectively, they have been hindered by a number of problems. With reference to the views of various democratic theorists, and from the perspective of this study, some factors crucial to strengthening political parties' institutional frameworks and for accelerating Ghana's democratic consolidation are stable and predictable political institutions that promote participation and democratic values. It also includes independent electoral institutions that promote free and fair elections and produce results that are acceptable to all parties and the public and vocal civil society to monitor public officials' abuse of power. It further includes a supportive political culture that enhances political

participation in decision-making and government institutions that are committed to promoting democratic principles. In order to sustain public support for the democratic system and avoid Ghana's bitter experiences with political destabilization of constitutional governments, the political parties should be more committed to expanding the ideals of democracy to their members by promoting the political principles of democracy. The parties should also make efforts to drastically reduce corruption, promote internal party democracy. The election processes should be made freer and fairer and other internal reforms should be implemented that could lead to effective structural transformation in all the political parties. The study further argues that exploring the potential strengths of democratic initiatives "from below and within" by empowering the grassroots members of the parties can help Ghana's democratic consolidation process. The process of consolidating democracy also requires addressing external constraints and removing policy bottlenecks such as the harsh conditionalities from Ghana's external donors that could hinder the strengthening of Ghana's democracy, in order to make the democratic process more meaningful to the ordinary people.

The consolidation of Ghana's democracy, and for that matter, the third-wave democracies in Africa requires strengthening public accountability through the institutionalization of political parties. The scope and potential of the society to exert pressure on political institutions and parties in decision-making processes contributes significantly toward democratic consolidation. This includes strengthening relations between government institutions and society and institutional reforms. Government institutions must be guided by a basic set of institutional checks and balances provided in the constitutional provisions and a need for consensus on constitutional arrangement. All public officials must be subject to the rule of law, promote transparency in the performance of their functions and be accountable to the people in the discharge of their duties. State institutions such as the police should treat suspects fairly and people should

be free from intimidation, physical violation, arbitrary arrest, and detention without trial. Citizens must have equal and secure access to justice, due process and redress in court where their rights and freedoms are infringed upon, and the justice system should observe due rules of impartiality and equitable treatment of all cases to promote confidence in the legal system to deliver fair and effective justice.

There should be a clear-cut parliamentary and judicial independence from the government without any interference from the executive branch in the performance of their duties and horizontal accountability among the branches of government to promote checks and balances and effective separation of powers and reconciliation of constitutional and political arrangements that are satisfying to all groups within the society. As suggested by the Country Review Mission of the African Peer Review Mechanism, in order to further strengthen Ghana's democracy, there should be a clear separation of powers between the legislature and the executive body by changing the constitutional provision that allows the appointment of majority of ministers from parliament, which weakens parliament's oversight functions. The process of consolidating democracy also needs to be understood in terms of the promotion of democratic values and the existence of a free and fair electoral process. There should be equal and effective protection of freedom of expression, information, association and assembly, and the need to develop powerful institutionalized parties to function within the framework of democratic principles.

To sustain a hegemonic democratic culture in Ghana, party leaders and government officials must be held accountable to the public through respect for civil liberties, human rights, drastic reduction in corruption, and building trust between the party leaders and the grassroots members. The study further contends that there is a need for social and political reforms in the political parties' internal organization such as internal party democracy, effective representation and participation strategies. As long as the political parties remain elite-based, there will be continued discontent at the grassroots of the parties, and members' increasing disillusionment with the leadership of the political parties could result in a sagging support for democracy and internal revolt within the political parties as has been happening in some parties' constituencies. Avoiding internal revolt and secession from the parties, as has happened on two different occasions in the NDC party, leading to the formation of the NRP and later the DFP, will depend on the capacity of the leaders of the political parties to move the political parties' organization from their elite-based focus to grassroots and societal based to increase participation and reduce possible tension between the national and regional leaders on the one hand, and the constituency and unit leaders on the other.

Although Ghana's electoral system and party organization are still not perfect, significant improvements have been made in the electoral system and improved upon its party development, and that has won the country's democratic development, local and international support. Compared to many fledgling democracies in Africa and other parts of the developing world, the prospects of consolidating multi-party democracy in Ghana is very high. For example, Freedom House's 2006 and 2007 international ratings on the level of democracy and freedom in countries placed Ghana in the category of countries promoting political rights, civil liberties and freedom of speech. People are gradually understanding and accepting the democratic culture after years of authoritarian rule. With two major and three minor parties contesting free and fair elections every four years, and the gradual reforms being implemented in the military and police service, coupled with the vigorous role played by civic groups, one can fairly argue that there is no imminent

threat to derail Ghana's democratic consolidation project. Nonetheless, given the history of President Rawlings' NDC government's lack of accountability to parliament and the judiciary between 1992 and 2000, these bodies should be increasingly vigilant of possible abuse of power by any future over-zealous executive. Ghana's democratic system appears to be relatively healthy, although there is a need for continued public demands for government accountability, and the ability of government to implement institutional reforms to address the needs of the people.

Despite the fact that Ghana's democracy is on the path of consolidation, it continues to face a number of problems. In the course of examining the organization of the political parties, and their role in promoting democratic development, it became evident that a number of problems continue to plague the party system and the consolidation of Ghana's democracy. While the parties and ruling governments under the Fourth Republic have taken some important steps toward promoting democracy in Ghana, it is necessary that the opposition and ruling parties are not complacent of their achievements so far, but see democracy as an ongoing process that require constant scrutiny and reforms to address the problems facing the people and the country in general. As Onwukike noted, "democracy as an organizational system, and like culture, is not static. With time, it grows and develops in form as well as in purpose. "While the role of public officials and the government is vital for the development of a viable democracy in Ghana, the role of the public institutions is complicated by low levels of public trust in the political institutions, the police service, the judiciary, the political parties and public officials, due to the widespread corruption, government accountability deficit, and lack of participation in decision-making. The present high public support for democracy in Ghana could therefore be attributed to the fact that the public regards democracy as "the only game in town," especially after years of suffering under military rule and oppression.

The underlying argument in the study is that for Ghana's democracy to be firmly consolidated, some of the weaknesses need to be recognized and addressed appropriately. The challenge is how to build sustainable democratic institutions and strengthen parties to achieve enhanced participation in decision-making and political accountability. The key role of the civic groups in the nurturing and consolidation of democracy show that public support for the development and consolidation of democracy is also vital and needs to be sustained over a long period of time. Evidence from the research on public interest in political activities show that the CSOs, the political parties and the general public are committed toward preserving the country's democratic gains made in the last sixteen years. For example, a recent article by Michael Bratton and Robert Mates confirmed that support for democracy is strong among the Ghanaian public. Nonetheless, until the political parties and the government show such a commitment toward strengthening Ghana's democratic gains, failure to addressing the issues highlighted in the preceding chapters, could lead to some major setbacks from public disillusionment in democracy, and probably create the environment for military intervention or political unrest.

This study argues that where there is favourable international support to help the state build its institutional and policy capacity, and the existence of an enabling environment for the participation of an effective and vociferous civil society in public policy to complement the role of the political parties, it is possible to consolidate democracy. Despite some institutional problems, such as the need to strengthen the police and legal system, which normally exist in new democracies, with the institutionalization of the party system and state institutions, coupled with the increasing role of civil society and the donors in Ghana's democracy, it is plausible to argue that Ghana's democracy is on the path to consolidation since it meets many of the basic tenets proposed by many democratic theorists, such as Linz and Stepan's behavioural and attitudinal models; the Przworski's turn-over criteria and Diamond's legitimacy approach of democratic consolidation. Based on the theoretical views in the literature review and the empirical evidence in the subsequent chapters, the study argues that Ghana is making significant strides in its democratic consolidation. For example, at the time of transition, Ghana was considered a pseudo-democracy because although the P/NDC held competitive elections, it failed to uphold the political freedoms, civil liberties and the rule of law essential in a liberal democratic system. However, with the power alternation and the strengthening of civil liberties and institutional frameworks, the country's political system moved into the realm of an electoral/liberal democratic system. The challenge of vulnerability and reversibility to militarism by anti-democratic actors, and erosion and regression to semi- democratic rule has gradually faded and been replaced with aspirations for sustainability, endurance, democratic continuity and persistence. Hence, the completion of the democratic transition to consolidation represents one important step in the country's democratic development. The study further contends that the African Peer Review Mechanism, the New Partnership for African Development, and the military and financial support from the donors to Ghana, present great opportunities for mounting popular vigilance against military intervention, and in support of democratic consolidation.

In conclusion, I wish to state that my analysis and criticism of the political parties, government officials and institutions in this study is not intended to undermine their role and effort to promote democratic development in Ghana, nor should it be seen as ignoring the progress that has been made since the 1992 transition. On the contrary, my motivation for conducting research in this area is that I believe the study will contribute to the literature and practice of democracy in Africa, and particularly Ghana. For Ghana's evolving democratic consolidation processes to continue to thrive and sustain its rapidly developing pace, the parties and government needs to develop strategies to meet the unique challenges such as corruption and lack of internal party democracy facing Ghana and other new democracies in the developing world. While the recommendations made on how to sustain Ghana's democracy is my belief that implementing the necessary reforms could greatly deepen the country's democratic development. Making the political parties rethink their organization and their role in Ghana's democratic development would help overcome some of the problems highlighted in the study. From this perspective, by critically analyzing the roles, organizational strategies, internal democracy and funding practices of Ghana's political parties, as well as their representation functions and their relations with civic groups and society in general, effective strategies and robust policies could be formulated to enhance the organization of the political parties and Ghana's democratic consolidation. Through these initiatives, the government and political parties can resolve some of the critical problems that need serious attention and reforms, and by successfully dealing with these issues, Ghana's democratic consolidation process could move forward to a whole new and unprecedented level.

www.ingramcontent.com/pod-product-compliance
Lightning Source LLC
Chambersburg PA
CBHW031056080526
44587CB00011B/702